Sara's Secrets for Weeknight Meals

Also by Sara Moulton

SARA MOULTON COOKS AT HOME

Sara's Secrets

for Weeknight Meals

SARA MOULTON

Recipes developed with
Joanne Lamb Hayes

Photographs by Dana Gallagher

BROADWAY BOOKS

NEW YORK

BROADWAY

PRINTED IN CHINA

BROADWAY BOOKS and its logo, a letter B bisected on the diagonal, are trademarks of Random House, Inc.

Visit our Web site at www.broadwaybooks.com

First edition published 2005

Book design by Maria Carella

Library of Congress Cataloging-in-Publication Data
Moulton, Sara, 1952–
    Sara's secrets for weeknight meals / Sara Moulton.—1st ed.
        p.   cm.
    Includes index.
    1. Quick and easy cookery. 2. Dinners and dining. I. Title.
TX833.5.M68 2005
641.5'55–dc22   2004062882

ISBN 0-7679-1659-X

10 9 8 7 6 5 4 3 2 1

To my Mom

CONTENTS

Acknowledgments

In addition to the greater Moulton and Adler families, who contributed many ideas and recipes to this book, I have a raft of important people to thank:

Joanne Lamb Hayes, my stalwart partner on this book

Judith Weber, my hard-tackling agent

Jennifer Josephy, my wise editor

Jennifer Webb, my sous chef, who kept the *Gourmet* dining room running smoothly when I was off writing this book—and retested many of these recipes besides

Helen Baldus and Jennifer Baum, my able publicists

Todd Coleman, my food producer on *Sara's Secrets,* who helped with research

My kids, Ruth and Sam, for putting up with a year's worth of weird meals (although they were happy to eat breakfast and sandwiches for dinner)

My husband Bill . . . there are no words

Introduction

On the road promoting *Sara Moulton Cooks at Home* in 2002, I heard the same lament over and over again: Everyone swore they wanted to cook at home more often, but no one could find the time. What they dreamed of was a cookbook for meals that take fifteen minutes or less to prepare.

At first, frankly, this notion offended both the chef and the home-maker in me. My first cookbook was a compendium of virtually every recipe I'd ever loved, without too much thought given to how much time any of them took to prepare. Now all anyone was talking about was getting dinner made in fifteen minutes or less. Fifteen minutes?! What's the big rush? Cooking is fun. Cooking is therapeutic. Cooking is creative. Cooking concludes with a wonderful meal that brings the whole family together.

Then I remembered a little fantasy of mine from several years earlier—how much rosier my life was going to be the minute I stopped doing a live TV show every night and started taping them instead. I was sure I'd amble home from my day job at *Gourmet,* grab a magazine and a glass of wine, prop up my feet, and chill. That's when reality smacked me in the face. All the time that had been freed up for me was instantly consumed by the need to help my kids with their homework . . . and make dinner.

Suddenly I got it. If I could write a book that concentrated on getting dinner on the table on a weeknight and doing so quickly and intelligently—if not quite in fifteen minutes or less—I might indeed produce something very useful. This is that book.

However, this book is not only about making dinner quickly. It is also about making it good—and exciting. My friend and colleague Arthur

Schwartz, who was the longtime host of *The Arthur Schwartz Show* on radio station WOR in New York, has pointed out that most of us make the same ten recipes over and over again. If that's true—and I think it is—it's no wonder that most of us consider making dinner a chore. We're bored.

Accordingly, this cookbook reflects my efforts to rethink dinner. To begin with, I focus (with the exception of only two chapters) on nothing but entrées, including chapters devoted to dishes not normally considered the main course: "Soup for Supper," "Breakfast for Dinner," "The Substantial Sandwich," and "Entrée Salads."

I've also done my best to *internationalize* the thinking of the home cook, which can't help but enrich our options at dinnertime—although even these recipes have been streamlined. In truth, there's almost no way for us to make them with absolute authenticity, no matter how much time we have, if only because at least some of the authentic ingredients are too hard to find. Still, many of the recipes in this book indeed possess international pedigrees, with the advantage that almost all of the ingredients are available at our local supermarkets. I've listed mail-order or Internet sources for any ingredient that isn't quite that handy—and proposed alternative ingredients as well.

Speaking of alternatives—and of ways to bust out of the ten-recipes-ad-infinitum box—I've taken the trouble to suggest, one by one, how to recast any number of this book's two hundred recipes with substitute ingredients. In effect, then, here are far more than two hundred recipes at your disposal.

Meanwhile, the clock is always ticking. That's why every recipe here lists the "hands-on time" and the "total preparation time," which includes the hands-on time. The vast majority require twenty to thirty minutes hands-on time and thirty to forty-five minutes total cooking time. This is not an unreasonable amount of time to devote to a home-cooked dinner on a weeknight. (I'm hardly the first person to write a quick-prep cookbook, of course. My own model is Pierre Franey, whose *60-Minute Gourmet*—the product of a more leisurely era—still inspires me.)

Technique-wise, I've dispensed with what the French called *mise en place,* which means prepping all of your ingredients before beginning to cook a recipe. That's a smart way to go for a restaurant chef, who has to cook hundreds of dishes to order on any given night. But it's definitely not the fastest plan for a home cook, who can certainly wait to chop up the garlic and peppers while the onions are browning. Just make sure you read the whole recipe for a given dish before you start cooking, so you can anticipate which tasks you can do while something else is in progress.

Likewise, it was during the making of this book that the food processor became my best friend. That machine's grating and slicing disks reduce the time required for those tasks to almost nothing— although I turned to the grating disk in the first place because I knew that it's much quicker to cook grated vegetables than whole ones.

In my quest for speed I also rely quite a bit on the modern supermarket, now more super than ever. Many of these recipes take advantage of the prerinsed and/or presliced vegetables available in the supermarket's vegetable section or salad bar. And a simple walk down the aisle to the deli counter is all it takes to pick up rotisserie chicken or sliced-to-order turkey, ham, or roast beef.

In effect, this book takes dead aim at how to get dinner on the table Monday through Thursday nights with the barest minimum of muss and fuss, although many of the recipes would be great on the weekend, too. But if, in fact, you have a little more time to cook on the weekend—the time to shift gears, so to speak—I'd like to direct your attention to the chapter entitled "Cooking Ahead." The recipes there will absolutely repay the time and effort you sink into them. Having written a cookbook devoted to speed, I must confess that I could never discount the joys of slow food.

In fact, I can't help but think of Julia Child, who was strictly anti-fad and anti-rush-rush-rush. She advised us to cook dinner, dine with friends and family, and eat everything you want. (But no seconds!) This was her recipe for a long, sane, pleasurable life. Given that she didn't die until she was two days short of her ninety-second birthday, I can't see any reason to argue with her.

It is to my mother, however, that I am dedicating this book. At the helm of our home in the early sixties she was unavoidably inspired by the example of the Kennedys. She'd heard that Joseph P. had taken advantage of the dinner table to lead his eight children—including the future president, attorney general, and senator—in high-energy discussions of the Great Topics of the Day. My mom, in her turn, not only cooked dinner, she also encouraged my sister and brother and me—we were roughly thirteen, eleven, and four at the time—to join my father and her in a kind of suppertime symposium. You might say that she was a little too hopeful. Then again, I am her daughter, doing my best to follow in her footsteps. If the dinner conversation with my own husband and kids never quite reaches Kennedyesque heights, well, there we all are, together, chatting about our daily adventures and eating well.

Please read every recipe from start to finish before you begin cooking so that you can plan your time. Get that pot of water on to boil, preheat that oven, and then proceed. If you find that three ingredients are listed as chopped in the ingredient list, but they don't all go into the skillet at the same time, chop the one you will need first and get it into the pan. Then while that is cooking, chop the second ingredient, and so on. Likewise, if you see that a part of the dish simmers for twenty minutes, use that time to prep and measure the remaining ingredients. If you plan your time this way the recipe will get done even faster. As I mentioned in the introduction, this book, with a few exceptions, is all about quick weeknight entrées. Here is a summary of the chapters.

Basics

I had a bunch of little recipes and techniques that didn't fit elsewhere and yet were crucial to many recipes in the book. So they ended up in this chapter.

Soup for Supper

Hearty soups have always struck me as meals in themselves. They're not only substantial, they're easy to make. After all, you can toss nearly anything and everything into a broth and call it soup. My soups fall into the nearly-everything category. In each of them all the usual dinner food groups are present—protein, starch, and vegetable. The difference, of course, is that this time they're not lying on a plate; they're floating in a bowl of flavorful broth. (The broth becomes flavorful as the soup cooks—it requires no extra time.) As a finishing touch, many of these soups are garnished with an extra ingredient—nuts, grated cheese, some vegetables, or a sauce.

Entrée Salads

Like soup, a salad can be built up into an eminently respectable stand-alone entrée with a minimum of muss and fuss. Indeed, most of my entrée salads, like my soups, contain all of the usual dinner food groups. (And none of them is the kind of simple green salad that my meathead husband disdains as "rabbit food.") To dress them, use one of your bottled favorites or try my homemade vinaigrette, which is in the "Basics" chapter.

The Substantial Sandwich

A well-made sandwich is a thing of beauty, but most of us don't think of it as dinner. Here are twelve recipes that may change your mind—from melted cheese to the hearty meatball to the scampi hero and beyond. Many of them are complete in themselves; some of them just need a side dish or tossed green salad to round them out.

Breakfast for Dinner

Lots of folks prefer breakfast to any other meal. These range from the relative few who pour themselves a bowl of cereal in the evening and call it dinner to the zillions of restaurant-goers who order breakfast no matter what time of day it is. This chapter, then, is devoted to stick-to-your-ribs breakfast entrées that anyone might be happy to see at 7 p.m.

Despite the warnings of the food police, many of these dishes feature eggs. The dietary wisdom of the past—don't eat eggs because they're too high in fat and cholesterol—is passé. Today we understand that some fat is fine, and it is mostly saturated fat—not dietary cholesterol—that raises our cholesterol level. So eggs it is—although I also had fun exploring such other breakfast possibilities as knishes and quiche.

Pasta and Grains

For many of us a day without pasta is like a day without sunshine, which is why it was a dark day indeed when the low-carb fanatics convinced us that we'd have to kick pasta out of our pantheon of healthy food choices. Me, I've decided to live dangerously. Pasta is just too tasty, too versatile, and too affordable to do without. In this chapter I stick to the quicker-cooking pasta and grains, which means no recipes calling for wheat berries or brown rice. But regular dried pastas are there in force, as are wonton wrappers, basmati and other white rice varieties, and pearl couscous. And all of these recipes are substantial enough to make them worthy of entrée status.

Poultry, From the Meat Department, and From the Sea

I've lumped these three chapters together because there's nothing remarkable about them in a book like this; when you're trying to get dinner on the table quickly and healthfully, you'll often reach for recipes using poultry, meat, or fish. But though they're made with standard fare, each of these recipes offers a delicious new twist or two. I've used different cuts and varieties in each category—beef, lamb, and pork, steaks, scaloppine, and ground meats, chicken thighs and wings as well as breasts, whole fish and fish fillets; and all kinds of shellfish. I've also spiced up everything with ingredients from around the world.

Vegetable Plates

These meatless but intensely-flavored entrées should appeal to vegetarians and carnivores alike. They are certainly among my favorite recipes in the book. There are casseroles, kabobs, patties, pies, and stews—none of which requires too much else to round out a meal. But these are not the only vegetarian dishes in the book. Others, labeled with a *V* , are peppered throughout.

Shop and Serve

If the convenience of a meal's preparation is your prime consideration, this is the chapter for you. The sheer number of time-saving, preprepped ingredients at today's supermarkets—sliced vegetables from the salad bar, prepared pizza and polenta dough, packaged sauces—is amazing. In truth, it's a new world to me. (As a trained chef, I tend to make everything from scratch, although I understand that working this way takes me a lot less time than it would a home cook.) I was introduced to the glories of the modern supermarket by Joanne Hayes, my partner on this book. She found all sorts of prepared ingredients that I didn't know existed or had never paid attention to. The resulting recipes may seem too simple to be all that tasty, but they are delicious. And they are certainly some of the quickest in the book

Just Open the Pantry

Though we imagine that the pantry went out with the hoop skirt, most of us keep a ready supply of dry goods. When I talk about a pantry I mean not only the dried goods in your cupboard, but the vegetables you keep in a basket or bin at room temperature, the regular items you keep in your fridge at any given time, and the frozen goods you should keep in your freezer. I've assembled a pantry listing (page 11) to give you some guidance (although you may discover you already stock most of the items I suggest). All of the recipes in this chapter can be assembled entirely out of your pantry.

Cooking Ahead

Why devote a chapter to slow-cooked recipes in a book whose prime purpose is speed? Because if you cook one of these dishes in advance on a weekend, when you have a little extra time, there's nothing left to do on a weeknight but pull it out of the fridge and heat it up. And it's delicious. The beauty of most slow-cooked dishes, stews, and pot roasts (besides the fact that slow cooking develops great depth of flavor) is that they actually taste even better a day or two later and they freeze well. They also recycle nicely—the first night the dish might be a stew, the next a topping for pasta or polenta. And even though the total cooking time for all of these recipes is significant, I have made sure that none of them occupies too much of your hands-on time.

Side Dishes Take Center Stage

As far as I'm concerned, Americans eat too much protein and too few vegetables. I've always imagined that if we spent more time preparing exciting side dishes, the proportions would flip. Suddenly, the so-called side dish would take center stage and the so-called entrée would be playing a supporting role. This is the chapter where I test my little theory. Here is a raft of new ideas for great side dishes, including salads, starches, quick vegetable sautés, and oven-baked recipes. As accompaniment, toss a piece of meat or chicken on the grill.

Quick Sauces

The idea here is that if you have a good sauce, you don't have to fuss so much over what you put it on. Just grill or sauté a piece of meat, poultry, or seafood and top it with one of these quick sauces. All of them stand alone, meaning they don't depend on pan juices for their flavor. Rather, they're based on high-quality mayonnaise, olive oil, tahini (sesame paste), or miso. These recipes top off many of the entrées in this book, but I've also made suggestions for many other dishes they could dress up and make dinner-worthy.

Easy Desserts

Even a book devoted to weeknight entrées needs to pay *some* attention to weeknight desserts. We just made sure that they were as quick to prepare as the entrées. (We had a lot of fun doing it, too, especially Joanne, whose sweet tooth is more ferocious than mine.) Many of these desserts start with fresh fruit, which needs very little fixing up. We also provide two basic recipes, a cake and a cookie, both of which come with several variations. And that's not to forget about chocolate. If you try nothing else, you must make the Baked "Alaskan." It is a knockout.

I've included icons throughout the book for recipes that are vegetarian. Look for $\mathcal{V}$ for vegetarian choices.

Unless otherwise indicated:

Salt is kosher.

Black pepper is freshly milled.

Butter is unsalted.

Flour is unbleached all-purpose.

Vanilla extract is pure.

Vegetable oil is whichever brand you prefer.

Olive oil is extra virgin.

Brown sugar is firmly packed when measured.

Bay leaves are from Turkey.

Avocados are from California (also known as Hass avocados).

Maple syrup is Grade B. (See Sources, page 346.)

Fresh bread crumbs are homemade (page 23.) Dried breadcrumbs are homemade (page 24) or packaged.

Milk and yogurt are whole. (If you want to slim down the recipe, you can use lower-fat alternatives. However, you should stay away from no-fat products. I think they have no flavor.)

Mayonnaise, cream cheese, and sour cream are whole or low-fat, not fat-free.

Heavy cream is pasteurized, not ultrapasteurized. (The latter tastes cooked to me and tends to break faster than the pasteurized when whipped.)

Lemon, lime, and orange juice are freshly squeezed.

Lemon, lime, and orange zests are freshly grated. (The best tool for this job is called a Microplane. It is sold in many kitchenware stores. See Sources, page 346.)

Parmigiano-Reggiano is freshly grated. (Cup measurements are for cheese grated on a box grater. If you use a Microplane, the same weight of cheese will measure about twice as much.)

Eggs are large.

A few recipes in this book call for raw egg whites. These should be fresh. Although the risk of salmonella is real, it is minuscule. However, if you are cooking for one of the high-risk groups—the immune-impaired, the elderly, or the very young (under five years old)—you should reach for alternatives. Pasteurized egg whites or powdered egg whites (I've used a brand called Just Whites with great success) are both available at many supermarkets.

One tablespoon fresh herbs equals one teaspoon dried herbs.

Poultry is organic, "natural" (minimally processed), or kosher, if possible.

Meat is "natural" (minimally processed) or organic, if possible.

The fish used are not endangered. Overfishing, wasteful practices, and habitat destruction have endangered many species of fish. The fish I chose to use were not in the high-risk category at the time I was writing this book. But the situation keeps changing.
It's not always easy to know if a fish is or isn't endangered. For up-to-date information on the status of any fish, please go to the Seafood Choices Alliance Web site at www.seafoodchoices.com, or call (866) 732–6673. If the fish of your desire is indeed endangered, the Seafood Choices Alliance will provide you with alternatives.

Wine is drinkable. Don't ever use "cooking wine."

I am loosely defining the pantry as things you should keep on hand—not only in your cupboard (the literal pantry), but also in the fridge, the freezer, the dry vegetable bin, and the bread drawer, and I have broken down the list that way. However, many things that start in your cupboard end up in your fridge (such as ketchup, mustard, peanut butter, etc.). I have put them in the cupboard because that is where they start. This is a basic list of the kind of items that really help me to get dinner on the table during the week. Of course, you should adjust it to your preferences.

The Cupboard

OILS AND VINEGARS

   Extra virgin olive oil

   Vegetable oil

   Assorted vinegars—at least balsamic, white wine, and cider; I would add red wine, rice wine, and sherry vinegar

BOTTLED ITEMS

- Marinated artichoke hearts

- Roasted red peppers

- Italian pickled vegetables (olive salad, peperoncini, giardiniera)

- Pitted, brine-cured olives such as kalamata

- Pimiento-stuffed olives

- Sun-dried tomatoes

- Capers

- Tomato sauce

- Ketchup

- Dijon mustard

- Worcestershire sauce

- Hot sauce

- Peanut butter

- Jelly

CANNED OR SHELF-STABLE GOODS

- Assorted beans—kidney, white, chickpeas, black (I like the Progresso and Goya brands)

- Canned whole and chopped tomatoes (I like the Muir Glen brand)

- Canned or boxed chicken (I prefer Swanson Natural Goodness), vegetable, and beef broth

- Tuna (packed in oil for more flavor or in water for fewer calories)

- Salmon

- Anchovies

- Chipotles in adobo sauce

- Chopped green chiles

- Tahini

ASIAN INGREDIENTS

Soy sauce

Hoisin sauce

Fish sauce

Toasted sesame oil

Canned unsweetened coconut milk (available in low-fat and regular versions)

Water chestnuts

Rice vinegar

Rice wine (available at liquor stores and Chinese grocery stores)

Star anise

Dried wasabi powder

Soba noodles

GRAINS, PASTAS, AND DRIED GOODS

Assorted pasta—spaghetti, macaroni, linguine, orzo, and other varieties of your choice

Egg noodles

Long-grain white rice

Couscous

Bulgur

Cornmeal

Rolled oats

Lentils

Dried porcini or other dried mushrooms

Assorted crackers

Ramen noodles

BAKING INGREDIENTS

- Unbleached all-purpose flour
- Instantized flour (Wondra)
- Cornstarch
- Granulated sugar
- Brown sugar
- Corn syrup
- Honey
- Maple syrup (Grade B)
- Baking powder
- Baking soda
- Cream of tartar
- Pure vanilla extract
- Quick-rising yeast
- Assorted chocolate (unsweetened, bittersweet, semisweet, chips)
- Unsweetened cocoa
- Powdered egg whites (the brand I get is Just Whites)
- Powdered buttermilk
- Unflavored gelatin

SWEET SPICES

- Ground allspice
- Whole and ground cinnamon
- Nutmeg
- Ground cloves
- Ground ginger
- Crystallized ginger

SAVORY HERBS AND SPICES

Black peppercorns

Thyme

Rosemary

Sage

Turkish bay leaves

Oregano

Cumin seeds and ground cumin

Whole and ground coriander

Curry powder

Caraway seeds

Fennel seeds

Assorted paprikas—sweet, hot, smoked

Red pepper flakes

Cayenne

Chili powder

Kosher salt

Table salt (for baking)

Dried bread crumbs (I have a recipe in the "Basics" chapter)

Panko bread crumbs (I have a recipe in the "Basics" chapter)

ALCOHOL

Dry white wine

Dry vermouth

Dry Marsala or Madeira

Dry sherry

Brandy

Vegetable Bin

Onions

Garlic

Shallots

Russet (baking) potatoes

Boiling potatoes (red or white)

Bread Basket

Sandwich bread

Pita with pockets

Refrigerator

Lemons, limes, oranges

Mayonnaise

Sour cream

Plain yogurt

Milk

Large eggs

Bacon

Fresh ginger

Carrots

Chiles (jalapeño or serrano)

Miso paste

Rinsed lettuces

Parmigiano-Reggiano

Sharp Cheddar

Bottled horseradish

Unsalted butter

Freezer

- Puff pastry

- Shelled and deveined shrimp

- Wonton wrappers

- Flour and corn tortillas

- Corn, peas, lima beans, spinach, edamame

- Nuts

- Vanilla ice cream

Basics

Creole Spice Mix

V

MAKES ABOUT 1/3 CUP

1 tablespoon plus 1 teaspoon
hot paprika (see pages 183
and 347)
1 tablespoon kosher salt
1 tablespoon garlic powder
1 1/2 teaspoons freshly milled
black pepper
1 1/2 teaspoons onion powder
1 1/2 teaspoons cayenne
pepper
1 1/2 teaspoons dried oregano
1 1/2 teaspoons dried thyme

I developed this recipe as a way of glorifying the Blackened Fish in my first cookbook. Usually, I am not a fan of onion and garlic powder—nine and a half times out of ten I'll reach for the fresh—but we're talking about a dry spice mix here, and these powders meld in just fine. Use this spice mix to season fish, meat, or fowl before you cook them. You might even make up a big batch of Creole Spice Mix and parcel it out as gifts for the holidays.

Combine the paprika, salt, garlic powder, black pepper, onion powder, cayenne, oregano, and thyme and transfer to a small airtight container. Use within 3 months.

Todd's Garam Masala

V

MAKES ABOUT 2/3 CUP

Hands-on time:
6 minutes

Total preparation time:
8 minutes
plus cooling time

Todd Coleman, the former food producer of *Sara's Secrets* and a dear friend of mine, contributed two recipes to this book, both of them Indian. In typical Todd fashion, he also contributed notes about each recipe. Here are his thoughts about the spice mix called garam masala: "Masala is what gives Indian food its tone and feeling. According to *Hobson-Jobson,* the quirky Anglo-Indian dictionary, *masala* means 'materials, ingredients . . . or things . . . conducive to good.' Masala most commonly refers to a mix of spices, and garam means warm or hot in Hindi. The spices in garam masala are thought to be warming. Think gingerbread. Use these 'warm materials' to spice up your food and life."

2 tablespoons cumin seeds
2 tablespoons black
   peppercorns
1 1/2 tablespoons green
   cardamom pods
1 tablespoon coriander seeds
2 teaspoons whole cloves
2 teaspoons fennel seeds
1 cinnamon stick, 2 1/2 inches
   long
4 Turkish bay leaves
1 teaspoon ground ginger
1/2 teaspoon ground nutmeg

1. Combine the cumin, peppercorns, cardamom pods, coriander, cloves, fennel, cinnamon, and bay leaves in a large, dry skillet. Toast the spices over high heat, tossing or stirring them occasionally, until they have browned lightly and are fragrant, 3 to 4 minutes. Transfer the garam masala to a bowl to cool.

2. When the garam masala has cooled, grind it into a fine powder in a spice grinder, clean coffee grinder, sturdy blender, or mortar and pestle. Transfer the ground masala to a bowl and whisk in the ginger and nutmeg.

3. Store the garam masala in an airtight container, away from heat, light, and moisture, for up to 6 months.

STORING DRIED HERBS AND SPICES

A QUESTION I get asked a lot on my show is how to store dried herbs and spices. Both herbs and spices should be kept in a cool dark place, preferably a closed cupboard or drawer. They will last for about six months, depending on how long they were sitting on the shelf before you purchased them. You can tell by their color how fresh they are. Dried herbs go from green to gray as they age; dried spices also fade in color. (For example, paprika and cayenne should look red, not brown.) What happens after six months? It is not like spices and herbs go bad and will harm you; they just lose flavor, and it will take more of them to get the same effect in a dish. Whole spices have a longer shelf life than ground. You can purchase one of those little coffee grinders and use it exclusively for spices (unless you want your coffee to taste like cumin and coriander). You can even go one step further and intensify the flavor by toasting the spices in a small dry skillet over low heat until they are fragrant, and then grinding them. The best way to clean your spice grinder is to grind a little bread in it. Discard the bread and wipe the grinder out. The bread takes most of the spice aroma out of the grinder.

Bread Crumbs Four Ways

V

FRESH BREAD CRUMBS
MAKES ABOUT 2 1/2 CUPS

Hands-on time:
2 minutes

Total preparation time:
2 minutes

The bread crumbs you buy in the supermarket are certainly very convenient but often very stale, and will only get more so if you leave them on your shelf for a while. Most of us have leftover bread kicking around at any given time, so rather than toss it, why not turn it into homemade bread crumbs? It takes just two minutes from start to finish to make fresh bread crumbs. I am also including recipes for dried bread crumbs (four minutes of hands-on time), panko bread crumbs (again four minutes), and seasoned bread crumbs (a whopping nine minutes of your time). With the exception of the fresh crumbs, they all keep for several months in an airtight container in your cupboard. The fresh bread crumbs will also keep for several months if you wrap them tightly and freeze them.

1. Break 4 slices (4 ounces) homemade-style white toasting bread into quarters and process in a food processor fitted with the chopping blade until fine crumbs have formed, 45 to 60 seconds.

2. Store in an airtight container in a cool place and use within 2 days or wrap tightly and freeze.

Hands-on time:
4 minutes

Total preparation time:
24 minutes
plus 1 hour drying time

PANKO BREAD CRUMBS
MAKES ABOUT 1 CUP

1. Place 4 slices (about 4 ounces) homemade-style white toasting bread on a wire rack and set aside, uncovered, 1 hour, turning once.

2. Preheat the oven to 200°F. Grate the bread by hand on the coarsest side of a metal grater. Spread the crumbs on a rimmed baking sheet and place in the oven for 20 minutes, checking occasionally to make sure they don't begin to brown.

3. Turn off the oven and allow the crumbs to continue to dry as the oven cools. Once they are dry, store the crumbs in an airtight container and use within 2 months.

Hands-on time:
4 minutes

Total preparation time:
20 minutes
plus drying time

DRIED BREAD CRUMBS
MAKES ABOUT 2/3 CUP

1. Preheat the oven to 300°F. Break 4 slices (about 4 ounces) homemade-style white toasting bread into 1-inch pieces and spread them on a rimmed baking sheet. Bake 10 to 15 minutes or until they just begin to turn golden; stir occasionally and check to make sure they don't get too dark.

2. Turn off the oven and allow the bread to stay in the oven until completely dry, several hours or overnight. Once the toasted bread pieces are dry, process them in a food processor fitted with the chopping blade until fine crumbs have formed, 45 to 60 seconds. Store the crumbs in an airtight container and use within 2 months.

SEASONED DRIED BREAD CRUMBS
MAKES A SCANT 1 CUP

1. Combine the dried bread crumbs, Parmigiano-Reggiano, basil, oregano, and garlic powder in a small bowl; stir until thoroughly combined.

2. Store the crumbs in an airtight container and use within several days. For longer storage, add just the herbs and garlic powder with the crumbs; then add the cheese just before using.

Hands-on time:
9 minutes

Total preparation time:
25 minutes
plus drying time

Dried Bread Crumbs (page 24)
3/4 ounce Parmigiano-
   Reggiano cheese, finely
   grated (about 1/4 cup; see
   grating information, page
   10)
1/2 teaspoon dried basil
1/4 teaspoon dried oregano
1/4 teaspoon garlic powder

Hands-on time:
5 minutes

Total preparation time:
25 minutes
plus drying time

Croutons Four Ways

𝒱

MAKES ABOUT 2 CUPS

4 slices (about 4 ounces)
homemade-style white
toasting bread
1/4 cup extra virgin olive oil
Seasoning (see Variations)
1/4 teaspoon salt

This is a little more of a stretch than making your own bread crumbs. I doubt that most people are going to whip up a batch of homemade croutons after they get home from work. Maybe this is more of a weekend project; admittedly, it is the side of me that really loves to cook, as opposed to the busy working mom, who wanted to put Croutons Four Ways in here. They just taste so much better and so much fresher than store-bought, and if you do have some bread kicking around that is getting a little stale around the edges, this is the perfect use for it.

1. Preheat the oven to 300°F. Trim off the bread crusts; cut the bread into 3/4-inch squares.

2. Combine the oil, seasoning for the variation you are making, and salt in a large bowl. Add the bread and toss until the pieces are evenly coated. Spread the croutons out on a large, ungreased, rimmed baking sheet.

3. Bake until the bread begins to brown on the edges, about 20 minutes; stir occasionally and check to make sure they don't get too dark. Turn off the oven and allow the croutons to stay in the oven until thoroughly dry, several hours or overnight. Store as directed for the variation you are using.

Herb-Garlic:

Add 4 minced garlic cloves (about 4 teaspoons), 1 teaspoon paprika, 1/2 teaspoon dried thyme, and 1/2 teaspoon crumbled dried rosemary to the basic recipe. Use within 1 day. For storage up to 1 month, substitute 1/2 teaspoon garlic powder for the fresh garlic cloves.

Greek:

Add 2 teaspoons grated lemon zest, 1 tablespoon fresh lemon juice, and 1 1/2 teaspoons dried oregano to the basic recipe. Store in an airtight container and use within 1 month.

Italian:

Add 1 teaspoon dried basil, 1/2 teaspoon dried oregano, and 1/2 teaspoon garlic powder to the basic recipe. Store in an airtight container and use within 1 month. If desired, toss with another tablespoon oil and then 2 tablespoons very finely grated Parmigiano-Reggiano (see grating information, page 10) just before using.

Southwestern:

Substitute corn or peanut oil for the olive oil and add 2 teaspoons chili powder, 1 teaspoon ground cumin, 1/2 teaspoon dried marjoram, and 1/2 teaspoon onion powder to the basic recipe. Store in an airtight container and use within 1 month.

All-Purpose Vinaigrette

V

MAKES ABOUT 1 CUP

1/4 cup white wine, red wine,
balsamic, sherry, or your
favorite vinegar
1 teaspoon Dijon mustard
1/2 teaspoon kosher salt
1/4 teaspoon freshly milled
black pepper
3/4 cup extra virgin olive,
canola, or vegetable oil

As a salad-aholic I keep a jar of homemade vinaigrette handy at all times. Who cares if the local supermarket offers row upon row of ready-made dressings? There is simply no excuse for not making your own—all you have to do is throw together a few ingredients and stir. (Sometimes I'll add chopped shallots to the mix, which gives it a nice crunch and slight sweetness.)

I make my vinaigrette once a week and keep it in the fridge. If the oil hardens from being chilled, just set your container in a pot of hot water or on top of the stove and let it warm up while you're making the rest of the meal.

1. Whisk together the vinegar, mustard, salt, and pepper in a 1-cup glass measuring cup or jar until the salt is dissolved. Gradually whisk in the oil.

2. Cover and store in the refrigerator.

Food Processor Pizza Dough

v

MAKES ABOUT 4 SERVINGS

Hands-on time:
10 minutes

Total preparation time:
45 minutes

Making pizza dough in the food processor is a snap. You don't have to know how to knead; the machine does all the work. What's left is the fun—tossing in the herbs or spices. Chopped fresh rosemary or thyme, cracked black pepper, cumin seeds, and chili powder—these are all good ideas.

1. Combine 1 3/4 cups of the flour, the yeast, sugar, and salt in the bowl of a food processor fitted with the chopping blade. Add 3/4 cup very warm water (120° to 130°F) and the oil; process until a soft dough forms. Add as much of the remaining flour, 1/4 cup at time, as necessary to make the dough manageable..

2. Shape the dough in a ball and place in an oiled bowl, turning so an oiled surface is up. Cover and let rise in a warm place until double in size, about 35 minutes. Use as directed in a recipe.

2 to 2 1/2 cups unsifted, unbleached all-purpose flour

One 1/4-ounce package quick-rising yeast (about 2 1/4 teaspoons)

1 teaspoon sugar

1 teaspoon table salt

1 tablespoon extra virgin olive oil

Roasted Peppers or Chiles

Hands-on time:
5 minutes for 1 pepper; 1 extra
minute for each additional pepper

Total preparation time:
15 to 20 minutes plus cooling time
for 1 pepper; 1 extra minute for
each additional pepper

*Red, yellow, or orange bell
peppers or poblano chiles,
rinsed and dried*

V

MAKES A SCANT 1/2 CUP, CHOPPED OR JULIENNED,
PER PEPPER USED

I call for roasted peppers in several recipes, but they are also a great stand-alone side dish. Why bother to roast peppers—or chiles—in the first place? To remove the skin and to enhance their flavor with a smokiness they'd otherwise lack. Although there are several ways to skin a pepper, all of them are a tad messy. On the other hand, none of them requires very much work. Whichever method you choose, do not rinse the peppers with water to remove the skins or you'll end up washing away some of the flavor. Just peel off the skins with your hands. For a tasty marinated side dish, season your peppers with salt and pepper, drizzle a little balsamic vinegar and olive oil over them, and finish them with a sprinkling of fresh herbs.

1. If you have a gas stove, turn on 1 burner to a low flame for every 4 peppers you are using. If you have an electric stove, place an oven rack 4 inches from your broiler's heat source and preheat the broiler to high.

2. Place the peppers on the grate over the gas flame or on a rimmed baking sheet under the broiler. Using tongs, turn often, until the skins are blackened on all sides, 10 to 15 minutes. Transfer the peppers to a large bowl, cover tightly with plastic wrap, and set aside until the peppers are cool enough to handle.

3. When the peppers are cool, quarter each pepper, working over a bowl to catch the juices. Discard the stem and seeds, and peel off and discard the skin. Use as desired. Reserve the juice in the bowl for sauces or soups.

Beer Batter

V

MAKES ABOUT 1 3/4 CUPS, ENOUGH TO COAT 4 SERVINGS MEAT,
POULTRY, SEAFOOD, OR VEGETABLES

Beer batter is my favorite coating for deep frying, not because I want my fried foods to taste like beer (in fact, the beer flavor in a fried batter is pretty faint), but because it produces the crispiest crust. I use it for both Fish Tacos (page 199) and Fried Clam Sandwiches (page 94), but I encourage you to use it for other dishes, including onion rings, zucchini sticks, and shrimp.

One note: The beer batter will slither right off whatever you're battering if you don't first dust that item lightly with seasoned flour. So don't omit that step.

1. Whisk together 1 cup beer, 1 cup flour, and 1/2 teaspoon salt until almost smooth. Strain the batter through a sieve and let rest, covered, at least 15 minutes and up to 1 hour. Check the consistency; it should resemble a slightly thick pancake batter. If it doesn't, add more flour or beer.

2. Combine the remaining 1/2 cup flour with 1/4 teaspoon salt and 1/4 teaspoon pepper in a soup plate or plastic bag. Dip the item to be fried in the seasoned flour, shaking off the excess before coating it in the batter.

3. Most items should be fried at a temperature of 365° to 375°F and sprinkled with salt right after they are removed from the hot oil.

*Hands-on time:
10 minutes*

*Total preparation time:
25 minutes*

1 to 1 1/2 cups beer, any kind; the darker the color the more beer flavor will come through
1 1/2 to 1 3/4 cups unbleached all-purpose flour
Kosher salt and freshly milled black pepper

5 pounds chicken wings
2 medium onions, quartered
2 small carrots, halved
2 celery stalks, halved
4 rinsed and dried fresh flat-
leaf parsley sprigs
2 rinsed and dried fresh thyme
sprigs
1 Turkish bay leaf
1 teaspoon whole black
peppercorns

Chicken Stock

MAKES ABOUT 8 CUPS

I understand that most people are going to reach for a can of chicken stock on a weeknight (and yes, let's be honest, even on a weekend). But I am hoping that one weekend, when you have a little time on your hands, you'll plan ahead and pick up some chicken wings and the appropriate vegetables at the supermarket, and make a batch of the homemade stuff. The flavor is superior, and because it is made with chicken and bones, it contains gelatin, which contributes body to any recipe you put it in. I have tried boiling down several brands of canned stock to see what happens. If they had actually been made from bones, the liquid would eventually become very viscous. Instead, I can boil the broth down until it disappears, and poof, there is nothing left in the pan. My theory is that they simmered water and chicken fat to come up with the flavor in canned stock and then removed the fat. I don't know how else they got chicken flavor in there. I like to use chicken wings because they have equal parts of chicken (flavor), bones (gelatin), and fat in the form of skin (more flavor)—more of all three put together than any other part of the chicken. You will be very happy to have it on hand. We refer to it as liquid gold. This stock will keep for three days in the refrigerator or a few months in the freezer.

1. Rinse the chicken wings. Put them in a stockpot and add enough cold water to cover by 2 inches. Bring the mixture just to a boil over high heat, skimming and discarding the surface skim with a slotted spoon. Reduce the heat to medium-low and simmer, skimming frequently, for 20 minutes.

2. Add the onions, carrots, celery, parsley, thyme, bay leaf, and pepper-corns; simmer for 2 1/2 hours. Strain the stock and skim off all the fat that rises to the surface. (Alternatively, cool the stock and refrigerate it over-night. The fat will harden on top of the stock and is much easier to remove.)

3. Return the stock to the pot and simmer until reduced by one-third, about 30 minutes. Divide the stock among several resealable plastic bags and freeze it.

Quick Sides

Hands-on time:
5 minutes

Total preparation time:
10 minutes

2 tablespoons extra virgin
olive oil
Two 5-ounce packages rinsed
baby spinach
1 garlic clove, minced (about 1
teaspoon)
Kosher salt and freshly milled
black pepper

SAUTÉED SPINACH WITH GARLIC
MAKES 2 TO 4 SERVINGS

1. Heat the oil in a large skillet over high heat until hot. Add half of the spinach and cook, stirring, for 30 seconds. Add the remaining spinach and cook, stirring, until almost completely wilted, about 3 minutes.

2. Add the garlic to the spinach and cook, stirring, for 2 minutes. Remove the skillet from the heat, add salt and pepper to taste, and serve.

ROASTED VEGETABLES
MAKES 4 TO 6 SERVINGS

1. Preheat the oven to 450°F. Toss the vegetables with the oil and salt and pepper to taste.

2. Arrange the vegetables in one layer on a rimmed baking sheet and roast them in the middle of the oven for 10 to 15 minutes or until just tender.

Hands-on time:
3 to 10 minutes
(depending on
the vegetable)

Total preparation time:
13 to 25 minutes
(depending on
the vegetable)

1 head broccoli or cauliflower, cut into 1 1/2-inch florets; or one 1-pound bag baby carrots; or 5 medium parsnips (about 1 1/4 pounds), cut into 2 x 1/2-inch sticks; or 1 pound asparagus, trimmed; or any combination
1 tablespoon extra virgin olive oil
Kosher salt and freshly milled black pepper

Hands-on time:
5 minutes

Total preparation time:
50 minutes

1 large butternut squash
  (about 3 1/2 pounds) or
  2 packages peeled and
  cubed butternut squash
  (about 20 ounces each)
2 tablespoons unsalted butter
Kosher salt and freshly milled
  black pepper

BUTTERNUT SQUASH PUREE
MAKES 4 SERVINGS

1. Preheat the oven to 400°F. Cut the squash in half lengthwise; scoop out and discard the seeds. Arrange the two halves, cut sides down, on a lightly oiled rimmed baking sheet and bake in the middle of the oven for 45 minutes or until the squash is very tender.

2. Alternatively, if you are using the precut squash, arrange it in one layer on a lightly oiled rimmed baking sheet; cover tightly with aluminum foil and bake 25 to 30 minutes or until tender.

3. Remove the squash from the oven and let cool slightly. If using halved butternut squash, scrape out the pulp. Transfer the pulp or cubed squash to the bowl of a food processor fitted with a chopping blade. Add the butter and salt and pepper to taste; puree until smooth.

HERBED PEA MEDLEY
MAKES 4 TO 6 SERVINGS

1. Cook the frozen peas in boiling salted water according to the package instructions.

2. At the same time, bring a large saucepan of salted water to a boil. Add the sugar snap peas and cook for 30 seconds; drain immediately. Toss the peas and sugar snap peas with the butter, herb, and salt and pepper to taste.

Hands-on time:
10 minutes

Total preparation time:
15 minutes

One 10-ounce package frozen peas
Kosher salt
8 ounces sugar snap or snow peas, trimmed
1 tablespoon unsalted butter
1 tablespoon rinsed, dried, and shredded fresh mint or basil, or chopped fresh dill
Freshly milled black pepper

V

COLE SLAW
MAKES 4 TO 6 SERVINGS

1. Combine the mayonnaise, chili sauce, lemon juice, 1 tablespoon water, and salt and pepper to taste in a large bowl.

2. Add the cole slaw and toss until well coated with the mayonnaise mixture; cover and refrigerate until ready to serve.

Hands-on time:
5 minutes

Total preparation time:
5 minutes

1/2 cup low-fat mayonnaise
3 tablespoons chili sauce
2 teaspoons lemon juice
Kosher salt and freshly milled
 black pepper
One 16-ounce package cole
 slaw mix

V

SMASHED POTATOES
MAKES 4 TO 6 SERVINGS

1. Combine the potatoes and salted water to cover by 1 inch in a large saucepan. Bring the water to a boil over high heat; reduce the heat to low and simmer the potatoes for 15 to 20 minutes or until tender.

2. Drain and return the potatoes to the saucepan. Add 1/3 cup milk and the butter; smash with a potato masher until mashed enough to hold together. Add more milk until the desired consistency is reached. Season with salt and pepper to taste.

Hands-on time:
5 minutes

Total preparation time:
30 minutes

2 pounds small (1 1/2-inch) red
 potatoes, scrubbed
Kosher salt
2/3 to 1 cup milk, heated
3 to 4 tablespoons unsalted
 butter or to taste
Freshly milled black pepper

V

BEAN SALAD
MAKES 6 SERVINGS

Toss the beans, tomatoes, celery, vinaigrette, and garlic together in a large bowl. Add salt and pepper to taste.

Hands-on time:
10 minutes

Total preparation time:
10 minutes

Two 19-ounce cans white beans (Great Northern, cannellini, etc.), kidney beans, chickpeas, or pinto beans, drained, rinsed, and patted dry (about 4 cups total)

2 cups chopped (preferably by pulsing in a food processor) cherry tomatoes (about 5 ounces)

4 celery stalks, chopped

1/2 cup bottled vinaigrette or All-Purpose Vinaigrette (page 28, add prep time)

1 garlic clove, minced (about 1 teaspoon), optional

Kosher salt and freshly milled black pepper

GARLIC BREAD
MAKES 4 SERVINGS

1. Preheat the oven to 350°F. Place the bread, flat side down, on a cutting board. Cut the bread crosswise from the top almost to the bottom of the loaf (but don't cut through the bottom) to make 1/2-inch partially attached slices.

2. Combine the butter, garlic, and salt and pepper to taste in a small bowl. Spread the butter mixture evenly between the slices. Wrap the bread in aluminum foil and bake for 20 minutes or until heated through. Remove the foil from the top and bake for 10 minutes more.

Hands-on time:
5 minutes

Total preparation time:
35 minutes

One 10-inch loaf Italian or
French bread
3 tablespoons unsalted butter,
softened
1 to 2 garlic cloves, minced (1
to 2 teaspoons), or to taste
Kosher salt and freshly milled
black pepper

SIMPLE BOILED RICE
MAKES 4 TO 6 SERVINGS

1. Bring a large pot of salted water to a boil over high heat. Gradually pour in the rice and return to a boil. Boil rapidly until the rice is tender, about 17 minutes.

2. Drain the rice well and return it to the pot. Cook over low heat for 1 minute, stirring, to dry it out. Add butter, salt, and pepper to taste; serve immediately.

Hands-on time:
3 minutes

Total preparation time:
22 minutes

Kosher salt
1 cup long-grain white rice
2 tablespoons unsalted butter
or to taste
Freshly ground black pepper

PARMIGIANO-REGGIANO COUSCOUS
MAKES 4 TO 6 SERVINGS

1. Bring the chicken broth and butter to a boil in a medium saucepan. Stir in the couscous and cover. Remove from the heat and let stand 5 minutes.

2. Fluff the couscous with a fork; stir in the Parmigiano-Reggiano and add salt and pepper to taste.

Hands-on time:
5 minutes

Total preparation time:
10 minutes

2 cups chicken broth, Chicken Stock (page 32), or water or a combination
2 tablespoons unsalted butter
One 10-ounce package plain couscous
2 1/2 ounces Parmigiano-Reggiano cheese, finely grated (about 3/4 cup; see grating information, page 10)
Kosher salt and freshly milled black pepper

Soup
for
Supper

Hands-on time:
20 minutes

Total preparation time:
1 1/4 hours

1/4 pound thinly sliced
    pancetta, chopped
3 tablespoons unsalted butter
3 pounds yellow onions, thinly
    sliced
1 cup red wine
Three 14- or 14 1/2-ounce cans
    (about 5 1/4 cups) low-
    sodium beef broth
Kosher salt and freshly milled
    black pepper
4 large eggs
1/2 cup white vinegar
3 tablespoons cognac,
    optional
1 1/2 ounces Parmigiano-
    Reggiano cheese, grated
    (about 1/2 cup; see grating
    information, page 10)
Freshly milled black pepper
Eight 1/2-inch-thick slices
    French bread

Italian-style Onion Soup

with a Poached Egg and Parmigiano-Reggiano Cheese

MAKES 4 SERVINGS

One of our favorite neighborhood restaurants is Beppe, where Chef Cesare Casella has created a menu bursting with the big sunny flavors of his native Tuscany. He makes a mean lemony fried chicken, succulent spareribs in tomato sauce, and French fries fried with fresh herbs. But I'm particularly partial to his onion soup with a poached egg on top. My version is much simpler, but very satisfying nonetheless. If you can't find pancetta (unsmoked Italian bacon) in your local market, you can substitute regular old American bacon. The key is to cook the onions slow and low. Serve with Grilled Radicchio Salad (page 306) and Garlic Bread (page 40).

1. Cook the pancetta in a large saucepan over medium heat until crisp, about 12 minutes; transfer it to a plate using a slotted spoon.

2. Melt the butter in the same pan over medium-low heat. Add the onions and cook, covered, stirring occasionally, until they are very soft, about 20 minutes. Remove the cover and cook, stirring frequently, about 30 minutes or until the onions are golden brown. Add the wine and boil until it is reduced by half. Add the broth and simmer for 20 minutes. Taste and add salt and pepper, if desired.

3. Meanwhile, poach the eggs in a mixture of 1 quart water, the vinegar, and 1 teaspoon salt (see sidebar).

4. To serve, stir the cognac into the soup, if using, and ladle into four soup plates. Top each serving with a poached egg, some of the pancetta and cheese, and pepper to taste. Toast the bread in a toaster or under the broiler and serve with the soup.

VERY fresh eggs make the best poached eggs because both the yolks and whites will set up much better when they are young and viscous than when they are old and watery.

The best pot to poach them in is a large skillet. The water should be at least 2 inches deep. For each quart of water, add 1/2 cup white vinegar and 1 teaspoon salt. That may seem like a lot of vinegar, but the vinegar helps the egg to set up, and I promise you won't taste it at all. Bring the water to a bare simmer. Working with 1 egg at a time, break it into a little bowl and drop it into the pot. If you want to get fancy, you can create a little whirlpool with a spoon and then drop the egg into the center of the whirlpool. This supposedly makes the white wrap neatly and completely around the yolk and it is sort of fun to do. Let the eggs cook gently, until they look like they are just set, 3 to 5 minutes. Remove them with a slotted spoon and serve. You can make them ahead using the same cooking method and then transfer them to a bowl of ice and cold water to stop the cooking. Trim off any strands of white with a pair of scissors when the eggs have cooled to neaten them up; then store them in the fridge until it is time to reheat. They reheat easily by dipping them for 1 minute or so into gently simmering water.

HOW
TO MAKE A
PERFECT
POACHED
EGG

Hands-on time:
25 minutes

Total preparation time:
25 minutes
plus chilling time

3 tablespoons vegetable oil

1 medium onion, finely
chopped (about 1 cup)

3 cups shelled fresh or
defrosted frozen peas

2 1/2 cups canned chicken
broth or Chicken Stock
(page 32)

1 to 2 tablespoons rinsed,
dried, and chopped fresh
mint leaves or to taste

2/3 cup well-shaken buttermilk

Kosher salt and freshly milled
black pepper

1/2 cup unsalted dry-roasted
peanuts or raw cashews

1 pound medium shrimp,
peeled, deveined, and
halved crosswise

1 1/2 tablespoons salt-free
packaged garam masala,
curry powder, or Todd's
Garam Masala (page 21,
add prep time)

2 medium carrots, coarsely
shredded (about 1 cup)

2 teaspoons fresh lime juice

1 teaspoon toasted sesame oil

Chilled Pea Soup

with Mint, Curried Shrimp, and Peanuts

MAKES 4 SERVINGS

Cold soups generally leave me cold. They just seem like an excuse
for a cold drink. But this one is an exception. Prepared with all the
prescribed accoutrements—curried shrimp, shredded carrots, and
toasted nuts—this dish is a perfectly refreshing warm-weather
meal. Serve with Cole Slaw (page 38) or Radish and Orange Salad
with Peppery Orange Dressing (page 303).

1. Heat 1 tablespoon of the oil in a medium saucepan over high heat until
hot. Reduce the heat to medium; add the onion and cook, stirring
occasionally, until softened, about 5 minutes. Add the peas and broth;
bring to a boil over high heat. Reduce the heat to medium, and cook,
uncovered, until the peas are tender, 2 to 5 minutes. Transfer half of the
soup mixture to a blender and puree with half of the mint; strain through
a medium sieve into a medium bowl. Repeat with the remaining soup and
mint. Stir in the buttermilk and salt and pepper to taste. Cover and
refrigerate until ready to serve.

2. Just before serving, heat the peanuts in a large skillet over high heat,
stirring frequently, until they begin to toast, about 3 minutes. Remove
them to a bowl and set aside. Toss the shrimp with the garam masala until
evenly coated. Heat the remaining 2 tablespoons of oil in the same skillet
until hot. Reduce the heat to medium, add the shrimp, and sauté until
golden and just cooked through, about 3 minutes. Set aside in the skillet.

3. Toss the carrots with the lime juice, sesame oil, and salt and pepper to
taste. Ladle the soup into chilled bowls and top each portion with some of
the carrot salad, some of the shrimp and oil from the skillet, and the
peanuts.

WHENEVER you have a bottle of wine or a liquid that you want to chill quickly, the easiest and absolutely fastest way to do so is to put it into another container of ice and water. You can chill a bottle of champagne in about 15 minutes flat by almost completely submerging it in a bucket of ice and water. For a soup, just put it in a bowl, preferably metal, and set that in another bowl of ice and water. If you stir it every so often, you will speed up the process even more.

HOW
TO QUICK
CHILL

*1 cup canned chicken broth or
Chicken Stock (page 32)*
1/3 cup white wine
*2 medium boiling or Yukon
gold potatoes (about 12
ounces), peeled and thinly
sliced*
*1 medium onion, thinly sliced
(about 1 cup)*
2 celery stalks, thinly sliced
*8 thin slices Canadian bacon
(about 6 ounces), chopped*
*1 teaspoon rinsed and dried
fresh thyme or 1/3
teaspoon dried*
*Kosher salt and freshly milled
black pepper*
*2 tablespoons unsalted butter,
thinly sliced and quartered*
1 Turkish bay leaf
*1 1/2 pounds cod, scrod, or
halibut fillet*
1/2 cup half-and-half
*1/4 teaspoon paprika (see
pages 183 and 347)*

Oven-baked Chowder

MAKES 4 SERVINGS

I was born and bred in New York, but my roots are in New England, so you might say that chowder is in my blood. My family has always made it by starting with whole cod or haddock on the bone, because the bones are the key to big, big flavor. On a weeknight in the twenty-first century, however, I know most of us just don't have the time. So here's a simpler version. (OK, this recipe requires an hour and a quarter from start to finish, but only fifteen minutes of that is actual hands-on time.) And because all the ingredients are tightly sealed in one casserole, you can't boil off the flavor. It'll all be there to smack you in the face the instant you sit down to your bowl. Serve with crackers and Cole Slaw (page 38).

1. Preheat the oven to 375°F. Spray a shallow 2-quart baking dish with vegetable cooking spray. Bring the broth and wine to a boil in a small saucepan over medium heat.

2. Layer the potatoes, onion, celery, and bacon in the baking dish, seasoning with thyme, salt, and pepper between the layers. Pour the hot broth mixture over all, dot with butter, add the bay leaf, and cover tightly with a lid or aluminum foil. Bake 30 to 35 minutes, or until the potatoes are tender.

3. Remove the bay leaf from the potato mixture; add the fish and bake, covered, until the fish is just cooked through, about 30 minutes. Meanwhile, gently heat the half-and-half.

4. To serve, drizzle the hot half-and-half over the fish. Spoon the chowder into bowls, breaking the fish into flakes with the spoon; sprinkle each serving with some paprika.

Egg Lemon Seafood Soup

Hands-on time:
20 minutes

Total preparation time:
35 minutes

MAKES 4 TO 6 SERVINGS

I love the Greek *avgolemono*—chicken rice soup thickened with eggs and flavored with fresh lemon juice. I also love fish or shellfish with lemon. So I thought I'd marry the two and turn a great soup into a substantial supper. Get your fishmonger to shuck the clams, and make sure that he or she saves all the clam liquor. Serve with crusty bread and a tossed green salad.

1. Bring the broth to a boil in a large saucepan over high heat; reduce the heat to low, add the scallops and clams and their juice, and barely simmer for 3 minutes or until almost cooked through. Transfer the scallops and clams with a slotted spoon to a bowl.

2. Add the rice and mushrooms to the broth in the saucepan and simmer, uncovered, 15 to 17 minutes or until the rice is just tender (10 to 12 minutes if using orzo).

3. In a medium bowl whisk together the eggs and lemon juice. When the rice is cooked, add 1 cup of the hot broth to the egg-lemon mixture in a slow, steady steam, whisking constantly. Return the egg-lemon-broth mixture to the saucepan and cook over medium-low heat until just thickened. Do not bring to a boil. Add the scallops and clams and any liquid that has accumulated in the bowl. Season with salt and pepper to taste.

4. Ladle the soup and shellfish into bowls and garnish each portion with some of the herbs and a few chile slices, if desired.

6 cups low-sodium canned chicken broth or Chicken Stock (page 32)
1 pound bay scallops
2 1/2 dozen shucked littleneck or cherrystone clams with their juice
3/4 cup long-grain white rice or orzo
6 ounces shiitake mushrooms, stems discarded, caps cleaned and sliced
4 large eggs, lightly beaten
1/4 cup fresh lemon juice
Kosher salt and freshly milled black pepper
1/4 cup rinsed, dried, and shredded fresh basil leaves or chopped fresh dill
2 small red or green chiles, thinly sliced crosswise, optional

12 plum tomatoes (about 2 1/2
pounds)
2 ears corn, husks removed
2 small unpeeled onions,
halved
6 garlic cloves, unpeeled
1 tablespoon vegetable oil
1 teaspoon chili powder
Kosher salt
Four 6-inch corn tortillas
2 cups shredded cooked
chicken (from rotisserie
chicken or leftover roast
chicken, or two 6-ounce
packages roasted chicken)
One 14- or 14 1/2-ounce can
chicken broth or 1 3/4 cups
Chicken Stock (page 32)
2 tablespoons fresh lime juice
Freshly milled black pepper
1 ounce sharp Cheddar cheese,
grated (about 1/4 cup)
2 tablespoons rinsed, dried,
and chopped fresh cilantro

Charred Tomato, Chicken, and Tortilla Soup

MAKES 4 SERVINGS

This is a robust chicken vegetable soup with great depth of flavor, which comes not only from its ingredients, but from the way they're cooked. The charring of the vegetables in the oven concentrates their natural sugars and adds smokiness. The thickening of the soup with a toasted tortilla, a classic Mexican technique, contributes a subtle corn flavor. Preparation-wise, this soup is a breeze. The vegetables, the tortillas, and all the parts of the base are thrown into the oven together and then just pureed, bulked up with cooked chicken, and finished with lime juice. Serve with Roasted Vegetables (page 35) and a tossed green salad.

1. Preheat the broiler to high. Arrange the tomatoes, corn, onions, and garlic in one layer on a rimmed baking sheet and broil 4 inches from the heat, turning occasionally, until they are charred on the outside, about 10 minutes for the corn and garlic and about 18 minutes for the tomatoes and onions. Transfer the vegetables to a cutting board as they finish cooking and let them cool.

2. Combine the oil with the chili powder and 1/4 teaspoon salt and brush over one side of each tortilla. Cut 3 of the tortillas in half and then into 1/4-inch strips. Arrange the strips and the whole tortilla in one layer on a rimmed baking sheet and place on the bottom shelf of the oven while the vegetables are under the broiler. If the tortillas are not crisp when the vegetables are charred, reduce the oven to 400°F and bake them for 6 to 7 minutes, until they are crisp.

3. Peel the tomatoes, onions, and garlic and transfer in batches to a blender or food processor to puree. Crumble the whole tortilla and add it to the blender with one of the batches. Cut the corn kernels from the cobs.

4. Transfer the pureed vegetables from the blender to a large saucepan; stir in the chicken, broth, and corn. Bring the soup to a boil over high heat; stir in the lime juice and salt and pepper to taste. Ladle into bowls and top each portion with some of the Cheddar, cilantro, and tortilla strips.

EVEN if you are going to serve a soup cold it is best to puree it while it is hot; it will come out much smoother. The best tool for this job is the blender. Years ago when the food processor was developed I retired my blender, thinking that the food processor could do everything a blender could and better. I was wrong. A food processor never gives the same silky texture to a soup or pureed dish that a blender does. But you must be careful or you will end up wearing it. You should fill the blender only about one-third full with hot liquid and then leave the lid very slightly ajar to allow the heat to escape. Cover the top of the blender with a kitchen towel and let it rip for quite a while to make sure you get that creamy texture. Then, if you want, you can pass the soup through a strainer to get rid of any residual tiny lumps.

BLENDING
HOT SOUPS

7 scallions (white and light
    green parts)
3 slices fresh ginger (each the
    size of a quarter)
Three 14- or 14 1/2-ounce cans
    chicken broth or 5 1/4 cups
    Chicken Stock (page 32)
1/2 cup rice wine, sake, or dry
    sherry
1 tablespoon vegetable oil
8 ounces medium fresh
    shiitake mushrooms, stems
    discarded, caps quartered
1 pound boneless, skinless
    chicken breasts, cut into
    1/2-inch cubes
1 small head Napa cabbage
    (about 3/4 pound), coarsely
    shredded
8 ounces firm tofu, cut into
    1/2-inch cubes
1 cup cooked rice or Simple
    Boiled Rice (page 40, add
    prep time)
3 tablespoons soy sauce
1 teaspoon toasted sesame oil
1/3 pound sugar snap peas,
    trimmed and sliced
    diagonally into thirds
Kosher salt and freshly milled
    black pepper

Chinese Chicken Soup

MAKES 6 SERVINGS

When you combine good old chicken broth with healing ginger, you end up with a soup that is truly restorative. Bulked up with chicken, shiitake mushrooms, rice, and vegetables, this dish is filling enough for dinner. Round it out with a tossed green salad. You'll feel like a new person.

1. Smash 3 of the scallions and the ginger lightly with the side of a knife and combine with the chicken broth and wine in a large saucepan; bring to a boil over high heat. Reduce the heat to low and simmer for 15 minutes. Thinly slice the remaining 4 scallions (about 1/2 cup) and set aside.

2. Meanwhile, heat the oil in a large skillet over high heat until hot; reduce the heat to medium, add the mushrooms, and sauté for 5 minutes or until just tender.

3. Remove the scallions and ginger from the broth with a slotted spoon and discard. Add the chicken to the broth and simmer gently for about 5 minutes or until the chicken is almost cooked through. Stir in the cabbage, tofu, rice, cooked mushrooms, soy sauce, and sesame oil and cook until the cabbage has wilted, about 1 minute. Stir in the sugar snap peas, add salt and pepper to taste, and simmer 30 seconds. Serve immediately, sprinkled with the reserved sliced scallions.

Smashed Potato, Leek, and Cabbage Soup
with Corned Beef

Hands-on time:
15 minutes

Total preparation time:
1 hour

MAKES 4 SERVINGS

Potato and leek soup is a classic, but making it requires a lot of fuss. By the time you've finished peeling and pureeing all the potatoes you're ready for bed. This recipe saves time because the potatoes aren't mashed, they're smashed, meaning they're mashed with their skins on. (Assure your family and friends that the resulting texture isn't lumpy; it's rustic). In my quest to turn this soup into a one-dish meal, I reached for corned beef, which you can buy already cooked and sliced. Prosciutto or kielbasa would be great, too. Serve with crusty bread.

3 medium leeks (white and light green parts)
2 tablespoons unsalted butter
1 1/2 pounds baking potatoes
1/2 pound thinly sliced cooked corned beef
4 cups canned chicken broth or Chicken Stock (page 32)
4 cups shredded napa cabbage
2 teaspoons caraway seeds
Kosher salt and freshly milled black pepper

1. Quarter the leeks lengthwise and cut into 1/2-inch lengths. Soak in several changes of water, lifting the leeks out of the water to let any sand sink to the bottom of the bowl; drain well. Melt the butter in a large saucepan over medium-low heat. Add the leeks and cook, stirring occasionally, until softened, about 8 minutes.

2. While the leeks are cooking, peel the potatoes and cut into 1-inch chunks and cut corned beef into strips. Add the broth and potatoes and bring the soup to a boil over high heat; reduce the heat to low and simmer for 15 minutes or until the potatoes are tender. Remove the pan from the heat and, using a potato masher or a large spoon or fork, mash the mixture until the soup has a chunky texture.

3. Return the pan to the stove; add the cabbage, corned beef, and caraway seeds, and bring the mixture to a simmer over low heat. Simmer until the cabbage is just tender, about 5 minutes. Taste and add salt and pepper, if desired.

Hands-on time:
35 minutes

Total preparation time:
45 minutes

2 tablespoons extra virgin
olive oil
10 ounces chorizo or andouille
sausage, sliced
1 medium onion, sliced (about
1 cup)
1 medium head cauliflower
(about 2 pounds)
1 small Yukon gold potato
(about 4 ounces)
4 cups canned chicken broth
or Chicken Stock (page 32)
1 bunch mustard greens, kale,
or spinach, or a mixture,
tough stems discarded,
rinsed, dried, and thinly
sliced
3 tablespoons fresh lemon
juice
Kosher salt and freshly milled
black pepper
Paprika, preferably smoked
(see pages 183 and 347), for
garnish
Grilled or broiled slices of
homemade-style bread,
rubbed with a cut garlic
clove, optional

Creamy Cauliflower Soup
with Chorizo and Greens

MAKES 6 SERVINGS

This is a very substantial and satisfying soup. Thickened by pureed
cauliflower and potato, it is luxuriously creamy without any cream.
The sausage, greens, and paprika give it heat, and the cauliflower
florets give it crunch. Serve this soup with Garlic Bread (page 40)
and a nice green salad, and you've got a meal in a bowl.

1. Heat the oil in a large saucepan over high heat until hot. Reduce the
heat to medium, add the chorizo, and cook, stirring occasionally, until the
pieces are lightly browned on both sides, about 5 minutes. Transfer the
chorizo with a slotted spoon to a plate. Add the onion to the pan and
cook, stirring occasionally, until softened, about 5 minutes.

2. Meanwhile, cut 2 cups of small florets from the cauliflower and chop
the rest. Peel and thinly slice the potato. When the onion has softened,
add the chicken broth, chopped cauliflower, and potato to the saucepan;
bring the mixture to a boil over high heat. Reduce the heat to low and
simmer for about 8 minutes or until the cauliflower and potato are very
tender. Transfer to a blender in three or four small batches and puree until
very smooth.

3. Measure the pureed soup and return it to the saucepan. Add water, if
necessary, to make 7 cups. Stir in the reserved cauliflower florets and
simmer for 4 minutes or until they are almost tender. If you are using
mustard greens or kale, add them to the soup with the florets. When the
florets are just tender, stir in the chorizo and lemon juice; add salt and
pepper to taste. If using spinach, stir it in with the chorizo. Ladle the soup
into bowls; sprinkle each with some paprika and serve with garlic bread, if
desired.

DEPENDING on where you live in this country, you will find one of two basic kinds of chorizo—Spanish or Mexican. If you live in the West or Southwest, it will most likely be Mexican; if you live in any other part of the country it will most likely be Spanish. What is the difference?

In Spanish the word *chorizo* means sausage and refers to a variety of dry cured sausages that have been produced in Spain since Roman times and possibly before. Spanish chorizo is usually made from ground pork, but it can also be prepared from beef and other meats. It is flavored with garlic, salt, hot or sweet paprika, and other spices and herbs; cured; and sometimes smoked. It needs to be heated only enough to cook the outer casing and warm the interior. Until recently the only kind of Spanish-style chorizo you could find in this country was domestically produced; finally a few years ago the government allowed the importation of chorizo from Spain. The Portuguese have their own version, called *chouriço,* and if you are lucky enough to live near a Portuguese neighborhood you will find all sorts of delicious sausages in the supermarket.

Mexican chorizo is fresh sausage prepared with ground meat (usually pork), fat, ancho or *pasilla* chiles, pure chile powder, cumin, and sometimes a bit of vinegar and tequila. The sausage is sold either in links or in bulk and must be cooked completely before serving. I have not yet met a chorizo I didn't like. They are wonderful as the main ingredient but equally important in a supporting role, giving depth of flavor to many dishes, much the way bacon, ham, or pancetta does. You should do a taste test to find your favorite style and brand.

2 tablespoons extra virgin
  olive oil
1 medium onion, finely
  chopped (about 1 cup)
4 cups canned chicken broth
  or Chicken Stock (page 32)
One 1-pound bag split peas,
  rinsed and picked over
2 smoked ham hocks
8 ounces ham steak, quartered
2 medium carrots, sliced
2 celery stalks, sliced
2 cups stone-ground cornmeal,
  preferably white (see
  Sources, page 346)
Kosher salt
1 teaspoon sugar
2 tablespoons vegetable oil
Freshly milled black pepper
1/4 cup dry sherry or Madeira
Softened butter for spreading
  on the Johnny Cakes,
  optional

Split-Pea Soup
with Ham and Johnny Cakes

MAKES 6 SERVINGS

Split pea soup with ham hocks is my definition of comfort food. Add Johnny Cakes and it instantly becomes a comfort *meal*. Johnny Cakes are cornmeal cakes, usually (and best) made from white stone-ground cornmeal. They've been around since Yankee Doodle was sniping at the redcoats and were reportedly George Washington's breakfast staple. (You can find the cornmeal in many supermarkets—or see Sources, page 346.) New Englanders love to argue about whether Johnny Cakes should be thick or thin, crispy or soft, sweet or savory. My Great Aunt Dee was a born and bred Rhode Islander and I make them the way she made them: crispy on the outside and creamy on the inside, spread with butter. They are the perfect accompaniment to this smoky hearty soup. Serve with Cole Slaw (page 38).

1. Heat the olive oil in a large skillet over high heat until hot. Reduce the heat to medium; add the onion, and cook, stirring occasionally, until softened, about 5 minutes. Add 4 cups water, the broth, peas, ham hocks, ham, carrots, and celery. Bring the soup to a boil over high heat; reduce the heat to low and simmer for 40 to 50 minutes or until the peas are very tender.

2. Meanwhile, make the Johnny Cakes. Preheat the oven to 200°F. Bring 2 cups of water to a boil. Stir together the cornmeal, 1 1/2 teaspoons salt, and the sugar in a large bowl; stir in the boiling water and mix well. Heat 1 tablespoon vegetable oil in a large nonstick skillet or griddle over high heat. Reduce the heat to medium and working in batches, drop slightly heaping tablespoonfuls of the cornmeal mixture onto the heated pan. Press down slightly. Leave the cakes for 6 minutes, then turn them and cook an additional 6 minutes. Transfer the Johnny Cakes to a rimmed baking sheet and keep warm in the oven. Repeat the procedure with the remaining oil and batter. You should end up with about 24 Johnny Cakes.

3. Remove the ham hocks and ham pieces; let cool until they can be handled. Shred or cube the meat into small pieces; set aside. Discard the bones. Working in batches, transfer half the soup to a food processor or blender and blend until very smooth. Return the pureed soup and the ham to the saucepan and add salt and pepper to taste. Heat until hot.

4. Stir in the sherry and ladle the soup into bowls. Serve each portion with some of the Johnny Cakes. (Split the Johnny Cakes horizontally and spread with butter, if desired.)

2 ounces Parmigiano-Reggiano
cheese, finely grated (about
2/3 cup; see grating
information, page 10)

3/4 pound ground veal, turkey,
or lean ground beef

3 small onions, finely chopped
(about 1 1/2 cups)

1/2 cup fresh bread crumbs
from Bread Crumbs Four
Ways (page 23)

1/3 cup rinsed, dried, and
chopped fresh flat-leaf
parsley

1 large egg, lightly beaten

Kosher salt and freshly milled
black pepper

4 tablespoons extra virgin
olive oil

2 garlic cloves, minced (about
2 teaspoons)

8 cups packed, coarsely
chopped escarole, rinsed
and dried

Three 14- or 14 1/2-ounce cans
chicken broth or 5 1/4 cups
Chicken Stock (page 32)

One 19-ounce can white beans
such as cannellini, navy, or
Great Northern, drained
and rinsed

Escarole and White Bean Soup
with Large Meatballs

MAKES 4 SERVINGS

This is an adaptation of a classic Italian "wedding" soup. The traditional recipe calls for tiny little meatballs. Mine are larger; it makes this soup less labor-intensive. You can substitute spinach for the escarole and leftover cooked rice or noodles for the beans. Serve with Garlic Bread (page 40) and a tossed green salad.

1. Set aside 4 tablespoons of cheese. Combine the remaining cheese, the ground meat, 1/4 cup of the onions, the bread crumbs, parsley, egg, 3/4 teaspoon salt, and 1/4 teaspoon pepper in a medium bowl. Shape the mixture into 16 golf-ball-size meatballs.

2. Heat 2 tablespoons of the oil in a large, heavy saucepan over high heat until hot; reduce the heat to medium, add the meatballs, and brown them, turning until they are just firm to the touch and browned lightly, about 10 minutes. Transfer the meatballs with a slotted spoon to a plate.

3. Add the remaining oil and onions to the saucepan, and cook, stirring occasionally, until softened, about 5 minutes. Add the garlic and cook 1 minute. Add the escarole, broth, beans, and meatballs to the saucepan; bring to a boil and simmer until the meatballs are just cooked through, about 5 minutes. Add salt and pepper to taste. Divide the soup among 4 bowls; garnish each with 1 tablespoon of the reserved cheese.

Seared Beef in Autumn Broth
with Wasabi Cream

MAKES 4 SERVINGS

Hands-on time:
15 minutes

Total preparation time:
33 minutes

This dish began as a variation on a French recipe called *boeuf à la ficelle* (literally "beef on a string"), which requires the cook to tie a string around some filet mignon and lower it into a pot of barely simmering broth. I tried it and was stunned by its blandness. It struck me as a scandalous waste of a very expensive cut of meat, and I was ready to junk the whole idea. Then Joanne, my collaborator on this book, noted that though the meat was ruined, the broth was really delicious. So we switched to flank steak (which is much more affordable than filet mignon) and seared it separately. The result turned out to be a great cold-weather dish. Serve with crusty bread and Cole Slaw (page 38).

1. Halve the leek lengthwise and cut into 1/2-inch lengths. Soak according to step 1 on page 53. In a large saucepan, combine the leek with the broth, carrots, parsnips, turnips, garlic, thyme, and bay leaf. Bring to a boil over high heat; reduce the heat to low and simmer until the vegetables are tender, 15 to 18 minutes.

2. Meanwhile, heat the oil in a large skillet over high heat until hot. Reduce the heat to medium-high and add the beef seasoned with salt and pepper. Sauté until well browned on both sides and medium-rare in the center, 8 to 10 minutes total. Remove the beef to a plate; cover loosely with aluminum foil and let rest 5 minutes, then slice thinly against the grain.

3. Stir together the sour cream, any juices from the beef plate, and the wasabi; add salt and pepper to taste. Discard the thyme sprig and bay leaf; divide the vegetables and broth among 4 soup bowls. Arrange one-fourth of the beef in the center of each bowl and top each portion with a spoonful of the wasabi cream.

1 medium leek (white part only)
6 cups canned chicken broth or Chicken Stock (page 32)
2 medium carrots (about 6 ounces), peeled and sliced 1/2 inch thick
2 medium parsnips (about 10 ounces), peeled and sliced 1/2 inch thick
2 small turnips (about 8 ounces), peeled, quartered, and sliced 1/2 inch thick
2 garlic cloves, sliced (about 2 teaspoons)
1 sprig rinsed and dried fresh thyme or 1 teaspoon dried
1 Turkish bay leaf
2 teaspoons extra virgin olive oil
1 pound beef flank steak
Kosher salt and freshly milled black pepper
1/3 cup sour cream or crème fraîche
1 teaspoon prepared wasabi

Kosher salt

2 tablespoons vegetable oil

4 medium shallots, thinly
   sliced (about 1/2 cup)

Three 1/8-inch-thick slices
   ginger

1 to 1 1/2 tablespoons
   chopped fresh serrano
   chiles

3 cups canned low-sodium
   beef broth

3 cups canned chicken broth
   or Chicken Stock (page 32)

2 star anise

8 ounces rice vermicelli or
   capellini

3/4 pound flank steak, sliced
   very thin at an angle

2 tablespoons Asian fish sauce

2 tablespoons fresh lime juice

Accompaniments: Lime
   wedges, 1 1/2 cups bean
   sprouts, 1/4 cup each
   rinsed, dried, and shredded
   fresh basil, mint, and
   cilantro, and 3 serrano
   chiles, sliced thin

Vietnamese-style Beef and Noodle Soup

MAKES 4 SERVINGS

My brother Peter visited Vietnam in the summer of 1993, shortly after it reopened to tourism. He was knocked out not only by the country's lush physical beauty, but also by its cuisine. Back in New York, he took me to a little noodle shop in Chinatown to taste the famous Vietnamese noodle soup called *pho* (pronounced *fuh*). The broth is beef-based, long-simmered, and complex. The soup is finished with noodles and many delicious garnishes. My version, being a quick one, is nowhere near as deep as the original, but good old Pete—that paragon of objectivity—loved it. Serve with Butter-steamed Broccoli with Soy (page 296) or Asian Spiced Roasted Baby Carrots (page 292).

1. Bring a large pot of salted water to a boil over high heat. Meanwhile, heat the oil in a large saucepan over high heat until hot. Reduce the heat to medium; add the shallots, ginger, and chopped chiles and sauté, stirring occasionally, until the shallots are golden, 7 to 8 minutes. Add the broths and star anise and simmer for 10 minutes, uncovered.

2. Meanwhile, add the vermicelli to the pot of boiling water and cook it for 5 minutes. Drain the vermicelli and divide it among 4 bowls.

3. Remove and discard the shallots, ginger, chiles, and star anise from the broth using a slotted spoon. Add the meat to the simmering broth, return the mixture to a boil, and cook the meat 1 minute.

4. Transfer one-fourth of the meat to each bowl using a slotted spoon. Stir the fish sauce, lime juice, and salt to taste into the broth. Ladle the hot broth over each bowl of noodles and meat. Serve with bowls of the accompaniments on the side.

WHENEVER a recipe calls for raw meat to be sliced very thin I throw the piece of meat into the freezer for twenty to thirty minutes if I have the time; then it becomes just hard enough to be easy to slice. A really sharp knife helps, too.

SLICING
MEAT
THIN

Entrée
Salads

Hands-on time:
20 minutes

Total preparation time:
35 minutes plus
15 to 20 minutes
cooling time

3 large eggs

4 small boiling potatoes such
as red bliss (5 to 6 ounces
each), scrubbed

Kosher salt

1 cup fresh or frozen peas

1 pound skinless salmon fillet

2 tablespoons fresh lemon
juice

1 tablespoon extra virgin olive
oil

Freshly milled black pepper

1/4 cup low-fat sour cream

1/4 cup low-fat mayonnaise

2 tablespoons rinsed, dried,
and chopped fresh dill

1 tablespoon Dijon mustard

1/4 pound smoked salmon, cut
into strips

1 small head Boston or butter
lettuce, rinsed and dried

Fresh and Smoked Salmon Salad

MAKES 4 SERVINGS

I think smoked salmon is a wonderful secret ingredient; it adds not only a unique salmon taste but also an appealing smokiness, and a little goes a long way. This is my favorite way to cook fresh salmon on a weeknight, drizzled with lemon juice and olive oil and baked in a hot oven. You could make just the baked salmon part of this recipe and then top it with any number of the quick sauces at the back of the book, such as Horseradish (page 316), Parsley Pesto (page 320), Quick Herb (page 312), Sautéed Cherry Tomato (page 319), Mediterranean Salsa Verde (page 317), or Sesame Miso (page 323). But if you are a salmon lover, you will be happy to find both fresh and smoked salmon in this salad, combined with peas and dill, two salmon-friendly ingredients.

1. Preheat the oven to 400°F. Place the eggs in a medium saucepan with enough cold water to cover by 1 inch. Bring to a boil over high heat. Remove from the heat, cover, and set aside for 15 minutes. Transfer the eggs to a bowl of half ice and half water. Cool completely, then peel under cold running water and cut in half lengthwise.

2. While the eggs are cooking, cover the potatoes with salted cold water in another saucepan. Bring the water to a boil over high heat; reduce the heat to low and simmer the potatoes until they are just tender, 15 to 18 minutes. Remove them from the water and set aside to cool. Cut them into wedges. If using fresh peas, cook them in boiling salted water until tender, 2 to 5 minutes depending on their maturity; drain well. If using frozen peas, thaw them and drain well.

3. Meanwhile, arrange the salmon in a shallow baking dish; drizzle it with 1 tablespoon of the lemon juice, the oil, 1/4 teaspoon salt, and 1/8 teaspoon pepper. Bake the salmon in the center of the oven for 10 to 12 minutes or until just cooked through. Set aside to cool; then flake into large chunks.

4. Whisk together the sour cream, mayonnaise, dill, mustard, remaining tablespoon of lemon juice, and salt and pepper to taste for the dressing. When the ingredients have cooled to room temperature, gently toss the chunked salmon, the peas, and smoked salmon with two-thirds of the dressing. Line 4 plates with the lettuce and top with a mound of the salmon salad. Arrange the eggs and the potatoes around the mound and drizzle with a little of the remaining dressing.

*1/2 pound small red potatoes,
scrubbed and halved or
quartered*
Kosher salt
*1/2 pound green beans,
trimmed*
4 large eggs
*1 recipe Italian Tuna Sauce
(page 315)*
*2 tablespoons extra virgin
olive oil*
*1 pound medium shrimp,
shelled and deveined*
Freshly milled black pepper
*Four 3-ounce plum tomatoes,
cut into wedges*
8 anchovies, optional
*1/2 cup pitted, brine-cured
olives such as kalamata*

Shrimp Niçoise Salad

MAKES 4 SERVINGS

Niçoise salad, fairly well known in America these days, is a specialty from the city of Nice in the south of France. It consists of tuna, tomatoes, blanched string beans, boiled potatoes, hard-cooked eggs, and a vinaigrette dressing. I have adapted it by pureeing the tuna in the sauce and adding shrimp. You're welcome to replace the shrimp with the leftover cooked protein of your choice, including turkey, chicken, or ham. A cozy way to serve this salad is to arrange it on a big platter, set it in the center of the table, and invite people to help themselves.

1. Place the potatoes in a large saucepan with salted cold water to cover by 1 inch. Bring to a boil over high heat; reduce the heat to low and simmer until the potatoes are just tender but still hold their shape, 15 to 18 minutes, depending on their size. Transfer the potatoes to a bowl with a slotted spoon. Add the green beans to the same water and boil them for about 3 minutes or until crisp-tender. Transfer them with a slotted spoon to a bowl of ice and water to stop the cooking. Drain them well in a colander.

2. While the potatoes are cooking, place the eggs in a medium saucepan with enough cold water to cover by 1 inch. Bring just to a boil over high heat. Remove from the heat, cover, and set aside for 15 minutes. Transfer the eggs to a bowl of half ice and half water. Cool completely, then peel under cold running water and quarter lengthwise. Prepare the Italian Tuna Sauce.

3. Heat the oil in a large skillet over high heat until hot; reduce the heat to medium-high, add the shrimp, and sauté for 3 minutes, or until just cooked through. Season them with salt and pepper to taste.

4. To serve, arrange the potatoes, green beans, shrimp, tomatoes, eggs, anchovies if using, and olives on each of 4 plates; drizzle each salad with some of the sauce.

1/4 cup plus 3 tablespoons
   extra virgin olive oil
3 tablespoons fresh lemon
   juice
Kosher salt and freshly milled
   black pepper
1 1/4 pounds cleaned calamari
   (squid)
1 small garlic clove, minced
   (about 3/4 teaspoon)
1/2 pound small red potatoes,
   scrubbed and cut into
   3/4-inch chunks
1 large fennel bulb with
   fronds (about 1 1/4 pounds)
One 14 1/4-ounce can
   chickpeas, rinsed and
   drained

Grilled Calamari Salad

with Fennel, Potatoes, and Chickpeas

MAKES 4 SERVINGS

Calamari (we call it squid in English) is a natural candidate for a weeknight meal because it cooks so quickly. In fact, you *must* cook it quickly. There is this tiny little window of opportunity where you must get it into and out of the pan in a few minutes. Otherwise, you're forced to cook it for an hour in order to tenderize it. Anywhere in between, and you end up chewing on rubber bands. I decided to marinate and grill it to get a nice smoky taste. I've added fennel to the salad because, like calamari, it is a very popular ingredient in the Mediterranean. Fennel has a texture like celery with a faint taste of licorice. If you can't find it or don't like licorice, you can certainly use celery. The potatoes and chickpeas just round out the salad to make it dinner-worthy.

1. Preheat the oven to 450°F. Whisk together 1/4 cup plus 2 tablespoons of the olive oil, the lemon juice, 1 teaspoon salt, and 1/4 teaspoon pepper in a large bowl to make a dressing; set aside. Butterfly the calamari bodies and cut the tentacles in half if they are large. Toss the calamari with 2 tablespoons of the dressing and the garlic in a medium bowl and set aside for 10 minutes.

2. Toss the potatoes with the remaining 1 tablespoon oil and 1/4 teaspoon salt and arrange in one layer on a rimmed baking sheet. Roast on the upper rack of the oven for 20 minutes or until golden.

3. Meanwhile, trim off and discard the stalks from the fennel bulb, saving the fronds for garnish. Rinse the fronds and bulb; thinly slice the bulb and add to the dressing in the bowl along with the chickpeas.

4. Preheat a grill pan over high heat until hot. Drain the calamari. Working in batches, arrange the calamari on the grill pan; weight down with another skillet so the pieces don't curl. Grill for 20 seconds a side or until grill marks show and the calamari is just cooked through. Transfer the cooked calamari to a cutting board and cut the bodies into 1-inch pieces. Repeat until all the calamari have been cooked.

5. Add the calamari and hot potatoes to the fennel mixture and toss until well coated with dressing. Add salt and pepper to taste; garnish with the reserved fennel fronds and serve warm or at room temperature.

CALAMARI, or squid as it is called in English, is a mollusk related to cuttlefish and octopus. It has ten tentacles and a protective mechanism that releases dark ink into the water when it is in danger. It ranges in size from one inch to eighty feet, but the most common size used for cooking is twelve inches long. Its meat is firm and white with a slightly sweet taste. I recommend that you buy cleaned squid, which is readily available these days. Just make sure that it has no fishy smell and cook it within two days of purchase. Give it a quick rinse before cooking.

CALAMARI

1/2 cup plus 1 1/2 tablespoons
   vegetable oil
1 teaspoon chili powder
3/4 teaspoon ground cumin
Kosher salt
Four 6- or 7-inch corn tortillas
1/2 cup packed, rinsed, and
   dried fresh cilantro leaves
1/4 cup fresh lime juice
1/2 chipotle in adobo sauce,
   finely chopped, plus 1
   tablespoon adobo sauce*
   (see Note)
1 teaspoon sugar
Freshly milled black pepper
1 small head Romaine lettuce,
   rinsed, dried, and torn into
   bite-size pieces (about 4
   cups)
2 cups shredded or cubed
   cooked chicken
1 Hass avocado, cut into cubes
One 14 1/2- or 15-ounce can
   black beans, rinsed and
   drained
3 large plum tomatoes,
   chopped
4 ounces crumbled queso
   fresco or soft goat (about
   1/2 cup) or coarsely grated
   Monterey Jack cheese
   (about 1 cup)

Mexican Chicken Salad

MAKES 4 TO 6 SERVINGS

This is my favorite kind of salad because it has so many
ingredients—and each with a different texture, from the creamy
avocado to the crispy homemade tortilla chips. I have cheated
here by using leftover or rotisserie chicken. It would work just as
well with leftover cooked pork, shrimp, or beef. And if you really
want to speed up the recipe, here's another cheat: Swap store-
bought tortilla chips for the homemade kind.

Note: You can freeze the remaining chipotles in an ice cube tray (preferably metal, because plastic might pick up the heat from the chiles). Put
one chipotle into each slot with a little sauce, let them freeze completely,
then pop out the cubes and put them into a resealable plastic bag.

1. Preheat the oven to 400°F. Stir together 1 1/2 tablespoons of the oil,
the chili powder, cumin, and 1/4 teaspoon salt. Brush one side of each
tortilla with the mixture and cut each tortilla into 12 wedges. Arrange the
wedges in one layer on a rimmed baking sheet and bake them for 10 to 12
minutes or until crisp.

2. Puree the remaining 1/2 cup oil, the cilantro, lime juice, chipotle and
adobo sauce, and sugar in a blender; add salt and pepper to taste. Transfer
the cilantro dressing to a large bowl. Add the romaine, chicken, avocado,
black beans, tomatoes, and cheese to the cilantro dressing and toss well.
Divide the mixture among 4 bowls; top each with some of the tortilla
chips.

Smoked Chicken or Turkey Salad

Hands-on time:
20 minutes

Total preparation time:
25 minutes

MAKES 4 SERVINGS

This is an adaptation of a smoked chicken salad recipe sent to me by Mary Collette List of Kalamazoo, Michigan—a frequent visitor to my Web site—who tasted it for the first time at a friend's potluck dinner and then went home and figured it out. I added the option of using smoked turkey instead of smoked chicken. (Smoked turkey is more readily available.) I also decided to make the pecans spicy by tossing them in my Creole Spice Mix and then toasting them. Overall, a lot of nice textures and flavors come together here—and most of the ingredients are already prepared at the supermarket.

1 cup pecan halves
2 tablespoons unsalted butter, melted
2 teaspoons packaged Creole or Cajun spice mix or Creole Spice Mix (page 20, add prep time)
1/3 cup mayonnaise
1 teaspoon grated lemon zest
2 tablespoons fresh lemon juice
Kosher salt and freshly milled black pepper
1 pound fully cooked, boneless smoked chicken or turkey
1/2 cup small pimiento-stuffed olives, drained
4 cups mesclun
1/4 cup bottled vinaigrette or All-Purpose Vinaigrette (page 28, add prep time)

1. Preheat the oven to 300°F. Toss the pecans, butter, and Creole Spice Mix until the nuts are uniformly coated with the spices. Spread them on a rimmed baking sheet and toast them in the oven until they are crisp, 12 to 15 minutes, stirring occasionally. Transfer them to a plate to cool for 5 minutes.

2. Meanwhile, combine the mayonnaise, lemon zest, lemon juice, 1/4 teaspoon salt, and 1/8 teaspoon pepper in a large bowl. Remove and discard the skin from the chicken, if there is any, and cut the meat into 3/4-inch cubes. Toss the chicken, pecans, and olives with the mayonnaise mixture until completely coated.

3. To serve, toss the mesclun with the vinaigrette and divide among 4 chilled serving plates. Place the turkey salad on the mesclun and serve.

Hands-on time:
15 minutes

Total preparation time:
40 minutes

1 1/2 cups buttermilk
Kosher salt and freshly milled
*   black pepper*
1 pound thin-sliced chicken
*   breast cutlets*
4 ears corn, husks removed
1/3 cup low-fat mayonnaise
2 tablespoons rinsed, dried,
*   and chopped fresh mixed*
*   herbs (tarragon, chives,*
*   parsley)*
1/2 garlic clove, minced (about
*   1/2 teaspoon)*
2 beefsteak tomatoes, sliced
*   1/3 inch thick*
1/4 cup vegetable oil
1 cup dried bread crumbs from
*   Bread Crumbs Four Ways*
*   (page 23) or packaged*
6 cups loosely packed arugula
*   or your favorite lettuce,*
*   rinsed, dried, and torn into*
*   bite-size pieces*

Fried Chicken Salad

MAKES 4 SERVINGS

The chicken in this salad isn't really fried. It's soaked in buttermilk, breaded, and sautéed. It is, however, evocative of fried chicken. It's juicy. It's crispy. It's delicious—and much less caloric than actual fried chicken. I learned about the tenderizing effects of buttermilk from my Southern viewers, who soak their chicken in buttermilk before dusting it in flour and deep frying it. This recipe calls for boneless, skinless white meat chicken—which cooks up quickly but is difficult to keep moist. The buttermilk soak saves the day. The salad is filled out with fresh corn and tomatoes. It's nice and summery.

1. Combine 1 cup of the buttermilk, 1 teaspoon salt, and 1/4 teaspoon pepper in a medium bowl. Add the chicken and let marinate in the refrigerator for 20 minutes while you prepare the rest of the ingredients.

2. Preheat the oven to 250°F. Bring 2 quarts of salted water to a boil in a large kettle over high heat. Add the corn; return the water to a boil. Remove the corn immediately and set on a plate to cool slightly. Cut the kernels from the cobs.

3. Meanwhile, whisk together the remaining 1/2 cup buttermilk, the mayonnaise, herbs, and garlic; add salt and pepper to taste and set aside. Sprinkle the tomatoes on both sides with some salt and let drain on a rack.

4. Heat half the oil in a large skillet over high heat until hot; reduce the heat to medium-low. Place the bread crumbs on a pie plate; remove half the chicken from the buttermilk and dip it in the bread crumbs to coat well. Add to the skillet and cook until golden on both sides and just cooked through, 7 to 8 minutes. Transfer to a rimmed baking sheet and keep warm in oven. Repeat with remaining chicken and bread crumbs. Slice the chicken into 1/2-inch strips.

5. Arrange a bed of arugula on each of 4 plates; top with slices of tomato and a mound of chicken. Sprinkle with the corn and drizzle with the dressing.

CONTRARY to what you might think, buttermilk is very low in fat and calories. Originally, it was the liquid left over from the butter-making process, but these days it is a cultured product made by adding a bacteria to low- or nonfat milk. It is almost as thick as cream and has a taste reminiscent of yogurts. Buttermilk can be consumed straight up (it is an acquired taste), but it is especially useful in baking and cooking. It makes a good marinade for chicken because it is a tenderizer. Buttermilk keeps about two weeks in the fridge, but if you don't think you will use it up in that time you have a few alternatives. You can make your own for baking purposes by combining 1 cup milk with 1 tablespoon vinegar or lemon juice and letting the mixture stand for 10 minutes. You can also purchase buttermilk powder, which has a shelf life, unopened, of one year and lasts even longer when stored in the fridge. To use it in a recipe you can reconstitute it either by combining 1 cup of water with 4 tablespoons of the powder, or by adding the dry powder to the dry ingredients and the water to the wet ingredients.

WHAT
IS
BUTTERMILK?

Hands-on time:
20 minutes

Total preparation time:
20 minutes

Kosher salt

1 recipe Sesame Miso Sauce
(page 323)

1/2 pound sugar snap peas

8 ounces soba noodles
(Japanese buckwheat
noodles)

2 cups shredded or cubed
cooked chicken

2 medium carrots, peeled and
shredded, preferably using
the grating disk of a food
processor (about 1 1/4 cups)

One 8-ounce can sliced water
chestnuts, rinsed and
drained

1/2 cup unsalted roasted
peanuts

4 scallions (white and light
green parts), thinly sliced
(about 1/2 cup)

Freshly milled black pepper

Soba Noodle and Chicken Salad

MAKES 6 SERVINGS

Soba, or Japanese buckwheat noodles, are increasingly showing
up in the "international" aisle of many supermarkets. They cook
quicker than wheat pasta and have a uniquely earthy taste of
their own. You can substitute spaghetti for the soba, but make
sure you rinse it after it is cooked to get rid of the excess starch.
(Otherwise your salad will become quite gluey.) I was introduced
to the delights of this dish's miso sesame dressing in a fish dish
that ran in *Gourmet* several years ago. It is creamier and more
substantial than a regular sesame sauce, and I always figured it
could top off any number of relatively mild dishes, and not just
fish. My husband, no fan of soy-based products other than soy
sauce, loved this salad.

1. Bring a large pot of salted water to a boil over high heat. Make the
Sesame Miso Sauce.

2. Add the sugar snap peas to the boiling water and cook for 30 seconds.
Remove them with a slotted spoon and transfer them to a bowl of ice
water to stop the cooking. Drain them and pat them dry.

3. Add the noodles to the same pot of boiling salted water and cook them
until they are just tender, about 5 minutes. Drain noodles in a colander;
rinse under cold water to stop the cooking, then drain well.

4. Combine the Sesame Miso Sauce, peas, noodles, chicken, carrots, water
chestnuts, peanuts, and scallions; toss well. Add salt and pepper to taste.

Turkey Club Salad

Hands-on time:
25 minutes

Total preparation time:
30 minutes

MAKES 6 SERVINGS

This salad is composed of all the elements found in the classic turkey club sandwich, except that the bread has been turned into croutons and the mayonnaise into herb sauce. The bacon is cooked my favorite way—on a rack in the oven. The bacon turns out less greasy, and you end up making less of a mess than if you'd cooked it in a skillet on top of the stove.

1. Preheat the oven to 400°F. Trim off and discard the bread crusts. Cut the bread into 1/2-inch cubes; toss them with the oil, 1/4 teaspoon salt, and 1/4 teaspoon pepper and arrange them on a baking pan. Arrange the bacon on a rack on a baking pan. Put the bacon and croutons on separate shelves in the oven and bake 10 minutes. Switch shelves; bake the croutons 4 to 5 minutes longer or until crisp and browned on the edges, and the bacon until crisp, about 10 minutes longer. Set both aside to cool to room temperature.

2. Meanwhile, prepare the Quick Herb Sauce in a large bowl and add the lettuce, turkey, and tomatoes. When the bacon and croutons have cooled, crumble the bacon and add it to the salad along with the croutons. Toss until combined.

Six 1/2-inch-thick slices country bread
2 tablespoons extra virgin olive oil
Kosher salt and freshly milled black pepper
8 ounces bacon (8 to 9 slices)
3/4 cup Quick Herb Sauce (page 312)
8 cups shredded romaine lettuce
1 pound cooked turkey, cut into 1/2-inch cubes (about 3 cups)
1 cup cherry or grape tomatoes, halved lengthwise

3/4 pound small (about 1 1/4
  inches) red potatoes,
  scrubbed and quartered
Kosher salt
2 tablespoons sherry vinegar
2 teaspoons Dijon mustard
1/4 cup heavy cream
1 garlic clove, minced (about 1
  teaspoon)
Freshly milled black pepper
1/4 cup extra virgin olive oil
Two 15 1/2-ounce cans black-
  eyed peas, rinsed and
  drained
1 pound cooked deli or
  leftover ham, cut into
  1/2-inch cubes
3 medium stalks celery, split
  lengthwise, then sliced
  crosswise
One 5-ounce bag rinsed baby
  spinach
2 cups packaged croutons or
  from Croutons Four Ways
  (page 26, add prep time)

Ham, Potato, and Black-eyed Pea Salad
with Creamy Garlic Dressing

MAKES 4 SERVINGS

Here's where the American South (ham and black-eyed peas)
meets the classical French (creamy garlic dressing). In truth,
anything tossed in this dressing tastes good. Feel free to put it on
sautéed shrimp, roast chicken, or grilled vegetables. (It was
adapted from a *Gourmet* recipe for Grilled Quail Salad.) The only
ingredients you need to cook here are the potatoes. The rest are
waiting for you at the supermarket, already cooked or prepared.
If you don't want to make croutons, you can substitute quick
toasts made by running some slices of country bread under the
broiler.

1. Place the potatoes in a large saucepan with cold salted water to cover
by 1 inch and bring the water to a boil. Simmer the potatoes for 15 to 18
minutes, or until they are just tender. Drain.

2. Meanwhile, whisk together 1 tablespoon of the vinegar and 1 teaspoon
of the mustard in a medium bowl. Add the hot potatoes and toss until
well coated; set aside.

3. Combine the remaining vinegar and mustard with the cream, garlic, 1/4
teaspoon salt, and 1/8 teaspoon pepper in a large bowl. Gradually whisk
in the oil to make a dressing. Add the potatoes, black-eyed peas, ham,
celery, and salt and pepper to taste; toss to combine. Add the spinach and
croutons, toss again, and serve.

Kielbasa and Celery Root Salad
with Horseradish Sauce

Hands-on time:
30 minutes

Total preparation time:
40 minutes

MAKES 4 SERVINGS

When I came up with the idea for this salad I was focusing on the celery root part of it. Celery root, also known as celery knob or celeriac, is the thickened aromatic root of a variety of celery plant with a dense crunchy texture. In France it is often julienned or shredded and tossed in a mustardy vinaigrette, which was my inspiration for this dish. I decided to start with another sharp flavoring, horseradish, and enhance it with mustard. What goes nIcely with celery, horseradish, and mustard? Some kind of sausage like kielbasa. You could also use knockwurst or bratwurst or any other worthy German or Polish sausage.

*1 pound small red potatoes,
    scrubbed*
Kosher salt
1/4 cup cider vinegar
*1 recipe Horseradish Sauce
    (page 316)*
2 tablespoons Dijon mustard
*1 large celery root (12 ounces),
    peeled and cut into
    matchsticks*
*One 16-ounce package pork,
    beef, or turkey kielbasa*
*One 10-ounce package frozen
    baby lima beans*
*6 scallions (white and light
    green parts), chopped
    (about 3/4 cup)*
*2 tablespoons drained, bottled
    capers and/or 2 tablespoons
    chopped dill pickles,
    drained*
Freshly milled black pepper

1. Place the potatoes in a large saucepan with cold salted water to cover by 3 inches. Bring the water to a boil over high heat; reduce the heat to low and simmer the potatoes until just tender, 15 to 18 minutes. Transfer the potatoes from the pan to a cutting board with a slotted spoon and let them cool slightly. Leave the pot of water on the stove. Then quarter the potatoes and toss them with the vinegar and 1/4 teaspoon salt in a medium bowl.

2. Meanwhile, prepare the Horseradish Sauce. Combine the sauce with the mustard in a large bowl; add the celery root and toss to combine.

3. After removing the potatoes, cut the kielbasa into several sections and add it to the boiling water along with the lima beans. Return to a boil over high heat and cook 5 minutes. Drain the kielbasa and limas in a colander. When the kielbasa is cool enough to handle, slice it crosswise about 1/3 inch thick.

4. Stir the kielbasa, potatoes, limas, scallions, capers, and salt and pepper to taste into the celery root mixture and serve.

Two-Melon, Prosciutto, and Feta Salad

Hands-on time:
15 minutes

Total preparation time:
15 minutes

1 1/2 tablespoons fresh lime
juice
1/2 teaspoon smoked paprika,
sweet or hot (see pages 183
and 347)
Kosher salt and freshly milled
black pepper
5 tablespoons extra virgin
olive oil
1/8 medium watermelon
(about 2 pounds), peeled
and sliced 1/2 inch thick
1/2 medium cantaloupe (about
1 1/2 pounds), peeled and
sliced 1/2 inch thick
6 ounces feta or aged goat
cheese, thinly sliced
4 ounces thinly sliced
prosciutto

MAKES 4 SERVINGS

Melon and prosciutto is such a refreshing summertime appetizer
that I wondered if there was a way to make it entrée-hearty without ruining its essential appeal. I did it by adding watermelon and
feta cheese to the lineup. These two play together beautifully—the
sweet watermelon and the salty feta hand in hand, so to speak. And
the smoked paprika in the dressing (see Sources, page 347) pulls all
the elements together. (If you don't have the time to track down
the smoked paprika, you can substitute regular old sweet paprika
from the supermarket.) This is a summertime dish, perfect for those
warm nights when you don't even want to switch on the stove.

1. Whisk together the lime juice, paprika, 1/4 teaspoon salt, and 1/8
teaspoon pepper. Slowly whisk in the oil.

2. Arrange the melons, cheese, and prosciutto decoratively on a plate and
serve with the dressing.

Antipasto Salad
with Parmigiano-Reggiano Dressing

Hands-on time:
25 minutes

Total preparation time:
25 minutes

MAKES 6 TO 8 SERVINGS

This is the perfect lazy-day summer salad, since you don't have to use the oven. You could buy the blanched broccoli or cauliflower and prepared pasta salad at the salad bar and never even turn on the stovetop. But this salad would be equally good on any night, summer or winter, when you are pressed for time. Feel free to substitute other meats or cheeses for the ones suggested below.

1. Bring a large pot of salted water to a boil. Meanwhile, combine the parsley, oil, Parmigiano-Reggiano, vinegar, and mustard in a blender; puree until the dressing is smooth. Add salt and pepper to taste and set aside.

2. Ladle 1/2 cup of the boiling water over the tomatoes in a small bowl. Set them aside to soak for 10 minutes or until softened; drain and pat dry.

3. Add the broccoli to the boiling water and cook for 2 to 3 minutes or until crisp-tender. Transfer it with a slotted spoon to a bowl of ice water to stop the cooking.

4. Meanwhile, add the pasta to the same water and boil until al dente, 8 to 10 minutes. Drain the pasta and toss immediately with the dressing, broccoli, chickpeas, artichoke hearts, salami, tomatoes, and salt and pepper to taste. Cool slightly, then stir in the cheese and serve.

Kosher salt
1/2 cup packed fresh flat-leaf parsley leaves, rinsed and dried
1/2 cup extra virgin olive oil
1 ounce Parmigiano-Reggiano cheese, freshly grated (about 1/3 cup; see grating information, page 000)
3 tablespoons red wine vinegar
2 teaspoons Dijon mustard
Freshly milled black pepper
1 ounce sun-dried tomatoes, halved crosswise (about 1/2 cup)
2 cups broccoli or cauliflower florets
1/2 pound fusilli or rotini
One 15- or 15 1/2-ounce can chickpeas, rinsed and drained
One 6 1/2-ounce jar marinated artichoke hearts, drained and cut in half
1/4 pound sliced salami, prosciutto di Parma, or soppressata or a mix, cut into bite-size pieces
4 ounces smoked mozzarella, provolone, or Italian fontina, or a mix of these cheeses cut into 1/2-inch cubes

Thai-style Steak Salad
with Spicy Mint Dressing

MAKES 4 SERVINGS

This is a fun summertime meal. I have given instructions for cooking the steak in a skillet, but you could also just throw it on the grill or a grill pan for a little smoky taste. You can either give each person a plate with all the parts to make a lettuce wrap, as I have done here, or set up a platter as part of a buffet table.

1/2 cup freshly squeezed lime juice

1/3 cup rinsed, dried, and finely shredded fresh mint

1 to 2 jalapeños, seeded and thinly sliced crosswise

2 tablespoons soy sauce

3 to 4 teaspoons sugar

1 tablespoon Asian fish sauce

1 garlic clove, minced (about 1 teaspoon)

1 pound boneless sirloin steak, 1 1/2 inches thick

Kosher salt and freshly milled black pepper

1 tablespoon vegetable oil

2 heads Boston lettuce, rinsed and spun dry

2 large carrots, shredded (preferably in a food processor)

1 large red bell pepper, cut into strips

1/4 pound sugar snap peas, blanched in boiling salted water for 30 seconds and drained

1. Whisk together the lime juice, mint, jalapeños, soy sauce, sugar, fish sauce, and garlic until the sugar is dissolved. Let stand while you prepare the rest of the ingredients.

2. Season the steak on both sides with salt and freshly ground pepper. Heat the oil in a medium skillet over high heat until hot; reduce the heat to medium-high and add the steak. Sauté it to your desired doneness, 4 to 5 minutes a side for medium-rare. Transfer the steak to a plate and let it rest for 5 minutes, then cut it across the grain into very thin slices (the thinner the better). Add any juices from the steak plate to the sauce.

3. Arrange the lettuce, carrots, red pepper, and sugar snap peas on each of 4 plates. Divide the steak among the plates and spoon some of the sauce over each portion. Each person should use the lettuce as a wrapper and fill it with some of the meat and accompaniments.

FISH SAUCE is used in Southeast Asian cooking to provide salt and depth of flavor. It is made from fermented anchovies, salt, and water. In Vietnam fish sauce is called *nuoc mam* and in Thailand, *nam pla;* it is used much the same way the Chinese use soy sauce. Even though its aroma is quite overwhelming when you take off the lid, you will find that its intensity dissipates when combined with other ingredients. It can be found in Asian markets and some supermarkets, and I have given a mail-order source at the back of the book (page 346).

WHAT
IS FISH
SAUCE?

The
Substantial
Sandwich

Greek Salad Sandwiches

with Feta Dressing

V

MAKES 4 SERVINGS

4 ounces good-quality feta
cheese, crumbled (about
2/3 cup)
1/4 cup extra virgin olive oil
2 tablespoons mayonnaise
1 teaspoon fresh lemon juice
1 1/2 teaspoons fresh oregano
leaves or 1/2 teaspoon
dried
Kosher salt and freshly milled
black pepper
One 5-ounce package rinsed
baby spinach
4 medium plum tomatoes
(about 12 ounces), halved
and thinly sliced
6-inch piece English cucumber,
thinly sliced (about 1 1/2
cups)
1 cup canned chickpeas, rinsed
and drained
1/2 cup rinsed and dried fresh
mint leaves
1/3 cup pitted, brine-cured
olives such as kalamata
6 peperoncini (Tuscan pickled
peppers), chopped
Four 5- to 6-inch pita rounds,
cut in half

This is a slight twist on a Greek salad. I just put all the elements into a pita pocket and used the feta to make a dressing. If you like Greek salads you will love this more substantial sandwich. Serve with Oven Fries (page 295).

1. Combine the feta, oil, 3 tablespoons water, the mayonnaise, lemon juice, and oregano in a blender or small food processor and blend until smooth. Add salt and pepper to taste.

2. Combine the spinach, tomatoes, cucumber, chickpeas, mint leaves, olives, and peperoncini with the feta dressing. Divide the salad mixture among the 8 pita halves and serve.

Herbed Egg Salad Sandwiches

Hands-on time:
15 minutes

Total preparation time:
35 minutes

V

MAKES 4 SERVINGS

I love hard-cooked eggs moistened with a little mayonnaise and crunched up with celery or scallions. It reminds me of my elementary school days, when my little brown bag not infrequently contained one of my mom's egg salad sandwiches.

A quick way to chop a hard-cooked egg is with an old-fashioned egg slicer. First slice it the usual way—horizontally. Then slice it vertically. Finally—and this is a tad perilous, although you can pull it off if you move carefully—stand the egg straight up on its bottom and slice down the length of it. It's sort of fun, and a lot more efficient than chopping away at it with a knife.

Feel free to add smoked salmon to the sandwich to make it even more substantial. Serve with a salad of sliced tomatoes and cucumbers, topped with a few olives.

8 large eggs
1/2 cup low-fat mayonnaise
3 medium celery stalks, finely chopped (about 3/4 cup)
6 scallions (white parts only), finely chopped (about 3/4 cup)
1 1/2 tablespoons rinsed, dried, and chopped fresh tarragon or dill
1 tablespoon white wine vinegar
Kosher salt and freshly milled black pepper
8 large slices country bread
1 bunch watercress, coarse stems discarded, or 4 Boston or butter lettuce leaves, rinsed and dried

1. Place the eggs in a large saucepan with enough cold water to cover by 1 inch. Bring just to a boil over high heat. Remove from the heat, cover, and set aside for 15 minutes. Transfer the eggs to a bowl of half ice and half water. Cool completely, then peel under cold running water and chop them by hand, with an egg slicer (see headnote), or pulse them in a food processor.

2. Combine the chopped eggs with the mayonnaise, celery, scallions, tarragon, vinegar, and salt and pepper to taste, stirring gently. Mound one fourth of the salad on top of each of 4 slices of bread. Top each with some watercress and another slice of bread. Cut in half and serve.

Fried Green Tomato Sandwiches
with Goat Cheese

MAKES 4 SERVINGS

Being the ignorant Northerner that I am, I always thought that green tomatoes were transformed at the beginning of the season into fried green tomatoes because nobody could wait for those first tomatoes to ripen. I have been enlightened by my Southern friends and now understand that these tomatoes are actually harvested at the end of the season out of fear of the upcoming frost. I am happy to eat them at either end of the season, particularly gilded with Vidalia onion (pronounced *VIE-DAY-LI-A*, please; I got corrected on my Northern pronunciation by several Southern viewers), goat cheese, and a little herb mayonnaise. Serve with Cole Slaw (page 38) or Grated Carrot Salad (page 293).

1. Trim off and discard a thin slice from each end of the tomatoes. Cut each tomato into 4 slices. Sprinkle the slices on both sides with salt, using about 1/2 teaspoon total; drain in a colander 10 minutes.

2. Meanwhile, prepare the Quick Herb Sauce, thinly slice the onion, and slice the goat cheese 1/3 inch thick (use unflavored dental floss).

3. Pat the tomato slices dry, season with pepper, and dip in cornmeal to coat on both sides. Heat the oil with the garlic in a large skillet over medium heat until hot and the garlic just begins to turn golden; discard the garlic and set aside half the oil. Increase the heat to medium-high and brown half the tomatoes on both sides, about 5 minutes total. Repeat with the reserved oil and tomatoes.

4. Spread half of the Quick Herb Sauce over 4 slices toasted bread. Top with onion, goat cheese, fried tomatoes, remaining herb sauce, and remaining bread. Slice each sandwich in half and serve.

Hands-on time:
30 minutes

Total preparation time:
30 minutes

3 large green tomatoes (10 to 12 ounces each)
Kosher salt
1/2 recipe Quick Herb Sauce (page 312)
1/2 large sweet onion
8 ounces soft goat cheese
Freshly milled black pepper
1/3 cup yellow cornmeal
2 tablespoons extra virgin olive oil
1 large garlic clove, sliced (about 1 1/2 teaspoons)
8 slices country bread, toasted

Welsh Rabbit with Broiled Tomatoes and Toasted Walnuts

V

MAKES 4 SERVINGS

1 beefsteak tomato (about 12
    ounces) or 4 plum tomatoes
    (about 3 ounces each),
    sliced 1/3 inch thick
Kosher salt
1/4 cup chopped walnuts
6 ounces sharp Cheddar
    cheese, grated (about 1 1/2
    cups)
1/4 cup beer or dry sherry
1 tablespoon Worcestershire
    sauce
1 teaspoon dry mustard
1/8 teaspoon cayenne pepper,
    optional
Freshly milled black pepper
4 slices rye or whole wheat
    bread, toasted

Welsh rabbit (or rarebit) is a fancy name for a pretty prosaic, if delicious, dish—melted sharp Cheddar cheese on toast. Indeed, it is one of my favorite quick meals. I thought, however, that the recipe might be improved with the addition of tomatoes and toasted walnuts. The resulting sandwich is just the kind of comfort food I'd whip up after a bad day at the office. Serve with Cole Slaw (page 38) or a tossed green salad.

1. Preheat the oven to 350°F. Sprinkle the tomato slices lightly on both sides with salt; arrange them on a wire rack over a tray to drain for 10 minutes and then pat dry with paper towels.

2. Meanwhile, spread the walnuts in a pie plate or baking pan and toast in the preheated oven for about 10 minutes or until fragrant. Toss the cheese with the beer, Worcestershire sauce, mustard, cayenne, if using, and salt and pepper to taste.

3. Preheat the broiler to high. Arrange the toasted bread in one layer in a shallow baking dish; divide the tomatoes among the toast slices. Divide the cheese mixture and walnuts over the tomatoes. Broil about 4 inches from the heat source for 3 to 4 minutes or just until the cheese is melted. Serve immediately.

WHETHER you choose English walnuts, black walnuts, pecans, almonds, hazelnuts, peanuts, pine nuts, Macadamia nuts, or Brazil nuts, the addition of nuts to a recipe will bring crunch, flavor, and nutrition to the dish.

Freshness is the most important factor in selecting nuts in the market but it is sometimes not easy to determine because of the packaging. If you don't mind shelling them, nuts in the shell are often fresher than shelled ones. Look for large nuts with clean, unbroken shells. When choosing shelled nuts, look for plump, unbroken nut meats. There should be no shriveled or discolored nuts and no powdery residue in the bags. Vacuum-packed nuts are more likely to be fresh than those in other containers. If possible, sniff the container to see if there is any sign of rancidity.

Once you bring nuts home, store them in a cool, dry place. Although it isn't very dry, the fridge or freezer is often the best choice. Try to use the nuts within several months of purchase even if you are storing them in the freezer. Take the time to roast nuts lightly just before using them; it will bring out their flavor. Although nuts can be roasted at various temperatures—they can often go in the oven when you are baking something else—I suggest spreading them on a rimmed baking sheet and baking them in the center of a 350°F oven for about 10 minutes. Be sure to watch them carefully and remove them just as they start to color.

A
NUT
PRIMER

Hands-on time:
15 minutes

Total preparation time:
25 minutes

12 slices homemade-style
white or whole wheat
bread
8 ounces lightly salted
mozzarella cheese,
preferably fresh, cut into 12
thin slices
24 rinsed and dried large fresh
basil leaves
4 ounces thinly sliced
prosciutto di Parma
2 large eggs, lightly beaten
2 tablespoons milk
1/2 cup packaged dried bread
crumbs or from Bread
Crumbs Four Ways (page
23, add prep time)
1/4 cup pine nuts, finely
chopped
Kosher salt and freshly milled
black pepper
3 tablespoons extra virgin
olive oil

French-toasted Mozzarella and Prosciutto Sandwiches

MAKES 6 SERVINGS

Mozzarella en Carozza is a wonderful deep-fried Italian sandwich. At *Gourmet* we sautéed it instead, which makes the dish lighter but no less flavorful, and it's the *Gourmet* version that inspired this sandwich. I've "beefed it up" with prosciutto, but you're welcome to leave it out. Whichever, you'll be shaking hands with an extremely satisfying—if rather decadent—dinner. Serve with Grilled Radicchio Salad (page 306) or Bean Salad (page 39).

1. Preheat the oven to 200°F. Place six slices of bread on a flat work surface; arrange half of the mozzarella on the bread, trimming it and rearranging as necessary to cover each slice. Divide the basil and prosciutto di Parma over the mozzarella on each slice of bread; top with the remaining mozzarella and bread slices. Trim off and discard the bread crusts.

2. In a shallow bowl combine the eggs and milk. In another bowl combine the bread crumbs, pine nuts, and 1/8 teaspoon each salt and pepper.

3. Heat 1 1/2 tablespoons of the oil in a large skillet over high heat until hot. Dip the sandwiches into the egg mixture, letting the excess drip off, and then into the bread crumb mixture, coating them well.

4. When the pan is hot, reduce the heat to medium-low and add half the sandwiches. Cook them about 3 minutes on each side or until they are nicely golden and the cheese has melted. Place them in the oven to stay warm and repeat with the remaining oil and sandwiches. Cut the sandwiches in halves or quarters and serve.

Smoked Trout and White Bean
Brandade on Grilled Bread

MAKES 4 SERVINGS

Brandade is a spread from the south of France made essentially with salt cod, garlic, and olive oil. It is absolutely delicious but time consuming because you have to start by soaking salt cod for two to three days. It is not something you can just whip up on a weeknight. I am taking liberties by calling this brandade, but anyone who knows and loves the original will be happy with this quick substitute, which definitely mimics the texture and has a lovely, vaguely similar taste. Brandade is usually served with some kind of toast or bread on the side. I decided to just spread it on grilled bread, top it with roasted peppers, and turn it into a very satisfying sandwich. Serve with Radish and Orange Salad with Peppery Orange Dressing (page 303).

1. Thoroughly drain and quarter the jarred roasted peppers or prepare and quarter Roasted Peppers. Meanwhile, combine 2 tablespoons of the oil with the garlic in a small skillet. Cook over low heat until the garlic is softened but not browned, about 3 minutes. Set aside to cool.

2. Remove and discard the skin and bones from the trout. Combine the trout, beans, cooled oil and garlic mixture, and the lemon juice in a food processor or blender and puree until it becomes a very smooth spread. Add salt and pepper to taste.

3. Brush both sides of the bread with the remaining oil and toast on a grill pan until golden and well scored, about 4 minutes on each side.

4. Divide the brandade among four slices of bread (a generous 1/3 cup on each); top each with some pepper quarters and another slice of bread. Slice the sandwiches in half and serve with Niçoise olives.

Hands-on time:
25 minutes using Roasted Peppers;
20 minutes using bottled peppers

Total preparation time:
25 minutes using Roasted Peppers;
20 minutes using bottled peppers

One 12-ounce jar roasted red peppers in water, well drained, or 2 Roasted Peppers (page 30, add prep time)
3 tablespoons extra virgin olive oil
1 garlic clove, coarsely chopped (about 1 teaspoon)
One 8-ounce package smoked trout
1/2 cup canned white beans, drained and rinsed
1 1/2 teaspoons fresh lemon juice
Kosher salt and freshly milled black pepper
8 slices country bread
Niçoise olives

Scampi Heros

One 16- to 18-inch loaf Italian
bread
2 tablespoons extra virgin
olive oil
1 medium green bell pepper,
sliced (about 2 cups)
1 medium onion, sliced (about
1 cup)
6 garlic cloves, sliced (about 2
tablespoons)
One 8-ounce package sliced
white or crimini mushrooms
8 ounces shelled and deveined
large shrimp, split
lengthwise
1/3 cup pimiento-stuffed
olives, drained and sliced
2 tablespoons fresh lemon
juice
1/2 teaspoon kosher salt
1/4 to 1/2 teaspoon hot sauce

MAKES 4 SERVINGS

Nobody ever really gets enough shrimp, which is why the idea of a scampi hero seemed luxurious to me. (In Italy scampi is the name for the tail portion of any of several kinds of small lobsterlike creatures. In America scampi is the name for a dish of large shrimp cooked in butter or oil with garlic.) It'll cut your prep time way down if your local supermarket sells raw shrimp already shelled and deveined—but make sure they smell very fresh. Frozen shrimp are another option. I keep a bag in the freezer. I don't devein them, just defrost and peel them—it is very quick. This sandwich would work equally well with scallops, and they cook in about the same time. Serve with Bean Salad (page 39) or Grated Carrot Salad (page 293).

1. Preheat the oven to 225°F. Split the loaf of bread lengthwise, leaving one long side attached. Scoop out some bread to make a hollow in the bottom half. Close the loaf and place it in the oven to warm until ready to fill.

2. Heat the oil in a large skillet over high heat until hot. Reduce the heat to medium; add the pepper, onion, and garlic and cook, stirring occasionally, until softened, about 5 minutes. Add the mushrooms and cook, stirring, until all the liquid the mushrooms release has evaporated, 5 to 7 minutes.

3. Add the shrimp and sauté just until they are cooked through, about 3 minutes. Stir in the olives, lemon juice, salt, and hot sauce to taste; spoon the mixture into the loaf of bread. Cut into 4 pieces and serve.

Pressed Smoked Salmon or Turkey Reubens

Hands-on time:
15 minutes

Total preparation time:
27 minutes

MAKES 4 SANDWICHES

Built of corned beef, melted Swiss cheese, and Russian dressing, the Reuben sandwich is a masterpiece of heart-stopping excess, huge not only in flavor but in size. Indeed, as my father-in-law might say, the typical Reuben sandwich is "big enough to choke a horse." I suppose that trying to invent a less-than-Rubenesque Reuben was slightly sacrilegious—rather like dreaming of a low-cal version of foie gras—but I thought it might be worth a shot. I substituted both smoked salmon and smoked turkey for the corned beef and—wonder of wonders—found them to be equally delicious. So it's up to you—choose whichever one suits your mood.

By the way, you can make this sandwich on a panini grill. If you don't have one, the homemade press I suggest works just as well. Serve with Cole Slaw (page 38) or Sautéed Beets with Balsamic Vinegar (page 305).

1/4 cup low-fat mayonnaise

2 tablespoons chili sauce or ketchup

2 tablespoons finely chopped dill pickle

1 teaspoon fresh lemon juice

Kosher salt and freshly milled black pepper

8 slices rye bread

4 to 6 ounces Gruyère, Italian fontina, or Swiss cheese, thinly sliced

8 ounces smoked salmon or smoked turkey, thinly sliced

One 14 1/2-ounce can sauerkraut, drained, rinsed, and gently squeezed dry

2 tablespoons unsalted butter

1. Combine the mayonnaise, chili sauce, pickle, lemon juice, and salt and pepper to taste. Spread one side of each slice of bread with some of the dressing. Arrange half of the cheese on four of the slices. Divide the salmon, sauerkraut, and remaining cheese among the cheese-topped slices of bread and top each with one of the remaining bread slices, dressing side down.

2. Heat the butter in a large skillet over medium-low heat; add the sandwiches and something heavy (a cast-iron skillet, flat saucepan lid, or heatproof plate and a weight, such as a food can or a full kettle) to firmly press the sandwiches down. Cook for 6 minutes a side or until golden and the cheese has melted. Cut the sandwiches in half and serve.

Fried Clam Sandwiches

Beer Batter (page 31)
Quick Herb Sauce (page 312)
   or Rouille (page 314)
6 hot dog rolls, preferably
   top-split
2 tablespoons melted butter
Vegetable oil for deep frying
2 pints shucked (preferably by
   your fishmonger) littleneck
   clams
2 cups packed shredded
   iceberg or romaine lettuce
6 lemon wedges

MAKES 6 SERVINGS

I just love fried clams. Let me back up here—I actually love any-thing fried, but you can't always justify it from the mess and caloric point of view. Clams were made to be fried. Anybody who has been to Cape Cod or Ipswich, Massachusetts, or to one of the many little food shacks along the New England coast knows how special they are. The trouble is, when I asked my fishmonger about the availability of soft-shell clams (the usual suspect for this dish), he said they were not so easy to find and really quite expensive if you got them already shucked. I decided to go with littlenecks instead and, yes, littlenecks are a little chewy but the flavor is right there. Serve with Oven Fries (page 295) and Cole Slaw (page 38).

1. Make the Beer Batter, strain it, and let it rest while you prepare the Quick Herb Sauce. Combine the seasoned flour as directed in the Beer Batter recipe. Preheat the oven to 225°F.

2. Heat a griddle or cast-iron frying pan over high heat until hot; reduce the heat to medium-high. Brush the outsides of the rolls with melted butter and toast on the griddle, turning on all sides until golden, 4 to 6 minutes total. Keep the rolls warm in the oven while you fry the clams.

3. Heat 2 inches of vegetable oil in a deep saucepan to 375°F. Drain the clams and pat dry. Working with about one-fourth of the clams at a time, dip them in the flour mixture, shake off the excess, then dip them in the batter to coat them and let the excess drip off. Add the clams to the oil and deep fry until they are golden brown, 1 to 2 minutes. Transfer to paper tow-els to drain and keep warm in the oven. Repeat with the remaining clams.

4. Spoon a little Quick Herb Sauce on the toasted rolls. Divide the clams among the rolls. Top each with some lettuce and serve with a lemon wedge.

TWO main types of clams are found in the Northeast—quahogs (pronounced *ko-hogs)* and soft shells. Quahogs are classified by size. Littlenecks are 1 1/2 to 1 1/4 inches across and you get about 7 to 10 per pound. They are tender and have a sweet taste. Cherrystones are 2 1/4 to 3 inches across and come 5 to 7 a pound. They are chewier than the littlenecks. The largest clams are simply called quahogs or chowder clams and are chopped up and used for just that. Soft shells, also known as steamers, fryers, or long necks (after the black siphon that protrudes from their shells) are usually steamed or shucked and turned into fried clams. They really should be called "thin shells," because their shells are thinner, not really softer, than other clam shells.

CLAMS

Chicken Livers on Garlic Toasts

1 pound chicken livers

1 cup milk

Four 3/4-inch thick slices country bread

2 tablespoons extra virgin olive oil

1 large garlic clove, split lengthwise

2 tablespoons unsalted butter

1/3 cup Wondra or unbleached all-purpose flour

Kosher salt and freshly milled black pepper

4 large shallots, chopped (about 1/2 cup)

2 teaspoons rinsed and dried fresh thyme or 1/2 teaspoon dried

1/2 cup white wine

1 cup canned chicken broth or Chicken Stock (page 32)

3/4 cup heavy cream

2 tablespoons brandy

2 tablespoons coarse-grained Dijon mustard

1/4 cup rinsed, dried, and chopped fresh flat-leaf parsley

Rinsed and dried fresh flat-leaf parsley and thyme sprigs, optional

MAKES 4 SERVINGS

When I was the chef at Cybele's in Boston's Faneuil Hall in the late seventies, these chicken livers were a big feature on our Sunday brunch menu. Every so often I make them for the husband at home since he is rather addicted to them. Recently when we were up at the family farm I had a few chicken livers kicking around from those happy little packages that come in the roasting chickens. My sister-in-law, Chris Creatura, mentioned that one of her favorite hors d'oeuvres in Italy was chicken liver bruschetta (bruschetta is grilled bread), so I thought, why not put it all together and make a substantial sandwich? Serve with a tossed green salad and Sautéed Spinach with Garlic (page 34).

1. Combine the livers and milk in a bowl and refrigerate for 30 minutes.

2. Preheat a grill pan over medium heat or the oven to 375°F. Lightly brush the bread slices with oil on both sides, using about 1 tablespoon of oil. Grill or bake the bread until golden, turning once, about 5 minutes. Rub the toasted bread with the cut sides of the garlic while the bread is still hot.

3. Heat the butter and remaining tablespoon of oil in a large skillet over medium-high heat. Drain the livers well and toss with the flour, 1/2 teaspoon salt, and 1/4 teaspoon pepper, shaking off the excess.

4. Sauté the livers until they are well browned on the outside and just losing their pinkness in the center, about 6 minutes; transfer to a plate. Add the shallots and thyme and sauté until the shallots are golden, about 3 minutes. Add the wine and simmer until almost evaporated. Add the broth and cream. Simmer, stirring until thickened, 4 to 5 minutes. Add the brandy, mustard, and salt and pepper to taste. Stir in the livers and parsley; cook until hot. Serve over toast; garnish with parsley and thyme, if desired.

Middle Eastern Meatball Sandwiches
with Cucumber Yogurt Sauce

Hands-on time:
20 minutes

Total preparation time:
35 minutes

MAKES 4 SERVINGS

This is nothing more than a fancy hamburger on a skewer with a garlicky yogurt sauce, but boy, is it good. It was a hit with my family the very first time I made it. You're welcome to top it off with some sautéed peppers and onions, but it's pretty substantial all by itself. Serve with Grated Carrot Salad (page 293).

1. Preheat a grill or broiler. Combine the cucumber with the yogurt, 1 teaspoon garlic, and salt and pepper to taste; set aside. Combine the beef, onions, eggs, oregano, remaining garlic, 1 teaspoon salt, and 1/2 teaspoon pepper. Stir until the mixture holds together well. Form into 8 ovals about 3 inches long and 1 1/2 inches wide and thread them onto metal skewers.

2. Brush the meatballs with the olive oil and place the skewers on an oiled rack or a broiler pan. Grill or broil 4 inches from the heat source, turning to brown on all sides, until cooked through, about 8 minutes a side. Remove the skewers from the grill or broiler and slip the meatballs off the skewers.

3. Cut the pita breads in half and tuck a meatball into each half. Serve at once topped with some of the cucumber yogurt sauce and shredded lettuce.

Note: Greek yogurt is available in the dairy section of supermarkets. If you can't find it, purchase about a third more regular yogurt than the amount of Greek yogurt called for in the recipe and drain it in a coffee-filter-lined strainer in the refrigerator for about 4 hours or until it has reduced to the necessary amount. For example, drain 1 cup of regular yogurt to get 2/3 cup, or 3 cups of regular yogurt to get 2 cups.

4-inch piece English cucumber, grated in a food processor or by hand (about 3/4 cup)

1 3/4 cups plain whole-milk Greek yogurt or drained regular plain whole-milk yogurt (see Note)

3 garlic cloves, minced (about 1 tablespoon)

Kosher salt and freshly milled black pepper

2 pounds ground beef, lamb, or turkey

1 1/2 small onions, finely chopped (about 3/4 cup)

2 large eggs, lightly beaten

1 tablespoon rinsed, dried, and finely chopped fresh oregano or mint or 1 teaspoon dried

1 tablespoon extra virgin olive oil

4 pita breads with pockets, warmed

Shredded romaine lettuce for garnish

Breakfast
for Dinner

Brie, Bacon, and Spaghetti Frittata

Kosher salt
1/4 cup chopped walnuts
1/4 pound spaghetti
6 slices bacon, chopped
1 medium onion, sliced (about
    1 cup)
8 large eggs, lightly beaten
6 ounces Brie cheese, rind
    removed, cheese cut into
    small pieces
1/2 teaspoon freshly milled
    black pepper
1 tablespoon vegetable oil

MAKES 6 SERVINGS

Here's how to turn your leftover pasta into a new meal in the form of an Italian omelet. You can bulk it up with just about anything kicking around in the fridge—including leftover vegetables, meat, and poultry. If you have one of those great old cast-iron skillets, use it for this dish. Then you can bring the skillet to the table and serve your frittata family-style. Serve with a tossed green salad and crusty bread.

1. Bring a medium pot of salted water to a boil over high heat. Preheat the broiler to high. Spread the walnuts on a rimmed baking sheet and place under the broiler, about 5 inches from the heat source, until they just begin to brown, about 2 minutes.

2. Add the spaghetti to the boiling water and cook until just al dente, 8 to 10 minutes. Drain well.

3. Meanwhile, cook the bacon in a large, heavy, ovenproof skillet over medium heat until crisp, about 6 minutes. Transfer the bacon with a slotted spoon to paper towels to drain, leaving the fat in the pan. Add the onion and cook, stirring occasionally, until softened, about 5 minutes.

4. Combine the eggs with the cooked spaghetti, the Brie, bacon, walnuts, 1 teaspoon salt, and the pepper. Remove the onion from the skillet with tongs and stir it into the spaghetti and egg mixture.

5. Add the oil to the drippings in the skillet and heat over medium heat. Pour the spaghetti and egg mixture into the pan and cook until the frittata is almost set in the center, about 5 minutes. Broil the frittata just until the top is lightly browned and the center has set, 2 to 3 minutes.

THERE is a reason that the cast-iron skillet, a favorite pan going all the way back to colonial times, is still popular. Even though it takes time to heat up, once hot, it retains the heat evenly for quite a while. Moreover, if you take good care of it and keep it well seasoned, it will behave like a nonstick pan. The more you use it, the more nonstick it will become. Cast iron also happens to be extremely affordable, especially compared to all the new designer pans out there. When you first bring it home from the store, you must season it. Preheat the oven to 350°F. Wash the new pan with hot soapy water and a stiff brush. Then apply a thin coat of melted vegetable shortening to the entire surface, both inside and out. Place the pan upside down on the upper oven rack (put a piece of aluminum foil on the bottom rack to catch any drips) and bake for one hour. Turn off the oven and let the skillet cool before removing it from the oven. Never wash the skillet in the dishwasher, never use soap on it again (just scrub it with a brush and water), and always dry it immediately and apply a thin coat of vegetable oil. If it gets rusty (which it won't if you take good care of it), repeat the whole procedure.

HOW TO SEASON AND CARE FOR A NEW CAST-IRON SKILLET

Egg, Canadian Bacon, and Cheddar Biscuit Sandwiches

MAKES 4 SERVINGS

All right, I'll be honest. This is a takeoff on you-know-what served by that fast-food restaurant. Only they use English muffins, which actually makes for a pretty lean breakfast sandwich. You can use English muffins also if you want to cut back on time and calories. But these are the best biscuits you will ever eat. They are cream biscuits—the only fat and liquid in them is cream and they couldn't be simpler to make. Serve with Grated Carrot Salad (page 293) or marinated Roasted Peppers (page 30).

1. Preheat the oven to 425°F. Lightly grease a cookie sheet.

2. Stir together the flour, baking powder, and salt in a large bowl. Pour in enough of the cream to just form a dough. On a lightly floured surface, knead the dough gently several times and divide into 4 equal balls. Pat each ball to make a flat 3-inch round on the cookie sheet. Bake for about 20 minutes or until pale golden. Transfer to a rack and let cool slightly.

3. Meanwhile, in a large skillet over medium heat, cook the bacon, turning once, until just golden. Transfer the bacon to a plate and cover with aluminum foil to keep warm. Reduce the heat to low, add the butter to the skillet, and heat until the foam subsides. Add 1/4 teaspoon salt and 1/4 teaspoon pepper to the eggs and add them to the pan. Cook, stirring frequently, until the eggs just begin to set. Sprinkle the cheese on top, cover, and remove the pan from the heat. Let stand for 2 minutes.

4. To assemble the sandwiches, cut the biscuits in half horizontally with a serrated knife. Top the four bottom halves with a slice of bacon and one-fourth of the cheese-covered scrambled eggs. Top the eggs with another slice of bacon and the remaining biscuit halves.

Hands-on time:
20 minutes

Total preparation time:
30 minutes

2 cups unbleached all-purpose flour
1 tablespoon baking powder
1/2 teaspoon table salt
1 to 1 1/2 cups heavy cream
8 thin slices Canadian bacon (about 6 ounces)
2 tablespoons unsalted butter
8 large eggs, lightly beaten
Kosher salt and freshly milled black pepper
4 ounces Cheddar cheese, coarsely grated (about 1 cup)

1/2 large red bell pepper,
coarsely chopped (about
2/3 cup)

1 small onion, coarsely
chopped (about 1/2 cup)

1 large plum tomato, coarsely
chopped (about 1/2 cup)

1/2 cup packed rinsed and
dried fresh cilantro leaves

4 garlic cloves, coarsely
chopped (about 4
teaspoons)

Kosher salt and freshly milled
black pepper

8 thin slices Black Forest or
Virginia ham (without
holes; 6 to 8 ounces)

8 large eggs

2 ounces plain or jalapeño
Monterey Jack cheese,
grated (about 1/2 cup)

8 large tortilla chips (3-inch
triangles), coarsely crushed
(about 1/2 cup)

Eggs Baked in Ham
with Sofrito

MAKES 4 SERVINGS

Eggs baked in ham cups with creamed mushrooms underneath
appeared on the February 2002 cover of *Gourmet* magazine. I
made them on my show and was astonished (I don't know why—
everything is tested at the magazine a zillion times until it is
perfect) to find how easily they unmolded from the muffin tins
and held their shape. This is an adaptation using my Guatemalan
housekeeper Magda Alcayaga's sofrito in place of the mushroom
base. Once you have tried this recipe and marveled, as I did, at
how well it holds up, I guarantee you will start experimenting to
see what other items—cheese, spinach, tomatoes—might also go
nicely with the egg in its little ham cup. Serve with Smashed
Potatoes (page 38) or Oven Fries (page 295).

1. Preheat the oven to 400°F.

2. To make the sofrito combine the bell pepper, onion, tomato, cilantro,
garlic, 1/2 teaspoon salt, and 1/4 teaspoon pepper in a food processor and
process until smooth.

3. Fit a slice of ham into each of 8 lightly oiled muffin cups, custard cups,
or mini soufflé dishes (they must hold a scant 1/2 cup) with the ends of
the ham extending above the edges of the cups. Divide the sofrito among
the cups, shaping a hollow in the center. Crack 1 egg into each and top
with the cheese. If using custard cups or soufflé dishes, place on a rimmed
baking sheet for easy handling.

4. Bake in the center of the oven until the whites are cooked but the yolks
are still runny, about 15 minutes. Season the eggs with salt and pepper
and carefully remove (with the ham) from the muffin cups, using two
spoons or spatulas. Sprinkle with tortilla chips and serve.

Egg Foo Yung

Hands-on time:
15 minutes

Total preparation time:
25 minutes

MAKES 4 SERVINGS

When I was growing up, egg foo yung was a very popular item on Chinese take-out menus and in most Chinese restaurants. In recent years, however, it seemed to disappear. Reading a recipe for egg foo yung in an old cookbook not long ago, I was struck by its adaptability. It is, after all, a kind of Chinese omelet—and, as with any omelet, the filling possibilities are endless. I have done what I can, however, to improve on the old egg foo yung sauce, which I remember as pretty gluey. In the end, I think this recipe is a good example of how the old becomes new again.

1. Combine the chicken broth and the oyster sauce in a small saucepan. Whisk together the wine and cornstarch. Bring the chicken broth mixture to a boil and whisk in the cornstarch mixture. Simmer for 1 minute and keep warm on low heat.

2. Heat 3 tablespoons of the oil in a large, preferably nonstick, skillet over medium-high heat until hot. Reduce the heat to medium; add the celery, onion, and ginger and cook, stirring occasionally, until softened, about 5 minutes. Add the mushrooms and cook until all the liquid the mushrooms give off has evaporated. Add the water chestnuts and the protein and cook until just warmed through. Transfer the contents of the skillet to a platter and let cool slightly.

3. Combine the eggs, sesame oil, salt, and pepper; stir in the cooled vegetable and protein mixture. Heat the remaining 2 tablespoons oil in the skillet over medium heat. Add the egg mixture, let it set slightly, then lift up the sides to let the liquid egg slide underneath. Brown lightly on the first side, about 6 minutes. Divide into quarters and flip over one quarter at a time; cook until brown on the bottom, 4 to 5 minutes. Transfer to 4 plates and serve each portion topped with some of the sauce.

2/3 cup canned chicken broth or Chicken Stock (page 32)
1/4 cup oyster sauce
2 tablespoons rice wine or dry sherry
1 1/2 teaspoons cornstarch
5 tablespoons vegetable oil
2 celery stalks, sliced
1 medium onion, sliced (about 1 cup)
2 teaspoons finely grated fresh ginger (use a Microplane)
1 cup sliced fresh mushrooms
One 8-ounce can sliced water chestnuts, drained
1 cup finely shredded or chopped cooked protein such as rotisserie chicken, prosciutto di Parma, Canadian bacon, scallops, or shrimp, or a combination
6 large eggs, lightly beaten
1 teaspoon toasted sesame oil
1/2 teaspoon kosher salt
1/4 teaspoon freshly milled black pepper

Asparagus and Goat Cheese Souffléed Omelet

V

MAKES 2 SERVINGS

1/2 pound asparagus, trimmed
(see sidebar)
Kosher salt
3 ounces fresh goat cheese,
crumbled (about 1/3 cup)
2 teaspoons rinsed, dried, and
finely chopped fresh
tarragon or dill
Freshly milled black pepper
1 tablespoon unsalted butter
or vegetable oil
5 large eggs, separated
2 tablespoons unbleached all-
purpose flour

This is a cross between an omelet and a soufflé and doesn't take too much work as long as you have electric beaters. Make sure you beat your egg whites just to soft peaks; otherwise they won't fold properly into the egg yolk base. Any leftover cheese or vegetable such as broccoli, spinach, or the like would make a fine filling for this souffléed omelet, so consider this a clean-out-the-fridge dish. Serve with Radish and Orange Salad with Peppery Orange Dressing (page 303).

1. Preheat the oven to 375°F. Blanch the asparagus in a skillet filled with boiling salted water for about 2 minutes or until it is crisp-tender. Drain, pat dry, and cut crosswise into 1/4-inch pieces. Transfer to a bowl and toss with the goat cheese, tarragon, and salt and pepper to taste.

2. Melt the butter in a 10-inch nonstick skillet with a heatproof handle; tilt the pan to coat the bottom with the butter and remove from the heat. Whisk the egg yolks with the flour, 1/2 teaspoon salt, and 1/4 teaspoon pepper until the mixture is fluffy, about 3 minutes. Beat the egg whites with an electric mixer until they hold soft peaks; fold them into the yolk mixture gently but thoroughly, and pour the egg mixture into the skillet, spreading it evenly.

3. Bake the omelet in the center of the oven for 10 minutes, or until it is puffed and almost cooked through. Spoon the filling down the center, and with a spatula fold the omelet in half to enclose the filling. Bake the omelet in the center of the oven for 2 minutes more, or until the cheese is melted and the omelet is cooked through.

ASPARAGUS comes in all different thicknesses, from pencil-thin to nearly an inch. Some people are passionate about one size or another. I love all asparagus as long as it is fresh. How can you tell? The top will be tight and closed and the stalk will be completely smooth and firm. You should find asparagus in the supermarket standing on the stalk end in ice or a little water. I always cook it in a large skillet in two inches or so of salted boiling water. The bottom woody inch or two of any asparagus should be discarded; depending on the thickness of the stalk, the asparagus might also need to be peeled. (The larger the asparagus, the tougher the peel.) I usually do this when the asparagus is a half inch thick or more by laying it flat (so it doesn't snap) and running a peeler from just below the tip all the way down to the bottom of the stalk. This ensures that the asparagus cooks evenly from top to bottom.

TRIMMING ASPARAGUS

1 large or 2 small baking
    potatoes (about 12 ounces)
1/4 cup plus 2 tablespoons
    vegetable oil
Kosher salt and freshly milled
    black pepper
8 large eggs
4 ounces thinly sliced smoked
    salmon
1 recipe Horseradish Sauce
    (page 316), optional
Thinly sliced red onion and
    drained, bottled capers,
    optional

Potato Pancakes
with Smoked Salmon and Fried Eggs

MAKES 4 SERVINGS

I love smoked salmon with eggs. I love smoked salmon with potatoes and smoked salmon with horseradish. So I thought I would put it all together and garnish it with the perfect smoked salmon accompaniments, red onion and capers. I'm from New York—I know about smoked salmon. Serve with Grated Carrot Salad (page 293) or Sautéed Beets with Balsamic Vinegar (page 305).

1. Peel the potato and grate it, preferably using the grating disk of a food processor (or the coarse side of a box grater). Heat 3 tablespoons oil in a large nonstick skillet over medium-high heat until hot. Sprinkle the potatoes into the pan to form 4 pancakes, about 4 inches in diameter and 1/3 inch thick. Press them down with a spatula and cook them for 5 to 6 minutes or until the underside is golden brown. Season the top side with salt and pepper, turn the pancakes over, and cook them for 5 to 6 minutes more or until golden. Season the second side with salt and pepper.

2. When the potato pancakes are almost done, fry the eggs. In a large skillet heat the remaining oil over medium-low heat until hot. Gently break the eggs into the skillet, keeping yolks intact, and cook, covered, 5 minutes, or to desired doneness. Season with salt and pepper.

3. To serve, arrange 1 pancake on each of 4 plates; top with one-fourth of the salmon and 2 fried eggs. Spoon some of the Horseradish Sauce on top, if using, and garnish with the red onion and capers.

FOR MANY recipes what kind of potato you use makes a huge difference. There are two basic kinds: baking and boiling. Baking potatoes, also known as russets (the most famous being Idaho), are high in starch, and when cooked they come out soft and fluffy. Boiling potatoes, of which there are many varieties (the most famous being red bliss), are waxy and remain firm when cooked. Baking potatoes have a thick skin that is tough but very edible and full of nutrition (it is my favorite part of the baked potato); boiling potatoes have a thin skin that is so tender you can leave it on when you cook them. Baking potatoes are the candidate for any recipe where you want a lot of starch, such as shredded potato pancakes, mashed potatoes, or gnocchi; boiling potatoes are perfect for a recipe where you want the potato to hold its shape, such as potato salad. Just to confuse the matter, some potatoes are called "all purpose"; they can be used in any recipe.

WHICH POTATO?

Fried Eggs and "Refried" Beans Burritos

V

MAKES 4 SERVINGS

Four 7-inch flour tortillas
1/4 cup vegetable oil
1 small onion, finely chopped
*   (about 1/2 cup)*
1 teaspoon ground cumin
1/2 teaspoon chili powder
One 15-ounce can pinto beans,
*   drained and rinsed*
Kosher salt and freshly milled
*   black pepper*
8 large eggs
4 ounces Cheddar cheese,
*   grated (about 1 cup)*
1 cup bottled green salsa or 1
*   recipe Mexican Tomatillo*
*   Salsa (page 318, add prep*
*   time)*
1 cup crumbled tortilla chips

Eggs and beans are a happy match and substantial enough for dinner. These beans are "refried" in quotation marks because I've come up with a much lighter version of the classic recipe, which involves a fair amount of lard. Originally, I'd planned to serve the eggs and beans on top of crisped corn tortillas, but they were too hard to cut through. So I wrapped the whole concoction in warm flour tortillas, added crushed tortilla chips, cheese, and salsa to the filling—and turned the dish into a breakfast-for-dinner burrito. Serve with a sliced tomato and avocado salad.

1. Preheat the oven to 300°F. Wrap the tortillas in aluminum foil and set aside.

2. Heat 2 tablespoons of the oil in a medium skillet over high heat until hot. Reduce the heat to medium; add the onion and cook, stirring occasionally, until softened, about 5 minutes. Place the wrapped tortillas in the oven to warm.

3. Add the cumin and chili powder to the onion and cook 1 minute. Add the pinto beans and 1/2 cup water and cook for 5 minutes or until most of the water has evaporated. Remove from the heat and mash with a potato masher or fork until the beans are smooth with some lumps. Add salt and pepper to taste and keep warm while you cook the eggs.

4. Heat the remaining 2 tablespoons oil in a large skillet over high heat until hot. Reduce the heat to medium-low, break the eggs into the pan, and cook, covered, 5 minutes, or to desired doneness. Season with salt and pepper. To serve, spread some of the pinto bean mixture on each tortilla and top with 2 eggs, some of the cheese, salsa, and crumbled tortilla chips. Roll up and serve.

Mushroom Strata

V

Hands-on time:
20 minutes

Total preparation time:
1 1/4 hours

MAKES 6 SERVINGS

Strata is essentially a layered bread pudding. It is very substantial and a breeze to make. You can set it up ahead of time—the night before or in the morning before you leave for work—and then just pop it in the oven about fifty minutes before you want to serve it. Otherwise, you can certainly make it from scratch before dinner.

1. Preheat the oven to 350°F.

2. Grease an 8-inch square baking dish. Coarsely chop the mushrooms in several batches by pulsing once or twice in a food processor.

3. Melt the butter in a large skillet over medium-low heat. Add the shallots and cook, stirring occasionally, until they are softened, about 8 minutes. Add the mushrooms and cook over medium-high heat, stirring occasionally, until all the liquid the mushrooms give off has evaporated, about 7 minutes. Add the thyme and cook 2 minutes. Add the sherry, if using, and simmer until it has almost evaporated. Add salt and pepper to taste and set the mixture aside to cool slightly.

4. Whisk together the eggs, milk, 1/2 teaspoon salt, and 1/4 teaspoon pepper. Spread one-third of the mushroom mixture in the greased baking dish. Arrange 4 of the bread slices on top; spread with half of the remaining mushroom mixture and half of the cheese. Repeat with the remaining bread, mushroom mixture, and cheese. Pour the egg mixture over all.

5. Bake the strata in the center of the oven for 40 minutes, or until puffed and nicely browned. Remove from the oven and let stand 5 minutes before serving.

1 pound mixed exotic mushrooms such as shiitake (stems discarded), crimini, portobello, or oyster, cleaned

4 tablespoons (1/2 stick) unsalted butter

1/4 cup finely chopped shallots or onion

1 tablespoon rinsed and dried fresh thyme or 1 teaspoon dried

1/2 cup dry sherry, Madeira, or Marsala wine, optional

Kosher salt and freshly milled black pepper

6 large eggs

1 1/2 cups milk

8 slices homemade-style white or whole wheat bread

8 ounces Gruyère, Italian fontina, or aged Gouda cheese, coarsely grated (about 2 cups)

Fresh Corn Spoon Bread
with Broccoli and Sharp Cheddar

𝒱

MAKES 4 SERVINGS

2 cups whole milk
1 1/2 cups fresh corn kernels
   (from 2 to 3 ears corn)
1/3 cup yellow cornmeal
1 tablespoon unsalted butter
Kosher salt
1/8 to 1/4 teaspoon cayenne,
   optional
6 ounces extra-sharp Cheddar
   cheese, coarsely grated
   (about 1 1/2 cups)
4 large eggs, separated
2 cups small broccoli florets,
   blanched in boiling salted
   water for 3 minutes and
   drained

I have always loved Southern spoon bread—that creamy, airy cross between cornbread and a soufflé. I have added sharp Cheddar cheese and broccoli so that it becomes a substantial breakfast for dinner. One cup of any cooked vegetable would work here—cauliflower, peas, carrots, green beans, spinach, and so on—and three ounces of any good melting cheese would be fine too. Serve with Cole Slaw (page 38) and marinated Roasted Peppers (page 30).

1. Preheat the oven to 425°F. Generously grease a shallow 2 1/2-quart baking dish.

2. Combine the milk, corn, cornmeal, butter, 1 teaspoon salt, and the cayenne, if using, in a 3-quart saucepan and bring to a boil over medium-high heat, stirring frequently. Reduce the heat to low and simmer, stirring constantly, until thickened, 3 to 4 minutes. Remove from the heat, stir in the cheese, and let cool for 5 minutes. Whisk in the egg yolks and stir in the broccoli.

3. Beat the egg whites with 1/8 teaspoon salt with an electric mixer until they form soft peaks. Stir one-fourth of the whites into the cornmeal mixture and then fold in the remaining whites gently, until they are just incorporated. Spread the mixture evenly in the baking dish and bake in the center of the oven until it is puffed and golden, 15 to 20 minutes. Serve immediately.

Matzo Brei
with Creamed Spinach and Crispy Onions

V

Hands-on time:
20 minutes

Total preparation time:
20 minutes

MAKES 4 SERVINGS

I didn't know about matzo brei, that wonderful breakfast dish consisting of matzo and beaten eggs cooked in a lot of butter, until I started dating my now-husband (who is Jewish) in the mid-seventies. His mom, Esther, made it for me and I thought it was absolutely delicious. I always wondered if you could build on matzo brei, treating it much as you would treat an omelet or scrambled eggs and throw in any old ingredient. So I tried it and it worked surprisingly well. Boursin, an herb-flavored spreadable cheese that I have fond memories of from my childhood (it was very "gourmet" in the sixties), is a tad expensive, which is why I offer a few alternatives. Serve with Grated Carrot Salad (page 293) and Roasted Vegetables (page 35).

2 tablespoons vegetable oil
2 medium onions, thinly sliced (about 2 cups)
Kosher salt and freshly milled black pepper
3 whole matzos
6 large eggs, lightly beaten
2 tablespoons unsalted butter
Two 10-ounce packages defrosted frozen chopped spinach, excess water squeezed out
One 5.2-ounce package Boursin cheese or about 2/3 cup crumbled soft goat or cream cheese

1. Heat the oil in a medium skillet over high heat until hot. Reduce the heat to medium; add the onions and cook, stirring occasionally, until golden, about 8 minutes. Season with salt and pepper to taste and transfer to a bowl with a slotted spoon. Reserve the skillet and oil in which the onions were cooked.

2. Break up the matzos slightly and soak them in a bowl of cold water for 3 minutes. Drain the matzos well and combine them with the eggs, 3/4 teaspoon salt, and 1/4 teaspoon pepper.

3. Reheat the oil remaining in the reserved skillet with the butter over medium-high heat until hot. Add the matzo mixture and cook, stirring constantly, until the eggs are scrambled and the matzo has begun to crisp, about 5 minutes. Stir in the spinach and cheese and cook until just heated through. Top each portion with a mound of the onions.

Green Chile and Zucchini Quiche

v

MAKES 6 SERVINGS

4 tablespoons (1/2 stick)
unsalted butter, melted
24 whole-grain wheat crackers
(such as Triscuits), ground
in a food processor (about
1 cup) or 1 cup dried bread
crumbs from Bread Crumbs
Four Ways (page 23) or
packaged crumbs
1 medium zucchini (about 6
ounces)
Kosher salt
1 tablespoon vegetable oil
1 small onion, chopped (about
1/2 cup)
1/4 cup unbleached all-
purpose flour
1/2 teaspoon baking powder
3 large eggs
8 ounces Monterey Jack
cheese, coarsely grated
(about 2 cups)
8 ounces whole-milk cottage
cheese (1 cup)
One 4 1/2-ounce can chopped
green chiles, drained
Bottled salsa, optional

This quiche gets its Southwestern flair from Monterey Jack cheese and canned chiles. But if you have a little more time, you should lose the canned chiles and make it instead with roasted fresh poblanos, which are even more delicious. (See Roasted Peppers and Chiles, page 30.) I like the contrasting crunch of Triscuits, but just about any cracker would do. Then again, you could make this quiche without a crust and save a little time. Just put it in an oiled pie plate and bake it. Serve with Southwestern Sweet Potato Sauté (page 294) and a salad.

1. Preheat the oven to 375°F. Stir 2 tablespoons of the melted butter into the cracker crumbs. Press the crumb mixture into the bottom and 1 inch up the sides of a 9-inch glass pie plate. Bake the crust in the center of the preheated oven until it begins to brown, about 7 minutes. Remove the crust from the oven and reduce the oven temperature to 350°F.

2. Meanwhile, grate the zucchini, preferably using the grating disk of a food processor. Toss the zucchini with 1/2 teaspoon salt and let drain in a colander for 10 minutes. Heat the oil in a medium skillet over high heat until hot. Reduce the heat to medium; add the onion and cook, stirring occasionally, until softened, about 5 minutes. Squeeze the zucchini well with your hands to remove excess moisture. Add the zucchini to the onion and cook over high heat for 3 minutes.

3. Combine the flour, baking powder, and 1/4 teaspoon salt in a small bowl. In a large bowl with an electric mixer, beat the eggs until thick and fluffy, about 3 minutes. Add the Monterey Jack and cottage cheeses, the flour mixture, and remaining 2 tablespoons melted butter to the eggs and beat well. Stir in the zucchini mixture and chiles and pour the mixture into the crust. Bake the quiche in the center of the oven until the top is puffed and golden brown and a cake tester inserted in the center comes out clean, 35 to 40 minutes. Set aside at room temperature 5 minutes, cut into wedges, and serve with salsa, if desired.

Smoked Salmon Knishes

3 large baking potatoes,
    peeled and quartered (1 3/4
    pounds)
Kosher salt
1 1/4 cups unbleached all-
    purpose flour
1 teaspoon baking powder
1 large egg
1/4 cup vegetable oil
3 tablespoons unsalted butter
1 large onion, chopped (about
    2 cups)
1/4 pound thinly sliced smoked
    salmon, coarsely chopped

MAKES 4 KNISHES, SERVING 4

Hot, handy, and dense as lead, the classic potato knish was
considered a tasty little between-meals snack by the hard-hustling
American Jews of generations past. As a relatively fainthearted
twenty-first-century shiksa, I look at a knish and see not a snack
but the centerpiece of a whole meal.

In search of my own knish recipe, I sent Joanne on a pilgrimage to
Yonah Shimmel's, which has been selling great knishes from the
same address on Houston Street on New York's Lower East Side
since 1910. Shimmel's sets the standard. Their knishes are
handmade and baked, not fried. Diligent in our research, my
family and I sampled all of Shimmel's varieties: plain potato,
kasha, red cabbage, spinach, mushroom, sweet potato, vegetable,
and broccoli. Ultimately, in an effort to make this infamously
substantial dish even more substantial, protein-wise, we took the
basic potato knish and added salmon to it. Serve with Herbed Pea
Medley (page 37) and Sautéed Beets with Balsamic Vinegar (page
305).

1. Cook the potatoes in boiling salted water until tender, about 18
minutes; drain in a colander and let cool slightly. Mash, using either a
potato masher or a ricer, and set aside.

2. Meanwhile, stir together 1 cup of the flour, the baking powder, and
1/2 teaspoon salt in a medium bowl; stir in the egg, oil, and 2 tablespoons
water. Gradually knead in as much of the remaining flour as needed to
make a soft, yet not sticky, dough. Turn out on a board with any
remaining flour; divide into quarters and knead into 4 balls. Cover and set
aside while you make the filling.

3. Melt the butter in a medium skillet over medium-low heat. Add the onion and cook, stirring occasionally, until softened, about 8 minutes. Add the onion mixture, salmon, and salt to taste to the potatoes and mix well.

4. Preheat the oven to 400°F. Grease a cookie sheet. Roll out each ball of dough on a lightly floured surface into a 7-inch round. Put one quarter of the potato mixture in the center of each pastry round and shape the potato into a flat 4-inch cake about 1 1/2 inches thick. Bring the pastry up and around the potato mixture, leaving a 2-inch opening in the top center. Transfer the knishes to the cookie sheet and bake until golden, 15 to 20 minutes. Serve hot or at room temperature.

THERE are several different kinds of smoked salmon, ranging in salt content and in smoke. The regulations are a little hazy, however, so salmon can be mislabeled. Lox is supposed to be salmon that has been brine cured and then cold smoked. Nova or Nova Scotia lox is cured in a less salty brine than regular lox, so it is less salty. Lox is soft and supple and has a slightly oily texture.

If the salmon is just called smoked, it was brined and then cold or hot smoked. Hot smoking gives it a firmer, almost cooked texture and a smokier taste. Gravlax is made by a Scandinavian method that consists of curing salmon with salt, sugar, and dill. It is never smoked.

WHAT
IS SMOKED
SALMON?

Pasta
and
Grains

Kosher salt
1 small head cauliflower, cut
    into florets
1/4 cup extra virgin olive oil
Freshly milled black pepper
2 tablespoons unsalted butter
1 cup fresh bread crumbs from
    Bread Crumbs Four Ways
    (page 23)
1/4 pound pancetta or bacon,
    chopped
1 pound farfalle
One 14- or 14 1/2-ounce can
    chicken broth or 1 3/4 cups
    Chicken Stock (page 32),
    heated

Farfalle

with Cauliflower and Sautéed Bread Crumbs

MAKES 4 SERVINGS

At *Gourmet* my sous chef, Jennifer Webb, and I sometimes prepare the magazine's Cauliflower Steak for our lunch guests. (See page 000 for an adaptation of the recipe.) Afterward, we recycle the leftover cauliflower scraps by tossing them with a little olive oil and roasting them in a hot oven. This little dish simultaneously satisfies the permanent weight watcher and the passionate diner in both of us. Imagine drab virtuous cauliflower transformed into something intense, nutty, and quite satisfying— but no less virtuous than before. You don't need too much else here except the farfalle (or butterfly pasta), a few toasted bread crumbs, and some grated cheese. Serve with Sautéed Spinach with Garlic (page 34) or Grilled Radicchio Salad (page 306).

1. Preheat the oven to 450°F and put a large pot of salted water on to boil. Toss the cauliflower with 2 tablespoons of oil and sprinkle with salt and pepper to taste. Arrange in one layer in a shallow roasting pan and roast until caramelized and tender, about 15 minutes.

2. Melt the butter in a large skillet over medium heat until the foam starts to subside. Add the crumbs and sauté until golden, about 3 minutes. Transfer the crumbs to a plate. Add the remaining 2 tablespoons oil and the pancetta to the skillet and cook over medium heat until the pancetta is crisp. Set the pancetta and oil aside in the skillet.

3. Add the farfalle to the pot of boiling water and cook until just al dente, 8 to 10 minutes. Drain the farfalle and return it to the pot along with the cauliflower, chicken broth, and reserved pancetta and oil; add salt and pepper to taste and toss to combine. Stir in the crumbs and serve.

Fusilli

with Broccoli and Prosciutto

MAKES 4 SERVINGS

This recipe is adapted from a broccoli recipe that was sent to me by Richard D. Jehn, a personal chef and cookbook author from Shelton, Washington. I thought it was so tasty that I decided to add some pasta and turn it into a main dish. You could substitute sliced ham or Canadian bacon for the prosciutto di Parma if you want or leave it out altogether. One note on technique: I start the garlic in cold oil so that the oil can pull out more of the flavor from the garlic. It is similar to making a stock; you always start the bones in cold water and then bring the water up to a simmer to get the strongest-tasting stock. Serve with a tossed green salad and crusty bread.

1. Bring a large pot of salted water to a boil. Cut the broccoli into small florets; reserve the stems for another use. Add the broccoli to the boiling water and cook 2 minutes. Transfer the broccoli to a shallow bowl using a slotted spoon. Add the fusilli to the same boiling water and cook until al dente, 8 to 10 minutes. Drain, reserving 3/4 cup of the cooking liquid.

2. When the fusilli is almost done, combine the oil and garlic in a deep skillet. Place the mixture over low heat and cook until the garlic is fragrant and just beginning to turn light golden. Add the prosciutto di Parma strips and broccoli; sauté, stirring, 3 minutes. Add the fusilli, reserved cooking liquid, cheese, and salt and pepper to taste to the broccoli mixture; toss until combined and heated through. Transfer to a large serving bowl or 4 individual pasta bowls and serve.

Hands-on time:
15 minutes

Total preparation time:
25 minutes

Kosher salt
1 large head broccoli, rinsed
12 ounces fusilli (3/4 of
1-pound package)
3 tablespoons extra virgin
olive oil
3 garlic cloves, sliced paper-
thin (about 1 tablespoon)
1/4 pound prosciutto di Parma
(about 8 slices), cut into
strips
6 ounces Parmigiano-Reggiano
cheese, coarsely grated
(about 2 cups; see grating
information, page 10)
Freshly milled black pepper

*S*paghetti
with Beet and Goat Cheese Sauce

V

MAKES 4 SERVINGS

Kosher salt

1/2 cup walnuts

1 1/2 pounds beets, peeled

12 ounces spaghetti (3/4 of
1-pound package)

2 tablespoons extra virgin
olive oil

1 large red onion, sliced
(about 2 cups)

2 garlic cloves, minced (about
2 teaspoons)

10 ounces soft goat cheese
(about 1 1/3 cups),
crumbled

3 tablespoons fresh lemon
juice

Freshly milled black pepper

Beets, goat cheese, and walnuts are a combination made in heaven. Usually they find company in a salad. Here I have matched them in a pasta. Note that an ingredient of the recipe is reserved pasta cooking water. Italians often save part of the cooking liquid to toss with the sauce, which serves both to thin out the sauce and to bind it, since some starch is left in it from the pasta. Serve with a tossed green salad and Garlic Bread (page 40).

1. Preheat the oven to 350°F. Bring a large pot of salted water to a boil. Arrange the walnuts in one layer on a rimmed baking sheet.

2. Toast the nuts for about 10 minutes or until fragrant and slightly browned. Let cool, then coarsely chop. While the nuts are toasting, cut the beets into pieces that will fit through the feed tube of a food processor. Grate the beets using the grating disk, or grate by hand using the coarse side of a four-sided hand grater. (Be careful not to get the beet juice on your clothes.)

3. Meanwhile, add the spaghetti to the boiling water and cook until al dente, 8 to 10 minutes. Drain, reserving 1 cup of the cooking liquid. Transfer the spaghetti to a large bowl.

4. While the spaghetti is cooking, heat the oil in a large skillet over high heat until hot. Reduce the heat to medium-high and add the beets, onion, and garlic. Sauté, stirring frequently, for 4 to 5 minutes or until the beets are just crisp-tender. Add the reserved spaghetti cooking liquid and the goat cheese; cook, stirring, until the cheese softens into a sauce. Add the lemon juice and salt and pepper to taste.

5. Add the sauce to the spaghetti and toss well. Divide among 4 bowls and top each serving with the toasted nuts.

Hands-on time:
10 minutes

Total preparation time:
35 minutes

Kosher salt

1 tablespoon extra virgin olive
oil

8 ounces frozen breakfast
sausage, sliced 1/4 inch
thick (Note: do not defrost
sausages before cutting
them)

1 garlic clove, minced (about
1 teaspoon)

1 teaspoon rinsed, dried, and
chopped fresh sage or 1/4
teaspoon rubbed

1 teaspoon rinsed and dried
fresh thyme or 1/3
teaspoon dried

Two 14 1/2-ounce cans
chopped tomatoes

1 pound rotelle (cartwheel) or
other shaped pasta

2/3 cup heavy cream

Freshly milled black pepper

1 1/2 ounces Parmigiano-
Reggiano cheese, finely
grated (about 1/2 cup; see
grating information, page
10)

Annie's Favorite Pasta

(Cartwheel Pasta with Breakfast Sausage and Creamy Tomato Sauce)

MAKES 4 SERVINGS

When I told my sister Annie that I'd begun working on a new cookbook, she insisted that this time I had to include her all-time favorite pasta dish. Adapted from one of our most-loved Italian cookbooks, it is flavored with regular old breakfast sausages, tomatoes, and cream. In typical non-Italian fashion, I significantly increased the amount of sauce in the recipe, which will probably horrify all the Italian home cooks out there. But I see pasta as a vehicle for sauce, not the other way around. Serve with Herbed Pea Medley (page 37) and an arugula salad.

1. Bring a large pot of salted water to a boil. Meanwhile, heat the oil in a large skillet over high heat until hot; reduce the heat to medium, add the sausage, and sauté, stirring occasionally, until it is just cooked through, about 5 minutes. (Don't discard the fat released by the sausage.) Add the garlic, sage, and thyme; cook 1 minute. Add the tomatoes, reduce the heat to low, and simmer the sauce for 20 minutes.

2. During the last 10 minutes, add the pasta to the boiling water and cook until al dente, 10 to 12 minutes. Add the cream to the sauce and simmer just until the sauce has thickened slightly. Add salt and pepper to taste. Drain the pasta, reserving 2/3 cup of the cooking liquid. Stir the pasta cooking liquid into the sauce and toss with the drained pasta. Top each portion with some of the Parmigiano-Reggiano.

Bette's Macaroni and Cheese

Hands-on time:
20 minutes

Total preparation time:
55 minutes

𝒱

MAKES 6 SERVINGS

Here's another gem from our old family friend Bette Cohen, who debuted in my first cookbook as the author of Bette's Melba Toast. She says she serves this dish regularly to her friends and neighbors, noting, "Just add any green vegetable and it makes a meal." Indeed, you can't beat this recipe for convenience. You can prepare it in advance up through the addition of scallions and paprika; then refrigerate the whole dish. Pull it out of the refrigerator half an hour or so prior to dinner, drizzle the half-and-half over the top, and slide it into the oven. Serve with Butter-steamed Broccoli with Soy (page 296).

1. Cook the macaroni in boiling salted water until just tender, 8 to 10 minutes; drain thoroughly but don't rinse. Meanwhile, preheat the oven to 350°F. Coat a 2-quart shallow baking dish with 1 teaspoon of the butter.

2. Layer half the cheese, half the macaroni, all of the ham, the rest of the macaroni, and the rest of the cheese in the buttered dish. Sprinkle the potato chips over the top and dot with the remaining 2 teaspoons butter. Sprinkle the scallions and paprika over the casserole, then pour the half-and-half over all.

3. Bake the casserole in the center of the oven about 35 minutes, until bubbly and lightly browned on top.

2 cups macaroni

Kosher salt

1 tablespoon unsalted butter

8 ounces sharp Cheddar cheese, grated (about 2 cups)

8 ounces cooked ham finely chopped

1 1/2 cups crushed potato chips or crackers

3 scallions (white and light green parts), sliced (about 1/3 cup)

1 teaspoon paprika (see pages 183 and 347)

1 1/2 cups half-and-half or milk

Quick Asparagus Lasagna

V

MAKES 4 SERVINGS

2 teaspoons extra virgin olive
oil
Kosher salt and freshly milled
black pepper
1 pound asparagus, trimmed
1 medium onion, halved and
sliced (about 1 cup)
2 garlic cloves, sliced (about 2
teaspoons)
One 15-ounce container
ricotta cheese
2 teaspoons unbleached all-
purpose flour
18 refrigerated wonton skins
(see headnote on page 128)
8 ounces Italian Fontina
cheese, coarsely grated
(about 2 cups)

This is a recipe for spring, even though you can buy asparagus from South America out of season. Asparagus is tastier if you buy it locally and in season. All thicknesses are fine with me—from pencil-thin spears to thick stalks. However, I recommend that if the asparagus is thicker than, say, one-third of an inch, you should peel it from right below the tip to the end of the stalk. Break off the woody section of the stems first, which usually means the bottom inch or so.

By the way, there's no reason to put this recipe on the shelf when asparagus is out of season. It's just as delicious with broccoli florets or sautéed spinach. Serve with marinated Roasted Peppers (page 30) and a tossed green salad.

1. Preheat the broiler to high. Lightly oil a rimmed baking sheet and an 8-inch square pan. Combine the oil, 1/4 teaspoon salt, and 1/8 teaspoon pepper in a shallow bowl. Peel the lower stalks of the asparagus if they are thicker than 1/3 inch. Toss the asparagus in the oil mixture and arrange at one end of the oiled baking sheet. Toss the onion and garlic in any remaining oil in the same bowl and arrange them on the other end of the baking sheet. Broil until the edges just begin to brown, about 5 minutes.

2. Reduce the oven to 375°F. Combine the onion and garlic with the ricotta, flour, 1/4 teaspoon salt, and 1/8 teaspoon pepper in a blender; puree until smooth. Cut the asparagus into 1-inch pieces. Arrange 6 wonton skins in the bottom of the pan. Top with half the asparagus, one-third of the ricotta mixture, and one-third of the Fontina. Add another 6 wonton skins, the remaining asparagus, and another third of the ricotta mixture and Fontina. Top with the remaining wonton skins, ricotta mixture, and Fontina.

3. Bake the lasagna in the top third of the oven, 30 to 35 minutes, until bubbly and lightly browned. Cut into 4 servings.

Hands-on time:
20 minutes

Total preparation time:
55 minutes

1 teaspoon extra virgin olive
  oil
Kosher salt and freshly milled
  black pepper
1 medium onion, halved and
  sliced (about 1 cup)
2 garlic cloves, sliced (about 2
  teaspoons)
Two 12-ounce jars roasted red
  peppers in water, well
  drained, or 4 Roasted (red)
  Peppers (page 30, add prep
  time)
18 refrigerated wonton skins
8 ounces mozzarella cheese,
  coarsely grated (about 2
  cups)
4 ounces thinly sliced
  prosciutto di Parma, cut
  into strips
4 ounces Parmigiano-Reggiano
  cheese, coarsely grated
  (about 1 1/3 cups; see
  grating information, page
  10)

Roasted Red Pepper and Prosciutto Lasagna

MAKES 4 SERVINGS

Wonton skins, which can be found in the frozen-food section of
your supermarket, cook up beautifully, just like fresh Italian pasta.
I see no reason not to stock them in your freezer at home and
thaw them whenever you want to make "homemade" ravioli or
lasagna. Your family will think you are a culinary genius. Serve
with Radish and Orange Salad with Peppery Orange Dressing
(page 303).

1. Preheat the oven to 375°F. Lightly oil a rimmed baking sheet and an
8-inch square pan. Combine the oil, 1/4 teaspoon salt, and 1/4 teaspoon
pepper in a shallow bowl. Toss the onion and garlic in the oil mixture and
arrange on the baking sheet. Bake until the edges just begin to brown,
about 10 minutes.

2. Combine the peppers with the onion and garlic in a blender; puree
until smooth. Arrange 6 wonton skins in the bottom of the square pan.
Top with one-third of the roasted-pepper mixture and mozzarella cheese
and half of the prosciutto di Parma and Parmigiano-Reggiano. Add
another 6 wonton skins, another one-third of the roasted-pepper mixture
and mozzarella cheese, and the remaining prosciutto di Parma and
Parmigiano-Reggiano. Top with the remaining wonton skins, roasted-
pepper mixture, and mozzarella.

3. Bake in the top third of the oven 30 to 35 minutes, until bubbly and
lightly browned. Cut into 4 servings.

Crispy Pumpkin Ravioli

Hands-on time:
25 minutes

Total preparation time:
45 minutes

MAKES 4 SERVINGS

Stuff a wonton wrapper with something delicious and you're looking at nearly instant "homemade" ravioli. This recipe calls for a filling of super-quick canned pumpkin, but you could use fresh mini-pumpkin, butternut squash, or acorn squash purée. Just cut the pumpkin or squash in half, scoop out the seeds, and bake it until it is tender. Scoop out and season the flesh, then use in place of the canned pumpkin to stuff the wontons. Serve with Grilled Radicchio Salad (page 306) or Radish and Orange Salad with Peppery Orange Dressing (page 303).

1. Preheat the oven to 400°F. Spread the pine nuts on a rimmed baking sheet and bake until the nuts begin to brown, about 4 minutes. Remove the nuts to a bowl and return the pan to the oven to stay hot until the ravioli are ready to bake.

2. Melt 2 tablespoons of the butter in a small skillet over medium-low heat. Add the onion, garlic, and sage and cook until the onion has softened, about 8 minutes; transfer to a medium bowl. Add the pumpkin, Fontina, salt, and pepper to the onion mixture.

3. Working with 4 wonton skins at a time (keep the others covered with plastic wrap), arrange them on a lightly floured surface and place a mounded tablespoon of the mixture in the center of each. Lightly brush the edges of the wrapper with water and put a second wrapper over the first, pressing down around the filling to force out the air and seal the edges well. Make more ravioli with the remaining wrappers and filling in the same manner.

1/3 cup pine nuts

5 tablespoons unsalted butter

1 small onion, chopped (about 1/2 cup)

1 garlic clove, minced (about 1 teaspoon)

1 teaspoon rubbed sage

One 15-ounce can pumpkin puree

2 ounces Italian Fontina cheese, coarsely grated (about 1/2 cup)

1/2 teaspoon kosher salt

1/4 teaspoon freshly milled black pepper

48 square wonton wrappers, defrosted if frozen

2 tablespoons vegetable oil

One 14- or 14 1/2-ounce can chicken broth or 1 3/4 cups Chicken Stock (page 32)

Rinsed and dried fresh sage sprigs and chopped chives

3 ounces Parmigiano-Reggiano cheese, finely grated (about 1 cup; see grating information, page 10)

4. Remove the hot baking sheet from the oven, brush it with some of the oil, and arrange the ravioli in one layer. Brush the tops of the ravioli with the remaining oil. Return the pan to the oven and bake the ravioli for 8 minutes. Turn the ravioli over and bake another 8 minutes.

5. Meanwhile, heat the chicken broth in a small saucepan over high heat until hot and the remaining 3 tablespoons butter in a small skillet over low heat until it is nut brown. Arrange 6 ravioli in each of 4 bowls; spoon one-fourth of the broth over each portion. Top each serving with some of the butter, pine nuts, herbs, and Parmigiano-Reggiano.

Hands-on time:
25 minutes
with fava beans,
15 minutes
with lima beans

Total preparation time:
35 minutes
with fava beans,
25 minutes
with lima beans

4 tablespoons unsalted butter
1 small onion, finely chopped
   (1/2 cup)
1 garlic clove, minced
3/4 cup basmati rice
1/2 cup orzo
2 1/2 cups canned vegetable or
   chicken broth or Chicken
   Stock (page 32)
1 pound asparagus
Kosher salt
1/2 pound mushrooms,
   preferably morels, well
   cleaned and halved or
   quartered if large
1 cup blanched, peeled fava
   beans or frozen baby lima
   beans, defrosted
1 1/2 ounces Pecorino Romano
   cheese, grated (about 1/2
   cup; see Parmigiano-
   Reggiano grating
   information, page 10)
Freshly milled black pepper
Truffle oil, optional

Orzo and Basmati Pilaf
with Spring Vegetable Ragout

V

MAKES 4 SERVINGS

Orzo is a rice-shaped pasta from Italy. Basmati is a fragrant Indian long-grain rice with a wonderful nutty taste. The two of them combine to make a great side dish, but you can top it with anything and turn it into a main dish. Here we've chosen asparagus, mushrooms, and either lima beans or fava beans. By the way, some of the American versions of basmati would work well here too. Texmati is one that's pretty widely available. Serve with Asian Spiced Roasted Baby Carrots (page 292) and Garlic Bread (page 40).

1. Melt 2 tablespoons butter over medium-low heat. Add the onion and cook until softened, about 8 minutes. Add the garlic and cook 1 minute; add the rice and orzo and cook, stirring, until all the grains are coated with butter, about 2 minutes. Add 2 cups broth; bring the liquid to a boil over high heat, then turn it down to a bare simmer. Cover very tightly and cook for 15 minutes. Remove the pan from the heat and let stand for 5 minutes.

2. While the orzo is cooking, trim the ends off the asparagus and peel the bottom half if the asparagus stem is thicker than 1/3 inch. Bring a large skillet of salted water to a boil over high heat. Add the asparagus and cook for 2 to 4 minutes or until just tender. Drain, pat dry, and cut into 1/2-inch lengths.

3. Empty and dry the skillet; melt the remaining 2 tablespoons butter over medium heat. Add the mushrooms and cook until all the liquid the mushrooms give off has evaporated. Add the remaining 1/2 cup broth and the beans and cook for 3 minutes. Add the asparagus and cook until the mixture is just heated through. Stir in half the cheese and season with salt and pepper to taste. To serve, divide the pilaf among 4 bowls; top with the vegetable ragout and remaining cheese. Drizzle with truffle oil, if desired.

RICE is without a doubt the most consumed grain in the world. More than 40,000 varieties have been cultivated somewhere at some time, so it is no wonder that the rice choices in your supermarket are growing. Here are some you have to pick from.

Long-grain white rice is the most popular in the United States. The hull has been removed so it cooks in fifteen to twenty minutes and the grains tend not to stick together.

Medium- and short-grain white rices are less easy to find in the market but are available in ethnic markets, gourmet shops, health food stores, and by mail. These cook just as quickly as the long-grain rice, but release more starch and are more likely to stick together. *Arborio, Carnaroli,* and *Vialone Nano* are short-grain white rices imported from Italy. They are especially good for making risotto. The grains are rounder than most other rice in our market and when cooked, they become creamy and soft on the surface and al dente in the center.

Converted rice has been steamed before milling to preserve more of the nutrients once the hull is removed. This treatment also makes it easy to cook and less likely to stick together.

Aromatic rices such as *basmati,* which is imported from India; *jasmine,* which is imported from Thailand; and American aromatics such as *wild pecan, Wehani,* and *Delta Rose* have the flavor and aroma of popcorn when they are cooked.

Hybrid rices such as *Texmati* and *Jasmati* are American-grown varieties that have the aromatic qualities of the imported aromatic rice and the cooking qualities of American long-grain rice. They are easily available in supermarkets.

Brown rice can be any variety of rice that has not had the hull removed. It retains more of the nutritional value after cooking, but must be cooked 40 to 50 minutes to become tender.

Organic rice blends are now available in many supermarkets. The blends vary in the varieties of rice they include but are more likely to be medium-grain rice. They tend to need longer cooking than white rice, but are very attractive, crunchy, and higher in nutrients than many of the other choices.

Store boxes of rice in a sealed plastic bag to keep out bugs or, better yet, keep your rice in the fridge if you have room.

1 cup red wine

3 cups canned chicken broth
  or Chicken Stock (page 32)

1 Turkish bay leaf

2 tablespoons unsalted butter

1 medium onion, finely
  chopped (about 1 cup)

1 cup Arborio rice

2 medium legs and thighs (6
  ounces each) duck confit
  (see Sources, page 346)

2 medium sweet potatoes
  (about 12 ounces), peeled
  and cut into 1/2-inch cubes

1 teaspoon rinsed and dried
  fresh thyme or 1/3
  teaspoon dried

2 ounces Parmigiano-Reggiano
  cheese, freshly grated
  (about 2/3 cup; see grating
  information, page 10)

Kosher salt and freshly milled
  black pepper

Baked Risotto

with Red Wine, Sweet Potatoes, and Duck Confit

MAKES 4 SERVINGS

Risotto is a great one-size-fits-all dish because its sturdy creaminess provides the perfect backdrop for just about any foreground ingredient. But it needs to be nursed, stirred constantly so the rice absorbs the liquid at just the right pace. No one has the time for that on a weeknight. I discovered that if you bake the rice instead of cooking it on top of the stove, it requires much less tending. Baked Risotto isn't as creamy as the stirred version, but it's awfully good anyway.

Duck confit, or preserved duck, is rich and flavorful—and available at most gourmet food stores or through mail order (see Sources, page 346). If you prefer, substitute cooked chicken, pork, or turkey. Serve with a tossed green salad.

1. Preheat the oven to 375°F. Bring the wine to a boil in a saucepan over high heat; reduce the heat to low and simmer until reduced by half. Add the chicken broth and bay leaf to the wine and heat until hot.

2. Meanwhile, melt the butter in a skillet over medium-low heat. Add the onion and cook until softened, about 8 minutes. Add the rice, stirring until each grain is coated. Transfer the rice mixture to a 1 1/2-quart casserole; add the broth mixture with the bay leaf. Bake, covered, for 10 minutes. Remove from the oven and stir well. Bake, covered, for another 15 to 20 minutes or until the rice is tender.

3. While the rice is cooking, heat a medium skillet over medium-high heat. Add the duck confit, skin side down, and cook for 8 to 10 minutes or until the skin is very crisp. Remove the duck from the pan and let cool slightly, skin side up. Add the sweet potatoes and thyme to the duck fat in the pan and cook, stirring frequently, until the sweet potatoes are tender and slightly golden, about 8 minutes.

4. Remove the crisp skin from the duck and crumble; shred the meat and discard the bones. When the rice is done, remove the bay leaf and stir in the sweet potatoes, duck meat, and half the cheese; add salt and pepper to taste. Serve each portion topped with some of the crumbled duck skin and the remaining cheese.

WHEN a recipe calls for wine, it usually just says dry red wine or dry white wine, leaving the decision up to the cook. The most repeated advice on the subject is, "never cook with a wine you wouldn't drink," and that is a good place to start. I would revise that to "never cook with a wine you wouldn't drink with the dish you are preparing." The flavor intensity of the wine you select should match the flavor intensity of the other ingredients in the recipe. It should enhance the flavor of the main component of the dish rather than overpower it or disappear in its presence. You don't need to buy expensive wines for cooking, just wines that taste good to you. And be sure to avoid wines labeled "cooking wine."

SELECTING WINE FOR COOKING

Pearl Couscous and Shellfish Stew

4 tablespoons extra virgin
    olive oil
8 small sea scallops
8 medium shrimp, shelled and
    deveined
1/4 cup finely chopped shallots
2 garlic cloves, minced (about
    2 teaspoons)
3 plum tomatoes (about 8
    ounces), finely chopped
1 cup white wine
1 dozen mussels, scrubbed and
    debearded
1 dozen littleneck clams,
    scrubbed
1 to 1 1/2 cups canned chicken
    broth or Chicken Stock
    (page 32)
1 cup pearl or Israeli couscous
Kosher salt and freshly milled
    black pepper

MAKES 4 SERVINGS

Couscous is actually small grains of semolina pasta. It ranges in size from minuscule to pea-size balls known as pearl or Israeli couscous. I like the firmer texture of the larger couscous, which works well in a pilaf-based dish like this one. The liquid produced from cooking the shellfish is the base of the broth for the pilaf, augmented by chicken broth. It ends up being a very robust broth that not only flavors the couscous but also acts as the sauce for the stew. You can discard the shells from the clams and mussels before you serve the stew or you can just leave them on and let everyone shell as they eat. Serve with Grilled Radicchio Salad (page 306).

1. Heat 2 tablespoons of the oil in a large skillet over high heat until hot; reduce the heat to medium-high and add the scallops and the shrimp. Cook, turning once, until almost cooked through, about 2 minutes total. Transfer the shellfish with tongs to a strainer set over a bowl and set aside.

2. Add the shallots to the pan and cook over medium-low heat until softened, about 2 minutes. Add the garlic and cook, stirring 1 more minute. Add the tomatoes and cook for 3 minutes. Add the white wine, mussels, and clams. Cover and increase the heat to high. Steam for 3 to 5 minutes, transferring the mussels and clams as they open to the strainer with the shrimp and scallops. Discard any mussels and clams that do not open. Measure the tomato mixture in the skillet; add the liquid from the bowl under the shellfish and enough chicken broth to make 2 cups.

3. Heat the remaining 2 tablespoons oil in a saucepan over medium heat and add the couscous. Cook, stirring, for 3 minutes. Add the 2 cups liquid and bring to a boil. Turn it down to a simmer, cover the pan tightly, and cook for 5 minutes or until the couscous is tender.

4. Meanwhile, remove and discard the mussel and clam shells, if desired. Add all the shellfish to the couscous along with any more juices from the bowl; cook until just heated through. Add salt and pepper to taste and serve.

Ricotta Gnocchi

V

MAKES 4 TO 6 SERVINGS

Kosher salt

One 15-ounce container
whole-milk ricotta

3 large eggs, lightly beaten

1 cup unbleached all-purpose
flour

3 ounces Pecorino Romano
cheese, grated (about
1 cup; see Parmigiano-
Reggiano grating
instructions, page 10)

1 teaspoon salt

1/4 teaspoon freshly milled
black pepper

1/8 teaspoon nutmeg

2 cups of your favorite bottled
tomato sauce or 1/2 recipe
Sautéed Cherry Tomato
Sauce (page 319, add prep
time)

2 ounces Italian Fontina
cheese, coarsely grated
(about 1/2 cup)

These are a snap to make (especially compared to the more traditional potato gnocchi.) You put a pot of water on to boil, throw all the ingredients into the mixer, and then drop small mounds of dough into the water. It is a rustic dish; the gnocchi can be misshapen. If you have a very small ice cream scoop kicking around, that's the ideal tool for the job. Just dip it in warm water and pick up a mound of dough, which will fall easily into the water from the scoop. The homemade cherry tomato sauce is a delicious complement to the gnocchi, but your favorite storebought tomato sauce is just fine in a pinch. Serve with Garlic Bread (page 40) and a tossed green salad.

1. Preheat oven to 400°F. Bring a large pot of salted water to a boil. Beat the ricotta cheese and eggs together with an electric mixer until well combined. Stir in the flour, half of the Pecorino cheese, the salt, pepper, and nutmeg until just combined.

2. Scoop up a rounded tablespoon of the gnocchi dough, then use a second tablespoon to scoop the mixture off the spoon and into the boiling water. Repeat to make as many gnocchi as will fit in the saucepan without crowding. Simmer for 7 minutes. When they are cooked through, transfer the gnocchi with a slotted spoon to a shallow baking dish. Repeat until all the dough has been cooked.

3. Spoon the sauce over the gnocchi and top with Fontina and remaining Pecorino cheeses and bake for 10 minutes or until cheese has melted.

Poultry

Hands-on time:
20 minutes

Total preparation time:
50 minutes

4 chicken breast halves, with
skin and bone, halved
crosswise
Kosher salt and freshly milled
black pepper
2 tablespoons extra virgin
olive oil
1/2 pound sweet or hot Italian
sausage, cut into 1/2-inch
pieces
4 pickled cherry peppers,
quartered, stems and seeds
discarded
2 garlic cloves, minced (about
2 teaspoons)
1 cup white wine
One 14- or 14 1/2-ounce can
chicken broth or 1 3/4 cups
Chicken Stock (page 32)
Two 6 1/2-ounce jars
marinated artichoke hearts,
drained
1 1/2 tablespoons unbleached
all-purpose flour

Chicken with Sausage
and Hot Cherry Peppers

MAKES 4 SERVINGS

This is based on an Italian dish called *scarpariello*—sort of a "turf and turf." I love the combination of chicken and sausages to begin with, and when you throw in the pickled peppers, the whole dish takes on a lively peppery taste. When I first made this, I braised the chicken in the sauce and it came out a little tough (my stove is electric and it's hard to get the low temperature right.) The skin was rubbery, too. I decided I could achieve a crisper skin and a moister texture by searing the chicken on top of the stove and finishing it in the oven. This has the added benefit of speeding up the preparation time since you can make the sauce on top of the stove while the chicken is in the oven. If you are a glutton for very spicy food, use hot Italian sausage. If you are trying to cut back on fat, use turkey sausages. Serve with Mediterranean Orzo Pilaf (page 307) or buttered noodles.

1. Preheat the oven to 350°F. Season the chicken on all sides with salt and pepper. Heat the oil in a large skillet over high heat until hot; reduce the heat to medium-high and add the chicken to the skillet skin side down. Sauté until nicely browned, about 10 minutes. Place the chicken, skin side up, on a rimmed baking sheet; bake in the center of the oven 25 minutes or until just cooked through.

2. Meanwhile, add the sausage to the skillet in which you cooked the chicken. Cook over medium-high heat until lightly browned, about 8 minutes. Add the peppers and garlic; cook for 1 minute. Add the wine and cook until reduced by half, about 5 minutes. Add the broth and artichoke hearts and cook 5 minutes.

3. Whisk together 2 tablespoons of water and the flour; whisk into the sausage mixture and cook until thickened. Transfer the chicken to a serving platter; cover loosely with aluminum foil, and let rest 5 minutes. Stir any juices that have collected on the baking sheet into the sauce. Return the sauce to a boil and spoon over the chicken.

Balsamic Chicken

4 boneless chicken breast
halves, with skin (about
1 1/2 pounds)
Kosher salt and freshly milled
black pepper
2 tablespoons extra virgin
olive oil
1 medium onion, chopped
(about 1 cup)
1 garlic clove, minced (about
1 teaspoon)
4 plum tomatoes (about
1 pound), chopped
1/4 cup balsamic vinegar
1 cup canned chicken broth or
Chicken Stock (page 32)
2 tablespoons unsalted butter

MAKES 4 SERVINGS

The balsamic vinegar in this recipe—and you can use the regular old affordable supermarket variety—provides a sweet-and-sour base and great depth of flavor to this very quick sauce. This sauce would go nicely on sautéed pork chops or a flavorful fish such as salmon or bluefish as well. Serve with Smashed Potatoes (page 38) and Sautéed Spinach with Garlic (page 34).

1. Season the chicken with 1/2 teaspoon salt and 1/4 teaspoon pepper. Heat the oil in a large skillet over high heat until hot; reduce the heat to medium-high and add the chicken breasts, skin side down. Sauté for 6 minutes or until the skin is nicely browned. Turn the chicken over and sauté for 12 to 14 minutes, or until the chicken is just cooked through. Transfer with tongs or a slotted spoon to a plate and cover loosely with aluminum foil.

2. Reduce the heat to medium; add the onion to the skillet and cook, stirring occasionally, until softened, about 5 minutes. Add the garlic and cook 1 minute. Add the tomatoes and cook until softened slightly, about 3 minutes.

3. Add the vinegar and broth and simmer for 5 minutes. Add the butter and any juices from the chicken plate to the pan and heat just until the butter is melted. Transfer the chicken, skin side up, to each of 4 plates and top each serving with some of the sauce.

BALSAMIC vinegar is a reduction of crushed grapes that is combined with an older balsamic vinegar and transferred as it ages to a smaller barrel made from a different wood (including oak, cherry, chestnut, mulberry, acacia, juniper, and ash) each year. True balsamic vinegar can be made only in the regions of Modena and Reggio in Italy mainly from the white Trebbiano grape and must be aged at least ten years. The cost of a true artisan balsamic vinegar reflects the care that has gone into its production. However, there are less expensive balsamic vinegars; these have not been aged as long or are factory made and contain things other than grapes. If you are using a lot of balsamic vinegar in a recipe, it makes sense to take a look at less expensive brands, but read the label carefully to see what they contain.

ALL ABOUT BALSAMIC VINEGAR

4 boneless, skinless chicken
breast halves
4 ounces prosciutto di Parma,
thinly sliced
3 ounces Italian fontina
cheese, thinly sliced
1/3 cup Wondra or unbleached
all-purpose flour
Kosher salt and freshly milled
black pepper
1/3 stick unsalted butter
1/3 cup dry Marsala
3/4 cup low-sodium canned
chicken broth or Chicken
Stock (page 32)

John's Stuffed Chicken Breasts Marsala

MAKES 4 SERVINGS

My brother-in-law, John Murphy, invented this recipe because he knew his kids would love it (not to mention my sister Anne). He also liked the idea that you could complete the recipe to the point of browning the chicken breasts and then park them for up to an hour before finishing them in the oven. It is the perfect entertaining dish, but it also makes a simple elegant weeknight entrée. When you pour the Marsala and chicken broth mixture over the cooked breasts in the roasting pan, the liquid mixes with the melted cheese that leaks out of the chicken to form a delicious sauce. Serve with Parmigiano-Reggiano Couscous (page 41) and Herbed Pea Medley (page 37).

1. Preheat the oven to 350°F. Arrange the chicken breasts flat on a cutting board. Starting at one long side and cutting toward the other long side but not all the way through it, slice each breast almost in half horizontally so it opens like a book. Arrange a fourth of the prosciutto di Parma and a fourth of the cheese on one side of each chicken breast; fold the other side of each chicken breast over the filling. Combine the flour, 1/2 teaspoon salt, and 1/4 teaspoon pepper in a soup plate; dip each stuffed breast into the seasoned flour, coating it well on all sides.

2. Heat a skillet just large enough to hold the chicken breasts in one layer over high heat until hot. Add the butter and swirl as it melts. Add the chicken and sauté for 2 to 2 1/2 minutes a side or until golden. Transfer the breasts to a baking pan just large enough to hold them in one layer; bake 15 to 20 minutes or until just cooked through.

3. Add the Marsala to the skillet. Bring it to a boil, stirring to loosen any brown bits in the bottom of the pan. Add the broth and simmer for 3 minutes. Pour the sauce over the chicken and serve.

Lemon Chicken

Hands-on time:
15 minutes

Total preparation time:
35 minutes

MAKES 4 SERVINGS

For the longest time *torikatsu* chicken was one of my favorite Japanese takeout items. In fact, I loved this dish so much that I pretended it wasn't fried. Alas, one day I confirmed the awful truth. Heartbroken, I decided to invent a nondeep-fried version and add lemon to it. Here it is. The chicken comes out very moist from the marinade and crunchy from the coating. Serve with Simple Boiled Rice (page 40) and Butter-steamed Broccoli with Soy (page 296).

1. Combine the lemon juice and soy sauce in a large zippered plastic bag. Add the chicken and let marinate for 15 minutes at room temperature, turning occasionally.

2. Set up 3 bowls, one filled with the flour seasoned with 1/2 teaspoon salt and 1/4 teaspoon pepper, a second with the beaten eggs, and a third with the panko bread crumbs mixed with the sesame seeds. Remove the chicken from the marinade, letting all the liquid drip off; discard the marinade. Coat the chicken lightly with the flour, then dip it in the egg, letting the excess drip off. Coat it well with the panko mixture.

3. Heat half the oil in a large skillet over high heat until hot; reduce the heat to medium-low and add the chicken. Sauté for 6 minutes and add the remaining oil. Turn the chicken and sauté for 6 minutes more or until browned on the second side and just cooked through. Garnish with lemon slices.

1/2 cup fresh lemon juice (2 to 3 lemons)
1/4 cup soy sauce
1 to 1 1/4 pounds boneless, skinless, thin-sliced chicken breast cutlets
1/3 cup Wondra or unbleached all-purpose flour
Kosher salt and freshly milled black pepper
2 eggs, lightly beaten
1 1/4 cups packaged panko bread crumbs or panko from Bread Crumbs Four Ways (page 23, add prep time)
1/4 cup sesame seeds
5 tablespoons vegetable oil
Lemon slices for garnish

Hands-on time:
10 minutes

Total preparation time:
35 minutes

3 1/2 cups canned chicken
broth or Chicken Stock
(page 32)

1/2 cup white wine or
vermouth

1 1/2 pounds boneless, skinless
chicken breasts

1 recipe Italian Tuna Sauce
(page 315), using 2
tablespoons of the
poaching liquid from this
recipe rather than the 2
tablespoons chicken broth

Pitted, brine-cured olives such
as kalamata, optional

Poached Chicken Breasts
with Italian Tuna Sauce

MAKES 4 SERVINGS

What was the single most frequently asked question during the
run of *Cooking Live?* Probably, "Why is my white-meat chicken so
dry?" The answer is simple—"You overcooked it"—but the
solution is not. The problem is that you want to cook the white
meat long enough to kill any salmonella, but not a moment
longer. The chicken poaching method below is pretty foolproof.

This technique is especially good when cooking chicken for
chicken salad. You can take the poached chicken breast, cool it,
cube it, and then toss it with any number of sauces from the back
of the book, including Horseradish Sauce (page 316), Rouille (page
314), Tahini Sauce (page 324), or Quick Herb Sauce (page 312), for
a nice weeknight chicken salad. Here I have partnered it with
Italian Tuna Sauce (page 315). Typically, the Italians pour this sauce
onto veal to make *vitello tonnato*, but chicken is much less
expensive than veal and an equally great backdrop for the tuna
sauce. Chicken and tuna might seem like an odd combination on
paper, but you'll love it in your mouth. Serve on a bed of mesclun
with crusty bread, Bean Salad (page 39), and sliced tomatoes.

1. Combine the chicken broth and wine in a medium saucepan. Bring the
mixture to a boil over high heat. Add the chicken, reduce the heat to low,
and bring the liquid to a simmer. Simmer gently, uncovered, for 5 minutes.
Remove the pan from the heat, cover, and let stand for 10 minutes. Check
for doneness. If the chicken appears to be undercooked, return the broth
to boiling, cover, and let stand off the heat 5 minutes longer. Transfer the
chicken to a plate or platter and chill in the refrigerator for 10 minutes.
Reserve the chicken poaching liquid.

2. Meanwhile, prepare the Italian Tuna Sauce using 2 tablespoons of the chicken poaching liquid in place of the broth called for in the recipe. Reserve the rest of the cooking liquid for another use (such as in a soup or any recipe that calls for chicken broth).

3. Slice the chicken diagonally 1/2 inch thick and divide it among 4 plates. Drizzle one-fourth of the sauce over each portion. Garnish with olives, if desired.

Soy-braised Chicken

1/3 cup soy sauce

2 scallions (white and light
green parts), smashed with
a knife

3 tablespoons rice wine or dry
sherry

One 2-inch strip orange zest
(just the orange part, no
white pith)

Two 1/4-inch-thick slices
ginger, smashed with a
knife

1 teaspoon dark brown sugar

2 star anise

One 3 1/2-pound chicken, cut
into 8 pieces, skin removed

1 tablespoon cornstarch

MAKES 4 SERVINGS

Braising chicken or pork in an aromatic soy-based broth is a classic technique of Asian cuisine. It is also my favorite kind of recipe. You just throw a bunch of flavorings into a pot with the soy sauce, add the chicken, and braise it until done, either in the oven or on top of the stove. You don't even need a sauce. The chicken absorbs all of the flavor from the liquid. Serve with Simple Boiled Rice (page 40) and Butter-steamed Broccoli with Soy (page 296).

1. Preheat the oven to 325°F. Combine 1 1/2 cups water, the soy sauce, scallions, wine, orange zest, ginger, brown sugar, and star anise in an ovenproof saucepan or Dutch oven large enough to hold the chicken pieces in one layer; bring the mixture to a boil over high heat. Add the chicken, return the liquid to a boil, cover the pan tightly, and place in the center of the oven. Braise 15 minutes.

2. Remove the pan from the oven and turn the chicken pieces; cover and return to the oven. Braise 15 to 20 minutes longer or until the chicken is just tender. Remove the chicken with tongs to a platter; cover it loosely with aluminum foil and set aside. Whisk together the cornstarch and 2 tablespoons water. Bring the liquid in the pan to a boil, whisk in the cornstarch mixture, and simmer for 1 minute. Remove the scallions, orange zest, ginger, and anise with a slotted spoon. Serve the chicken drizzled with the sauce.

SOY SAUCE is made from fermenting soybeans with wheat, rice, or barley; salt; and water. *Chinese light soy sauce* is lighter in color and texture and slightly saltier than dark soy sauce. It is mainly used in cooking so that it does not darken the color of the food. *Chinese dark soy sauce* is darker, often has added caramel, and is sweeter in flavor and thicker in consistency than light. It is usually used as a condiment. *Japanese soy sauce (shoyu)* generally has a milder, sweeter, less salty taste than Chinese. *Tamari* is a Japanese soy sauce containing little or no wheat—so if you are cooking for someone with a wheat allergy, this is the soy sauce for you. Check the label first to make sure there is no trace of wheat. *Lite* soy sauce is lower in sodium.

The most important factor in your soy sauce selection is to choose one that is naturally fermented. If the bottle doesn't say that, it has probably been chemically produced from hydrolyzed soybeans, caramel coloring, and salt. There is a huge difference in flavor.

Soy sauce will keep in a cool dark place for several months after opening, but some manufacturers recommend keeping the lite soy in the fridge, since it has a lower sodium content.

ABOUT
SOY SAUCE

Hands-on time:
15 minutes

Total preparation time:
1 hour 10 minutes

4 slices bacon, chopped

1/3 cup Wondra or unbleached
all-purpose flour

Kosher salt and freshly milled
black pepper

8 bone-in chicken thighs
(about 3 pounds), skin
removed

1 tablespoon vegetable oil

1 medium onion, coarsely
chopped (about 1 cup)

1 tablespoon chopped fresh
rosemary or 1 teaspoon
dried

2 cups apple cider

1 unpeeled Granny Smith
apple, sliced 1/4 inch thick

3 tablespoons fresh lemon
juice

Cider-braised Chicken

MAKES 4 SERVINGS

This is one of those dishes that makes its own sauce as it cooks. In the course of an hour the bacon, cider, chicken, rosemary, and apple flavors all come together. The resulting liquid is thickened by the flour the chicken was dipped in so that the chicken, complete with sauce, is ready to go. I use chicken thighs on the bone because they have more flavor and are juicier than chicken breasts, but you could substitute breasts or use a mixture of white and dark meat. Serve with buttered noodles and Sautéed Spinach with Garlic (page 34).

1. Cook the bacon in a large, heavy skillet over medium heat until crisp, about 6 minutes. Transfer the bacon with a slotted spoon to paper towels to drain, leaving 1 teaspoon fat in the pan. Meanwhile, combine the flour, 1/2 teaspoon salt, and 1/4 teaspoon pepper in a soup plate. Add the chicken pieces, several at a time, and turn to coat evenly; shake off any excess.

2. Add the oil to the reserved bacon fat in the skillet and reheat over high heat until hot; reduce the heat to medium-high and add the chicken. Sauté the chicken until it is golden on both sides, about 5 minutes per side. Transfer the chicken to a plate with tongs.

3. Reduce the heat to medium; add the onion to the same skillet and cook, stirring occasionally, until softened, about 5 minutes. Add the rosemary and cook for 1 minute. Return the chicken and any juices from the plate to the pan. Add the cider and bring the mixture to a boil; reduce the heat to low and simmer the chicken, covered tightly, for 25 minutes.

4. Add the apple and cook 10 minutes longer, until the chicken has just cooked through and the sauce has thickened. If the sauce is not thick, remove the chicken and reduce the sauce. Stir in the lemon juice and reserved bacon; add salt and pepper to taste.

White Chicken Chili

4 tablespoons (1/2 stick)
   unsalted butter
1 medium onion, chopped
   (about 1 cup)
3 garlic cloves, minced (about
   1 tablespoon)
1/4 cup unbleached all-
   purpose flour
1 tablespoon chili powder
1 tablespoon ground cumin
1/4 to 1/2 teaspoon cayenne
   pepper
2 cups canned chicken broth
   or Chicken Stock (page 32)
1 cup white wine or additional
   chicken broth or stock
2 pounds ground chicken
Two 15- or 15 1/2-ounce cans
   cannellini or navy beans,
   drained and rinsed
2/3 cup sour cream or yogurt
Kosher salt and freshly milled
   black pepper
Accompaniments: salsa,
   chopped Hass avocado,
   grated cheese, and
   shredded lettuce

MAKES 6 SERVINGS

There is one good reason—other than chicken and chiles—why I love the white chicken chili on the menu at the burrito palace in our neighborhood: sour cream. This quick-to-make home version is delicious unadorned. Add the accompaniments and some homemade or store-bought cornbread, and it's over the top.

1. Melt the butter in a large saucepan over medium-low heat. Add the onion and cook, stirring occasionally, until softened, about 8 minutes. Add the garlic and cook 1 minute. Stir in the flour, chili powder, cumin, and cayenne to taste and cook 2 minutes longer. Gradually whisk in the broth and wine; bring to a boil and simmer 3 minutes.

2. Add the chicken and simmer gently until the chicken is just cooked through, about 8 minutes. Add the beans and sour cream and cook 15 minutes or until nicely thickened. Season with salt and pepper to taste. Serve with the accompaniments.

Mustard-chutney Roasted Chicken Thighs

Hands-on time:
10 minutes

Total preparation time:
45 to 50 minutes

MAKES 4 SERVINGS

When I was in my teens and on a perpetual diet, I was told that white-meat chicken is lower in calories than dark. That's true. But as a grown-up chef I know it's also true that dark meat is tenderer, juicier, cheaper, and more flavorful than the breast. (This is particularly true of the thighs, which do not have the tough sinews of the legs.) Everyone will love this dish. You can omit the jalapeños if you're not feeding chile lovers. Serve with Charred Onions and Peppers (page 297) and Coconut Rice (page 308).

1. Preheat the oven to 375°F. Lightly oil a rimmed baking sheet. Combine the chutney, mustard, mayonnaise, jalapeños, and lime juice in a large bowl; add the thighs and toss until completely coated.

2. Combine the crumbs and oil on a plate; add the thighs, one at a time, and coat with crumbs. Arrange on the baking sheet. Bake 35 to 40 minutes, until cooked through and the crumbs are golden brown. Transfer the thighs to a platter and serve.

1/3 cup mango chutney
  (preferably Major Grey's),
  finely chopped
3 tablespoons Dijon mustard
2 tablespoons mayonnaise
2 tablespoons finely chopped
  pickled jalapeños
2 tablespoons fresh lime juice
4 large bone-in chicken thighs,
  with skin (about 1 1/2
  pounds)
1 1/2 cups fresh bread crumbs
  from Bread Crumbs Four
  Ways (page 23)
1 tablespoon extra virgin olive
  oil

6 frozen breakfast sausages

2 small onions

4 slices homemade-style white
    bread, torn into small
    pieces

3 tablespoons unsalted butter,
    melted

1/4 teaspoon dried sage

1/4 teaspoon dried thyme

Kosher salt and freshly milled
    black pepper

4 Rock Cornish hens (1 to 11/4
    pounds each), rinsed and
    dried

1/2 cup white wine or
    vermouth, optional

One 14- or 14 1/2-ounce can
    chicken broth or 1 3/4 cups
    Chicken Stock (page 32)

3 tablespoons unbleached all-
    purpose flour

Thanksgiving Hens

MAKES 4 SERVINGS

Rock Cornish game hens, a cross between a White Rock hen and a Cornish hen, are underrated. Maybe this is because, ounce for ounce, they are a little more expensive than chicken, or perhaps they are a little scary for people who are used to chicken in parts. But they are delicious indeed, and their greatest attribute is that they are "mini." Each person gets his or her own bird. I thought it would be nice to come up with a recipe that mimics the Thanksgiving bird but can be made in one tenth the time. So these birds are stuffed à la Thanksgiving and served with a good old-fashioned pan gravy that you can whip up while the Cornish hens are resting. Serve with Southwestern Sweet Potato Sauté (page 294) and Herbed Pea Medley (page 37).

1. Preheat the oven to 375°F; arrange the frozen sausages in a shallow roasting pan and roast until cooked through, about 18 to 20 minutes. Set the sausages aside until they are cool enough to handle; then cut them into 1/4-inch slices. Reserve the pan. Turn up the heat to 475°F.

2. Meanwhile, finely chop one onion and coarsely chop the other. Combine the sliced sausages, bread, finely chopped onion, 2 tablespoons of the butter, the sage, thyme, 1/4 teaspoon salt, and 1/4 teaspoon pepper. Season the hens inside and out with an additional 1/4 teaspoon salt and 1/4 teaspoon pepper. Stuff each hen with one fourth of the bread mixture and tie the legs. Arrange the hens on a rack in the shallow roasting pan and drizzle the wine and remaining 1 tablespoon butter over them.

3. Roast the hens for 20 minutes. Add the coarsely chopped onion to the pan and continue roasting for 10 to 15 minutes longer, until a meat thermometer inserted in the thigh joint registers 170°F. Transfer the hens to a platter, cover loosely with aluminum foil, and let rest for 10 minutes.

4. Meanwhile, put the roasting pan on a burner; add the broth and bring to a boil, stirring to loosen any brown bits in the bottom of the pan. Whisk together 1/4 cup water and the flour; add to the roasting pan and bring to a boil, stirring constantly. Simmer 3 minutes. Serve the hens with the sauce.

Turkey Cutlets Milanese

1 pound thin turkey cutlets
2/3 cup Wondra or unbleached
all-purpose flour
Kosher salt and freshly milled
black pepper
2 large eggs
1 cup fresh bread crumbs from
Bread Crumbs Four Ways
(page 23)
1 ounce Parmigiano-Reggiano
cheese, finely grated (about
1/3 cup; see grating
information, page 10)
4 tablespoons extra virgin
olive oil
4 cups loosely packed baby
arugula, mesclun, or baby
spinach
1/4 cup bottled vinaigrette or
All-Purpose Vinaigrette
(page 28, add prep time)

MAKES 4 SERVINGS

Although one of my favorite dishes is Veal Milanese, I understand that not everyone is a fan of veal. Accordingly, I've cooked up an adaptation of the classic recipe that substitutes turkey for veal while still combining two of my favorite culinary elements: breaded sautéed meat and an acidic salad. Like breaded veal, breaded turkey needs an assertive counterpoint. My choice is peppery baby arugula tossed with a tart vinaigrette, which works like a spritz of lemon on a piece of fish.

If you are not a fan of arugula, substitute mesclun lettuce or baby spinach. If you are not a fan of turkey, substitute pounded pork or chicken cutlets. This is a perfect summertime dish, but I'd be happy to see it any time of the year. Serve with Oven Fries (page 295).

1. Sprinkle a small amount of water on a large sheet of plastic wrap. Place half of the turkey cutlets on top of the plastic and sprinkle again with water. Cover with another sheet of plastic wrap and pound with a rolling pin or meat pounder until about 1/4 inch thick. Repeat with the remaining turkey cutlets.

2. Using 3 soup plates, combine the flour, 1 teaspoon salt, and 1/2 teaspoon pepper in the first, lightly beat the eggs in the second, and combine the crumbs and cheese in the third. Lightly coat the turkey first with the flour mixture, then with the eggs, letting the excess drip off, and then with the crumbs.

3. Heat half the oil in a large skillet over high heat until hot; reduce the heat to medium-high and add half the cutlets. Sauté until they are golden and just cooked through, about 4 minutes a side. Transfer to a plate and cover loosely with aluminum foil. Repeat with the remaining oil and cutlets.

4. Meanwhile, toss the baby greens with the dressing. Transfer the turkey to plates, topping each portion with some of the salad.

ALTHOUGH there has been some debate about the relative safety of wooden versus plastic cutting boards, the Food and Drug Administration now recommends using either a hardwood such as maple or nonporous plastic for cutting boards. The FDA says the material used is not as important as the surface—it should be nonporous and smooth, with no cracks and grooves for bacteria to hide in.

Whichever material you use, scrub your cutting board regularly with hot water, soap, and a stiff brush. Plastic boards will get a good cleaning in the dishwasher, but don't put your wooden boards in there or they will warp. For more information go to *www.fda.gov/fdac/features/895_kitchen.html.*

CUTTING
BOARD
SAFETY

4 Pekin duck breast halves
Kosher salt and freshly milled
  black pepper
1 cup seedless grapes, halved,
  plus 4 small bunches for
  garnish
3 large shallots or 1/2 small
  onion, finely chopped
  (about 1/4 cup)
1 tablespoon finely grated
  fresh ginger (use a
  Microplane)
1/2 cup rice vinegar
1/2 cup canned chicken broth
  or Chicken Stock (page 32)
2 tablespoons Dijon mustard
1 tablespoon currant jelly

Sautéed Duck Breast
with Gingered Grape Sauce

MAKES 4 SERVINGS

Duck and fruit are a classic combination, humans having long ago figured out that the acid in oranges, apples, or pears acts as a great counterbalance to the richness of the duck. Here I've used grapes, because I think grapes are unjustly overlooked in cooking—they add sweetness, acidity, and crunch. And once they're cooked, they become even more grapey.

By the way, if you've never before tried duck, you might imagine it's too fatty and too gamey. Not necessarily true. Duck breast, at least, can be quite lean, and Pekin (a.k.a. Long Island) duck breasts aren't gamey at all. Maple Leaf Farms produces most of the duck you will find in the supermarkets. It comes whole, in halves, and in parts, and is pretty widely available these days. I suggest you cook the breasts with the skin still on, which guarantees better flavor and prevents them from drying out. If you want to avoid the extra fat, just remove the skin before serving. I also suggest you cook them medium-rare for maximum juiciness. Serve with Butternut Squash Puree (page 36) and buttered noodles.

1. Score the duck skin in a crisscross pattern and season the duck with salt and pepper. Heat a large skillet over high heat until hot. Add the duck, skin side down, reduce the heat to medium-high, and cook for 10 minutes, or until the skin is very crispy. Periodically remove and reserve any excess fat that the duck gives off. Turn the duck over and let it cook for 3 more minutes for medium-rare. Transfer to a plate, skin side up, and cover loosely with aluminum foil.

2. Add 2 tablespoons of the reserved duck fat to the skillet. Heat over high heat until hot; reduce the heat to medium and add the halved grapes, shallots, and ginger to the skillet. Cook for 3 minutes; add the vinegar and let it simmer until reduced by half. Add the broth, mustard, and jelly and simmer until thickened slightly, about 2 minutes. Add any juices that have accumulated on the duck plate and salt and pepper to taste.

3. Slice the duck at an angle into 1/4-inch slices and serve each portion topped with some of the sauce. Garnish each with a small bunch of grapes.

1 1/2 pounds ground turkey
   (white, dark, or mixed)
1 medium red bell pepper,
   finely chopped (about
   1 cup)
1/4 small head napa cabbage,
   finely shredded (about
   1 cup)
4 scallions (white and light
   green parts), finely
   chopped (about 1/2 cup)
1 large egg, lightly beaten
3 tablespoons rinsed, dried,
   and chopped fresh cilantro,
   mint, or basil, or a mix
2 tablespoons plus 1 teaspoon
   soy sauce
1 tablespoon finely grated
   fresh ginger (use a
   Microplane)
1 teaspoon toasted sesame oil
Kosher salt and freshly milled
   black pepper
2 to 3 tablespoons vegetable
   oil
1/4 cup plus 2 tablespoons
   mayonnaise
2 teaspoons prepared wasabi
6 hamburger buns, toasted if
   desired

Asian Turkey Burgers
with Wasabi Sauce

MAKES 6 SERVINGS

Sure, ground turkey is a nice lean alternative to ground beef, but its very leanness guarantees that it will usually be quite dry. How to juice it up? Vegetables—in this case Napa cabbage, which gives off moisture as it cooks.

The various Asian elements in the burger—soy sauce, ginger, and sesame oil—inspired me to complement it with a wasabi sauce. Although authentic Japanese wasabi is very hard to find in America, the supermarket brands available here still pack quite a punch. If you like spicy food, wasabi should become a staple in your pantry.

Serve this dish with Butter-steamed Broccoli with Soy (page 296) and Simple Boiled Rice (page 40).

1. Stir together the turkey, bell pepper, cabbage, scallions, egg, cilantro, 2 tablespoons of the soy sauce, the ginger, 1/2 teaspoon of the sesame oil, 1/2 teaspoon salt, and 1/4 teaspoon black pepper just until well mixed. Shape the mixture into six patties about 1/2 inch thick.

2. Heat 2 tablespoons of the vegetable oil in a large skillet over high heat until hot; reduce the heat to medium, add the burgers, and cook them for 5 minutes a side or until just cooked through, adding more oil if necessary.

3. Meanwhile, stir together the mayonnaise, wasabi, remaining 1 teaspoon soy sauce, and 1/2 teaspoon sesame oil.

4. Put a burger in each of the buns and top the burger with about 1 tablespoon of the sauce.

LIKE ginger, wasabi is an above-ground root, or rhizome. Native to Japan, it is a member of the Cruciferae family and is cultivated in cool mountain streams. Traditionally, the perishable condiment is produced by peeling and finely grating the bright green root on a grater just before serving, as the heat and flavor evaporate within fifteen to twenty minutes. In Japan, fresh and dried wasabi leaves are used for flavoring, and the rhizome is also pickled.

Unfortunately, authentic, fresh wasabi is hard to come by; it is very expensive and rarely found in the United States. Even in Japan, most of the wasabi served is made from powder or paste, reputedly pale imitations of the real thing, but plenty potent for Westerners who have never tasted the real stuff. Wasabi powder—a combination of dried and ground horseradish—was first made in Japan shortly before World War II. It stores well, is easily reconstituted with an equal amount of slightly warm water, and delivers the required punch.

The paste usually includes the same ingredients, but is ready to use when purchased. It is sold in tubes and should be kept in the fridge. It is often slightly milder than the powder and should be used shortly after opening for best flavor. Recent experiments in the Pacific Northwest of America have been successful in growing hydroponic wasabi, and although the fresh product is quite expensive and limited in production, it offers hope that someday the incendiary little mound on our plates will be freshly grated *Wasabia japonica*.

WHAT'S WASABI?

From
the Meat
Department

Hands-on time:
20 minutes

Total preparation time:
20 minutes

1 pound pork tenderloin, cut
   crosswise into 8 pieces
Kosher salt and freshly milled
   black pepper
2 tablespoons extra virgin
   olive oil
1 ounce prosciutto di Parma,
   cut into strips (about 1/3
   cup loosely packed)
1/2 lemon, peeled, cut into
   sections and the sections
   chopped
1 tablespoon drained, bottled
   capers
1 tablespoon rinsed, dried,
   and chopped fresh sage
2/3 cup canned low-sodium
   chicken broth or Chicken
   Stock (page 32)
2 tablespoons unsalted butter,
   sliced

Pork Tournedos
with Sage and Prosciutto

MAKES 4 SERVINGS

This is a takeoff on the Italian dish called *saltimbocca*, which literally means "jump into the mouth," because that is how tasty it is. The traditional dish has veal scaloppine, prosciutto, and sage. This variation, made with pork tenderloin, is just as good and a heck of a lot more affordable. The government advises us to cook pork to 160°F to prevent trichinosis (a disease that basically doesn't exist anymore). Considering that trichinosis is killed at 138°F, I always cook my pork to a medium doneness, about 145°F, and let the meat rest for five minutes, during which time its temperature goes up to 150°F. Pork is so lean these days it is best to cook it to medium so it will be juicy and tender. However, if you are cooking for anyone in one of the high-risk groups—the elderly, the immune-impaired, or children under five years old—you should probably cook your pork well done. Serve with Parmigiano-Reggiano Couscous (page 41) and Butternut Squash Puree (page 36).

1. Season the pork on both sides with salt and pepper. Heat the oil in a large skillet over high heat until hot; reduce the heat to medium-high; add the pork and sauté until well browned, about 4 minutes. Turn the pork and sauté until browned on the other side and the temperature has reached 145°F on a meat thermometer, about 4 minutes. Transfer the pork to a serving platter and cover loosely with aluminum foil.

2. Reduce the heat to medium; add the prosciutto di Parma to the skillet and sauté 30 seconds. Add the lemon, capers, and sage; cook, stirring, 1 minute. Return the heat to high; add the broth and cook until the liquid is reduced by a third, stirring to incorporate the browned bits from the pan. Stir in the butter and any juices from the serving platter. Bring the sauce to a boil and serve over the pork.

Pork Piccata

with Peperoncini

MAKES 4 SERVINGS

Hands-on time:
25 minutes

Total preparation time:
25 minutes

Lightly floured and sautéed and then finished with a lemony sauce, it is usually veal—not pork—that is given the piccata treatment. But veal is very pricey and, even so, not everyone likes it. So here's a version with pork instead. I've finished it off with one of my favorite ingredients, peperoncini, those wonderful little pickled hot peppers that typically adorn Greek salads (and yet are called Tuscan pickled peppers). They add a nice bite to this classic. Serve with Smashed Potatoes (page 38) and Roasted Vegetables (page 35).

*4 thin boneless pork chops
  (about 1 pound total)*
*3 tablespoons extra virgin
  olive oil*
*1/3 cup Wondra or unbleached
  all-purpose flour*
*Kosher salt and freshly milled
  black pepper*
*1 cup canned chicken broth or
  Chicken Stock (page 32)*
*2 tablespoons fresh lemon
  juice*
*2 tablespoons unsalted butter,
  cut into small pieces*
*1 tablespoon finely chopped,
  seeded peperoncini (Tuscan
  pickled peppers)*
*Thin lemon slices and rinsed,
  dried, and chopped fresh
  flat-leaf parsley, for garnish*

1. Sprinkle a small amount of water on a large sheet of plastic wrap. Place 2 of the pork chops on top of the plastic and sprinkle again with water. Cover with another sheet of plastic wrap and pound with a rolling pin or meat pounder until about 1/4 inch thick. Repeat with the remaining 2 pork chops.

2. Heat the oil in a large skillet over high heat until hot. Combine the flour with 1/2 teaspoon salt and 1/4 teaspoon pepper in a soup plate; coat the pork chops, shaking off the excess. Reduce the heat to medium-high and add the pork chops. Sauté the chops until they are golden, about 2 minutes per side. Transfer them to a plate and cover loosely with aluminum foil.

3. Pour off any fat and return the skillet to the heat. Add the broth and lemon juice. Increase the heat to high and bring to a boil, stirring to loosen any brown bits in the bottom of the pan. Reduce the heat to medium-low and simmer for 1 minute or until slightly thickened.

4. Return the pork to the skillet and simmer, turning often, until warmed through, about 2 minutes. Add the butter and peperoncini; heat just until the butter has melted. Season with salt and pepper to taste. Transfer the pork to plates, spoon some of the sauce over the top, and garnish with lemon slices and parsley.

Barbecued Kielbasa

Hands-on time:
20 minutes with
Tangy Barbecue Sauce,
10 minutes with bottled sauce

Total preparation time:
60 minutes with
Tangy Barbecue Sauce,
50 minutes with bottled sauce

*3 cups bottled barbecue sauce
or 1 recipe Tangy Barbecue
Sauce (page 321, add prep
time)*
*Two 16-ounce pork, beef, or
turkey kielbasas*
1 tablespoon vegetable oil
*2 medium onions (about 6
ounces each), cut into
wedges*
*3 medium celery stalks, cut
into 2-inch pieces*
*2 large green bell peppers, cut
into 1-inch squares*

MAKES 6 SERVINGS

In my research for this book I found a recipe for my grandmother Ruth's "Barbecued Frankforts" on a three by five-inch index card in an old metal box, handwritten in her own beautiful curly script. Granny was a superb ye olde New England cook, so I gave it a try. In the end I substituted kielbasa for hot dogs and used my own barbecue sauce recipe (although you're welcome to use your favorite supermarket brand). But what I kept of Granny's original recipe is the idea of throwing everything into a pan and then putting the pan into the oven for the flavors to marry. Serve with Simple Boiled Rice (page 40) and Cole Slaw (page 38).

1. Preheat the oven to 350°F. Prepare the Tangy Barbecue Sauce, if using.

2. Meanwhile, cut the kielbasa into eighths and pierce all over with the tines of a fork. Heat the oil in a large, ovenproof skillet over high heat until hot; reduce the heat to medium. Cook the kielbasa, onions, and celery, stirring occasionally, until they soften, about 5 minutes.

3. Add the barbecue sauce and bring to a boil. Cover the skillet tightly and bake in the center of the oven for 20 minutes. Uncover, stir in the bell pepper, and bake for an additional 20 minutes.

Ham Steaks
with Sweet-and-Sour Cabbage

Hands-on time:
15 minutes

Total preparation time:
45 minutes

MAKES 4 SERVINGS

Ham needs a counterpoint to balance all its smokiness and salt, and sometimes mustard alone doesn't do the trick for me. Given that pork and cabbage are a classic team, I thought that ham might go well with cabbage of the sweet-and-sour variety. Braising the cabbage in vinegar has the added benefit of turning the cabbage a beautiful deep red color. It looks to me like a jewel. Serve with Southwestern Sweet Potato Sauté (page 294) and a tossed green salad.

4 slices bacon, chopped
1 large onion, sliced (about 2 cups)
2 garlic cloves, minced (about 2 teaspoons)
1 teaspoon ground allspice
1/2 teaspoon ground cloves
1/2 cup balsamic vinegar
1/3 cup packed dark brown sugar
1 small red cabbage, shredded (about 4 cups)
One 14-ounce can Italian plum tomatoes, finely chopped, with juice (about 1 3/4 cups)
Kosher salt and freshly milled black pepper
2 tablespoon vegetable oil
1 1/2 pounds ham steak, cut into 4 pieces

1. Cook the bacon in a large heavy skillet over medium heat until crisp, about 6 minutes. Transfer the bacon with a slotted spoon to paper towels to drain, leaving the fat in the pan. Add the onion to the skillet and cook, stirring occasionally, until softened, about 5 minutes. Add the garlic, allspice, and cloves and cook for 1 minute. Add the balsamic vinegar and brown sugar and cook until the brown sugar has dissolved. Add the cabbage and tomatoes, bring the liquid to a boil, reduce the heat to medium-low, and cook, covered, for 30 minutes or until the cabbage is very tender. Add salt and pepper to taste and stir in the reserved bacon. Keep warm.

2. In another skillet heat the oil over high heat until hot; reduce the heat to medium-high and add the ham steak. Cook until lightly browned, 3 to 4 minutes on each side. Divide the steak among 4 plates and top each steak with some of the sweet-and-sour cabbage.

Asian Green Beans and Pork

1 pound lean ground pork,
  beef, or turkey
6 tablespoons soy sauce
1/4 cup rice wine or dry sherry
1 tablespoon sugar
1 large garlic clove, minced
  (about 1 1/2 teaspoons)
1 1/2 teaspoons finely grated
  fresh ginger (use a
  Microplane)
2/3 cup canned chicken broth
  or Chicken Stock (page 32)
1 tablespoon rice vinegar
1 tablespoon cornstarch
1 teaspoon toasted sesame oil
1 pound green beans, trimmed
3 tablespoons vegetable oil
Kosher salt and freshly milled
  black pepper

MAKES 4 SERVINGS

I have always loved the original version of this Chinese dish. The
only trouble is that the green beans are usually wok-fried in lots
of oil. I wanted to lighten it up a bit so I figured out a way to crisp
the beans without the fat—by broiling them. The result is a very
tasty, low-fat, easy-to-prepare dish. Serve with Butter-steamed
Broccoli with Soy (page 296) and Simple Boiled Rice (page 40).

1. Combine the ground pork with 3 tablespoons of the soy sauce, 3
tablespoons of the wine, 1 teaspoon of the sugar, the garlic, and ginger.
Combine the broth, vinegar, cornstarch, and sesame oil with the
remaining 3 tablespoons soy sauce, 1 tablespoon wine, and 2 teaspoons
sugar.

2. Preheat the broiler to high. Toss the green beans with 2 tablespoons of
the vegetable oil, 1/4 teaspoon salt, and 1/4 teaspoon pepper. Arrange the
beans in one layer on a rimmed baking sheet and broil, 4 inches from the
heat source, turning occasionally, for 10 to 12 minutes or until golden
brown and tender.

3. Meanwhile, heat the remaining tablespoon of vegetable oil in a large
skillet over high heat until hot; reduce the heat to medium, add the pork
mixture, and cook, stirring, until it is no longer pink, 3 to 4 minutes. Add
the broth mixture and cook for 2 minutes. Add the green beans and stir
until they are coated with the sauce.

Sausage, Lentil, and Spinach Stew

Hands-on time:
20 minutes

Total preparation time:
55 minutes

MAKES 4 SERVINGS

The Mediterraneans have long known that lentils and sausages are happy partners. Not only do they taste great together, they both cook up pretty quickly. In this recipe the sausages are browned first and then combined with the broth, flavorings, and lentils. Then everything simmers until the lentils are tender. The lentils absorb some of the juices from the sausages and the whole thing comes together—with the addition of the spinach—as a fragrant and satisfying little one-pot meal. Round it out with some grilled or toasted country-style bread, a green salad, and a glass of Chianti, and the world is a beautiful place. You can also transform this stew into a soup simply by adding more broth.

1. Combine the sausages and 1/4 inch water in a large saucepan. Bring to a boil over high heat. Reduce the heat to low, cover the pan, and simmer for 5 minutes. Remove the lid and cook until all the water has evaporated and the sausage has browned lightly.

2. Increase the heat to medium; add the onion, carrot, garlic, oregano, and bay leaf to the sausage and cook, stirring occasionally, until the vegetables have softened, about 5 minutes. Add the broth and lentils and bring the mixture to a boil over high heat. Reduce the heat to low; cook, partially covered, until the lentils are just tender, 30 to 35 minutes. Add the spinach and cook over medium heat until it is wilted. Discard the bay leaf and oregano sprig and add salt and pepper to taste. Add water and reheat if the stew is too thick.

1 pound Italian sweet or hot sausages, cut into 1-inch pieces

1 medium onion, chopped (about 1 cup)

1 medium carrot, chopped (1/2 cup)

2 garlic cloves, minced (about 2 teaspoons)

1 sprig rinsed and dried fresh oregano or 1/2 teaspoon dried

1 Turkish bay leaf

Two 14- or 14 1/2-ounce cans chicken broth or 3 1/2 cups Chicken Stock (page 32)

8 ounces dried lentils (about 1 cup), sorted and rinsed

One 5-ounce package rinsed baby spinach

Kosher salt and freshly milled black pepper

1 1/2 pounds New York strip
   steak (about 2 large steaks),
   1 1/2 inches thick, patted
   dry
Kosher salt
2 tablespoons coarsely
   crushed black peppercorns
   (see headnote)
2 tablespoons vegetable oil
1/2 cup red wine
2 large shallots, finely
   chopped (about 1/4 cup)
1 cup canned chicken broth or
   Chicken Stock (page 32)
1/3 cup heavy cream
3 ounces Roquefort or other
   blue cheese, crumbled
   (about 1/2 cup)
1 tablespoon brandy, optional

Pepper-crusted New York Strip Steak
with Blue Cheese Sauce

MAKES 4 SERVINGS

This is an old-fashioned French-style bistro steak glorified with blue cheese sauce. I happen to love Roquefort, but you could replace it with other tasty blues such as Gorgonzola, Stilton, Cabrales, or Maytag. In a pinch you could even use the precrumbled stuff.

The only tricky part of the recipe is coarsely grinding the pepper. You can't buy it that way—and I wouldn't want you to anyway, because it would lose its bite before it arrived at your table. Likewise, most pepper grinders don't have a coarse grind setting. So you have to grind it by hand. Here's how: Put the peppercorns on a cutting board, take a small skillet or saucepan, and crush them with the back of the pan, pushing down and away from you. That's all there is to it. Serve with Oven Fries (page 295) and Sautéed Spinach with Garlic (page 34).

1. Preheat the oven to 350°F. Season the steaks on all sides with salt, and press the peppercorns into the tops and bottoms. Heat the oil in a large skillet over high heat until hot; reduce the heat to medium-high and sear the steaks until well browned on both sides, 3 to 4 minutes. Transfer the steaks to a small roasting pan and place on the center shelf of the oven. Roast to desired doneness—10 to 12 minutes for medium rare. Transfer the steaks to a platter, cover them with aluminum foil, and let them rest for 5 minutes before slicing.

2. While the steaks are roasting, add the wine and shallots to the skillet in which the steaks were seared. Cook over low heat, stirring to incorporate the browned bits from the pan, until the wine has almost evaporated. Add the broth and cream and simmer until slightly thickened, about 5 minutes. Add the cheese, brandy, if using, and any juices that have accumulated in the roasting pan. Cook just until the cheese has melted, about 2 minutes.

3. Slice the steaks across the grain 1/4 inch thick; divide among 4 warm plates and top with the sauce.

PEPPERCORNS are actually berries that grow in grapelike clusters on the *Piper nigrum* plant, a climbing vine native to India and Indonesia. The berry is processed to produce three basic types of peppercorn—black, white, and green.

Green peppercorns are the soft underripe berries that are preserved by freeze-drying, dehydration, or by curing in vinegar or brine. They have a fresh flavor that is not as spicy-hot as black and white peppercorns. They can be used in any recipe that calls for black or white peppercorns.

Black peppercorns, the most common and intense of the three, are picked when the berry is not quite ripe, then dried until it shrivels and the skin turns dark brown to black. Among the best black peppers are the Tellicherry and the Lampong (see Sources, page 346).

White peppercorns are ripe berries whose skin has been removed, after which the berry is dried. They are tan and smooth and milder in flavor than black peppercorns. I was taught at cooking school to use white pepper in white or light-colored dishes where you don't want to see little black flecks. White pepper is also the choice for Chinese cooking. I actually prefer the taste of black peppercorns and throw them in everything, whether the food is white or not.

Pink peppercorns are not peppercorns at all but the dried berries of the Baies rose plant, which grows in Madagascar. They have a unique perfumed, almost sweet, taste. I like to add them to goat and mild cheeses.

PEPPERCORNS —A PRIMER

Korean-style Beef
with Spicy Cabbage

MAKES 4 SERVINGS

Skirt steak is one of those ingredients you would have to be very talented to mess up. It is a well-marbled (a butcher's way of saying significant fat runs through it), tough cut of meat that should be cooked rare to medium-rare and sliced thin across the grain. Skirt steak is the full-flavored cut of beef usually used for fajitas, and it takes very nicely to this Asian preparation. If you have time, make double the sauce and marinate the meat in half of it for an hour. I chose napa cabbage because it is more delicate than regular cabbage and provides the perfect crisp backdrop to the beef. Serve with Simple Boiled Rice (page 40).

3 tablespoons soy sauce
2 scallions (white and green parts), thinly sliced (about 1/4 cup)
2 tablespoons rice vinegar
1 tablespoon dark brown sugar
2 teaspoons finely grated fresh ginger (use a Microplane)
1 1/2 teaspoons toasted sesame oil
1 garlic clove, minced (about 1 teaspoon)
1 pound skirt steak
Kosher salt and freshly milled black pepper
4 tablespoons vegetable oil
4 cups thinly shredded napa cabbage (about 1 pound)
1/4 pound snow peas, halved diagonally
1 teaspoon red pepper flakes

1. Whisk together the soy sauce, scallions, vinegar, brown sugar, ginger, sesame oil, and garlic and set aside. Season the steak with salt and black pepper on both sides. Cut into pieces, if necessary, in order to fit all of it into the skillet.

2. Heat 2 tablespoons of the oil in a large skillet over high heat until hot; add the meat. Sear the steak on both sides, 4 to 6 minutes total for medium-rare.

3. Transfer the meat to a platter, cover loosely with foil, and let rest while you cook the cabbage. Discard the fat in the skillet; heat the remaining 2 tablespoons oil in the same skillet over high heat until hot. Reduce the heat to medium and add the cabbage and snow peas. Sauté for 3 minutes or until the cabbage is crisp-tender. Add the snow peas, red pepper flakes and salt to taste; sauté just until peas are hot, about 30 seconds.

4. To serve, slice the steak thin, against the grain, at an angle. Add any juices from the platter to the soy sauce mixture and toss the meat with the sauce in a bowl. Arrange a mound of cabbage on four plates; top with the meat and sauce.

IF YOU are going to splurge on an expensive steak, make sure you know what you are doing when you cook it. Steaks with fat running through them will be more flavorful, tender, and juicy, albeit more caloric. It is not the sort of thing you will be eating every day, so you might as well buy the best.

Pat the steak dry before you start and cut off any excess fat on the outside. Season the steak on both sides with kosher salt and freshly ground black pepper. Oil a skillet with just enough vegetable oil to barely cover the bottom. Heat the skillet over high heat until the oil almost begins to smoke; add the steak. Reduce the heat to medium-high and let the steak develop a crust. Many people do not get the pan hot enough to begin with and the steak steams rather than sears. Do not touch the steak until it has formed a crust; do not turn it over with a fork or press it down with a spatula (which lets out some of the juices). After it has properly seared, turn the steak over and repeat the procedure on the second side. Steaks that are thicker, 1 1/2 inches and over, might benefit from finishing in a 350°F oven so the crust does not get too dark.

Keep in mind that there will always be carryover cooking time, meaning that the meat will continue to cook after you have taken it out of the oven. So if you want your steak medium-rare, take it out when it is rare. I take a rare steak off the heat at 110° to 120°F, a medium-rare steak off at 130°F, and a medium steak off at 140°F. I wouldn't recommend cooking it any further as it will toughen and dry out.

Any steak, of any thickness, needs to rest for at least five minutes so that all the juices can redistribute. Transfer it to a plate or platter and cover it loosely with foil. Juices will accumulate on the plate as the steak sits; you can incorporate these into a pan sauce or just pour over the steak.

COOKING STEAK

Det Burgers

MAKES 4 SERVINGS

My first official cooking job was in the midseventies at a bar in Ann Arbor, Michigan (where I went to college), called the Del Rio. They featured live jazz on weekends. It was a democratic place; all decisions were made by common vote and it felt like one big family. The food we cooked was not all that sophisticated—chili, hamburgers, Greek salad, and soups based solidly on jars of soup base—but I got into it and prided myself on my soups in particular (the only item for which we did not have a formula). The most popular dish on the menu was a burger called the "Det" burger, which had been developed in the early seventies by one of the cooks, Bob Detweiler, when one day he got tired of making the same old burger on a bun. He topped the basic burger with what became the "Det" mixture—drained canned mushrooms, drained canned California olives, and reconstituted dried green pepper bits, covered with a slice of onion and cheese (his wife Julie, the manager, suggested the cheese). And here is the most important point—he steamed it in beer! It was really delicious, the sort of burger you dream about.

I have developed my own version here using fresh mushrooms, Mediterranean olives, and canned green chiles to add a little bite. Roasted peeled poblanos (see procedure for roasting peppers, page 30) are even better, but not everyone can go to that trouble on a weeknight. I made the Det burgers (with the poblanos) when I did a burger show on *Sara's Secrets,* and Michael Romano, the chef from New York City's three-star Union Square Café (who joined me to make his famous tuna burgers), insisted on taking the Det burger recipe home with him. Serve with Oven Fries (page 295) and Cole Slaw (page 38).

Det Burgers, continued

3 tablespoons vegetable oil

1 medium onion, sliced (about
1 cup)

Eight 1 1/2-inch crimini
mushrooms (about 4
ounces), sliced

Kosher salt and freshly milled
black pepper

One 4-ounce can sliced, peeled
green chiles, drained

1/3 cup pitted, brine-cured
olives such as kalamata,
sliced

1 1/2 pounds ground beef
chuck or round

6 ounces Cheddar cheese, cut
into 4 slices

1/3 cup beer

4 hamburger buns, split and
toasted

1. Heat 2 tablespoons of the oil in a large skillet over high heat until hot. Reduce the heat to medium; add the onion and cook, stirring occasionally, until softened, about 5 minutes. Increase the heat to medium-high; add the mushrooms and cook, stirring, until the mushrooms have browned and the liquid they release has evaporated, 4 to 5 minutes. Season the mushroom mixture with salt and pepper to taste and transfer it to a bowl; add the chiles and olives and set aside. Wipe out the skillet.

2. Gently shape the beef into four 4-inch burgers; season with salt and pepper. Heat the remaining tablespoon of oil in the skillet over high heat until hot. Reduce the heat to medium-high, add the burgers, and cook 3 minutes. Turn the burgers and cook 2 minutes. Top each with a quarter of the chile mixture and a slice of cheese. Add the beer to the skillet; cover and steam until the cheese has melted, about 3 minutes.

3. Transfer the burgers to the toasted buns and serve.

Meatloaf Burgers

Hands-on time:
25 minutes

Total preparation time:
30 minutes

MAKES 6 SERVINGS

Assembling a meatloaf and getting it into the oven is a breeze. Waiting an hour for it to cook is a drag. By contrast, these delicious burgers cook up in twelve minutes. When they're done you just glaze them with a quick chili sauce, run them under the broiler to finish, and—voilà!—mini meatloaf for everyone. Serve with Smashed Potatoes (page 38) and Herbed Pea Medley (page 37).

2 tablespoons vegetable oil
1 medium onion, finely chopped (about 1 cup)
1 celery rib, finely chopped
3 garlic cloves, minced (about 1 tablespoon)
1 pound ground beef chuck
1/2 pound ground pork
1/2 pound ground veal or turkey
1/2 cup sour cream
1/2 cup fresh bread crumbs from Bread Crumbs Four Ways (page 23)
1/4 cup Dijon mustard
2 teaspoons kosher salt
1 teaspoon freshly milled black pepper
1/3 cup chili sauce

1. Heat 1 tablespoon of the oil in a large ovenproof skillet over high heat until hot. Reduce the heat to medium; add the onion, celery, and garlic and cook, stirring occasionally, until softened, about 5 minutes. Transfer to a rimmed baking sheet, spreading out the mixture, and refrigerate to cool slightly. Combine the beef, pork, veal, sour cream, bread crumbs, 2 tablespoons of the mustard, the salt, and pepper; stir in the onion mixture. Shape into 6 equal burgers.

2. Heat the remaining tablespoon of oil in the skillet over high heat until hot; reduce the heat to medium and add the burgers to the pan. Cook the burgers for 6 minutes a side or until they are almost cooked through (nick and peek; they should be almost firm to the touch and have very little pink color inside). Transfer the burgers to a rimmed baking sheet.

3. Meanwhile, combine the chili sauce and the remaining 2 tablespoons mustard. Preheat the broiler to high. Spoon the chili sauce over each burger to cover well and place the skillet under the broiler. Broil for 2 minutes or until the topping begins to bubble.

Hands-on time:
30 minutes

Total preparation time:
30 minutes

3 slices bacon, chopped
2 large, unpeeled Yukon gold
   or boiling potatoes (about
   1 pound), cut into 1/2-inch
   cubes
1 1/4 pounds thin veal
   scaloppine
1/3 cup Wondra or unbleached
   all-purpose flour
Kosher salt and freshly milled
   black pepper
2 to 4 tablespoons vegetable
   oil
1/3 cup white wine
1/4 cup finely chopped shallots
   or onions
2 teaspoons paprika (see
   pages 183 and 347)
One 14- or 14 1/2-ounce can
   chicken broth or 1 3/4 cups
   Chicken Stock (page 32)

Veal Scallops

with Potato, Bacon, and Paprika Sauce

MAKES 4 SERVINGS

I have always been a fan of veal scaloppine, because it cooks so quickly and provides pan drippings for a very nice sauce. (I confess that I'm actually more interested in the sauce than the veal. To my way of thinking, the veal is just an excuse for the sauce.) I added the bacon to this dish for its smokiness and the potatoes for their substance. The sauce is made right in the pan. Deglaze it with white wine and add chicken broth. When you return the floured veal to the pan, the flour naturally thickens the sauce. Serve with Butter-steamed Broccoli with Soy (page 296).

1. Cook the bacon in a large heavy skillet over medium heat until crisp, about 6 minutes. Transfer the bacon with a slotted spoon to paper towels to drain, leaving 1 tablespoon of fat in the pan. Add the potatoes to the skillet and cook over medium heat, stirring occasionally, until golden and tender, about 8 minutes. Transfer the potatoes with a slotted spoon to a large plate, cover, and keep warm. Reserve the skillet.

2. While the bacon and potatoes are cooking, sprinkle a small amount of water on a large sheet of plastic wrap. Place half of the veal slices on top of the plastic and sprinkle again with water. Cover with another sheet of plastic wrap and pound with a rolling pin or meat pounder until about 1/4 inch thick. Repeat with the remaining veal.

3. Combine the flour with 1/2 teaspoon salt and 1/4 teaspoon pepper in a soup plate. Heat 1 tablespoon of the oil in the potato skillet over high heat until hot; reduce the heat to medium-high. Coat the veal with the flour mixture, shaking off any excess. and sauté (in batches, adding oil as necessary), 3 minutes a side. Transfer the veal with tongs to a plate and cover.

4. Add the wine, shallots, and paprika to the skillet; bring to a simmer, stirring to loosen any brown bits in the bottom of the pan. Add the broth and simmer until reduced by one third. Return the veal to the skillet and heat below a simmer until the veal is just heated through. Stir in the potatoes. To serve, divide the veal and potatoes among 4 plates, sprinkle with bacon, and spoon some sauce over each serving.

PAPRIKA is made by drying and grinding an aromatic red pepper, usually the tomato pepper. Although it is often associated with Hungarian cuisine, paprika is native to South America and didn't make it into Northern Europe until the seventeenth century. Today, Hungary and Spain are the major producers of paprika, which has evolved into a much milder form than its tropical ancestors. Most supermarkets have only one choice of paprika on the shelf; it is known as "sweet" paprika, which just means not hot. The degree of heat in paprika is determined by the heat of the peppers used as well as the percentage of ribs and seeds ground with the pods.

Semisweet and hot paprikas of varying intensities are available in specialty food stores and by mail. (See Sources, page 347.) Spanish smoked paprika includes the aromatic qualities of the woods over which the peppers were smoked. It can be purchased both hot and sweet. Paprika will keep its flavor for six months if stored in an airtight container in a cool, dry place. Although paprika is often used as a colorful topping to a finished dish, it does not release its full flavor and color until it is heated. You must treat it gently because of its natural high sugar content; if overheated, the sugars will burn and make any dish it is in taste bitter.

PAPRIKA

One 3 1/2-inch piece fresh
   ginger, peeled
6 garlic cloves, quartered
2 teaspoons plus 1 tablespoon
   salt-free packaged garam
   masala, curry powder, or
   Todd's Garam Masala (page
   21, add prep time)
3 whole dried chiles de arbol
1 Turkish bay leaf
1 teaspoon coriander seeds
1/2 teaspoon cumin seeds
2 tablespoons vegetable oil
1 medium red onion, chopped
   (about 1 cup)
2 tablespoons tomato paste
1 1/2 pounds ground lamb,
   beef, pork, turkey, or
   chicken
Kosher salt and freshly milled
   black pepper
3 medium plum tomatoes,
   cored and quartered
   lengthwise
1 cup well-stirred whole-milk
   yogurt, preferably Greek
1 cup defrosted frozen peas
1/2 cup rinsed, dried, and
   coarsely chopped fresh
   cilantro with stems

Todd's Keema Matar

MAKES 4 TO 6 SERVINGS

I have known many a "foodie," but Todd Coleman, the food producer of *Sara's Secrets*, takes the cake. In truth, his mania is contagious. He just gives me a quick tutorial and then—boom!—there I am on national television doing something I'd never even attempted before: rolling sushi or folding a napkin a tricky new way. I figure if I'm willing to try something for the first time on national TV, maybe the home cook will be inspired to give it a try in her own kitchen.

Todd is a big fan of Indian food, having traveled to India and cooked a lot with his Indian friends. I asked him to contribute a recipe to this book and here it is—in his own words: "Ground Lamb Fragrantly Luxuriating in Yogurt and Peas." If you use lamb in this recipe instead of beef, it will be more flavorful but more fatty. Todd's recipe for garam masala, a basic Indian spice mix, is in the Basics chapter (page 21). You might be able to find a generic version in the supermarket if you do not want to make his from scratch.

Serve with basmati rice, Grated Carrot Salad (page 293), and flatbreads.

1. Cut 1 1/2 inches of the ginger into matchstick strips and set aside; cut the remaining 2 inches into 1/8-inch crosswise slices. Combine 1/4 cup water, the ginger slices, garlic, and 2 teaspoons garam masala in a blender or mini food processor and puree until slushy; set aside. Combine the chiles, bay leaf, coriander, and cumin in a small dish; set aside.

2. Heat the oil in a large (preferably cast-iron) skillet over high heat until hot; reduce the heat to medium. Add the chile mixture and cook, stirring with a wooden spoon, until it splutters, turns lightly brown, and a wonderful fragrance wafts up to you, about 30 seconds. Immediately add the onion and cook, stirring occasionally, until softened, about 5 minutes. Quickly add the ginger mixture and tomato paste and cook, stirring continuously, until caramelized, about 2 minutes.

3. Add the lamb, 1/4 teaspoon salt, and 1/4 teaspoon pepper and cook, stirring occasionally, until it begins to brown, about 4 minutes. Add the tomatoes and cook, stirring occasionally, until the lamb is cooked through and the tomatoes are slightly wilted, about 4 minutes.

4. Remove the skillet from the heat and stir in the ginger matchsticks, remaining 1 tablespoon garam masala, the yogurt, peas, and cilantro. Season with salt and pepper to taste.

Hands-on time:
10 minutes

Total preparation time:
35 minutes

3 garlic cloves, minced (about
   1 tablespoon)
3 tablespoons fresh lemon
   juice
2 tablespoons extra virgin
   olive oil
1 tablespoon rinsed, dried,
   and chopped fresh
   rosemary or oregano or 1
   teaspoon dried
Kosher salt and freshly milled
   black pepper
2 pounds boneless leg of
   lamb, cut into 1 1/2-inch
   cubes
4 small onions (about 2 inches
   across), quartered
3/4 cup low-fat mayonnaise
1/4 cup pitted, brine-cured
   olives such as kalamata,
   finely chopped

Grilled Lamb and Onion Kabobs
with Olive Aioli

MAKES 4 SERVINGS

Lemon, olive oil, rosemary, and garlic—this is my favorite marinade for lamb, whether I am cooking a roast or skewering kabobs. They work well together because both the marinade and the lamb are products of the Mediterranean. The sauce, made of garlic and olive-flavored mayonnaise, is also Mediterranean—and a great shortcut, given that the mayo is premade. I love grilled onions with the lamb, but you can add other vegetables to the skewers. Serve with Mediterranean Orzo Pilaf (page 307).

1. Combine 2 tablespoons boiling water with 1 teaspoon of the garlic and set aside to cool slightly. Whisk together 2 tablespoons of the lemon juice, the oil, rosemary, the remaining 2 teaspoons garlic, 1/4 teaspoon salt, and 1/8 teaspoon pepper in a medium bowl. Add the lamb and onions and set aside, tossing gently several times, for 15 minutes. If using wooden skewers, soak 4 in water.

2. Meanwhile, combine the mayonnaise, olives, remaining tablespoon of lemon juice, 1/8 teaspoon salt, and 1/8 teaspoon pepper in a small bowl. Stir in the reserved garlic and water mixture.

3. Preheat the grill or the broiler. Thread the meat and onions on 4 skewers, alternating them. Drizzle with any marinade from the bowl. Grill or broil 4 inches from the heat source, 6 to 8 minutes a side for medium-rare.

4. Transfer the meat and onions from the skewers to plates and serve each portion topped with some of the olive sauce.

KABOB cooking has a lot going for it. Kabobs can be assembled ahead so they are ready to throw on the grill or under the broiler at the last minute. They make it possible to cook small pieces of meat and vegetables on a grill. They are a colorful way to present foods, and are easy to serve. Here are a few suggestions that will make the job even easier.

Selecting skewers: Metal skewers can be reused and help to conduct the heat to the inside of the food. Bamboo skewers are disposable but should be soaked in water for fifteen to thirty minutes before use to make them less flammable. What to cook: It is important to group items on each skewer that will cook in the same amount of time. If you want to use vegetables that take a while to cook, either precook them before assembling the kabob or put them on separate skewers from the quick-cooking items and start cooking them first. To keep skewered items from rolling around on the skewer when you try to move them, insert two parallel skewers through the foods.

KABOBS

Hands-on time:
15 minutes

Total preparation time:
35 minutes plus
thawing or rising time

1 pound defrosted frozen
pizza dough or 1 recipe
Food Processor Pizza Dough
(page 29, add prep time)
1/4 cup pine nuts
3/4 pound ground lamb or
beef
1 small onion, finely chopped
(about 1/2 cup)
1 medium plum tomato,
seeded and finely chopped
(about 1/3 cup)
1/4 medium green bell pepper,
finely chopped (about 1/4
cup)
2 tablespoons fresh lemon
juice
1 tablespoon red wine vinegar
1 tablespoon tomato paste
2 garlic cloves, minced (about
2 teaspoons)
1 teaspoon kosher salt
1/4 to 1/2 teaspoon cayenne
pepper

Middle Eastern Pizza

MAKES 4 SERVINGS

I discovered this recipe when I worked at La Tulipe restaurant in New York City in the early eighties. Once a week I was responsible for family dinner, the staff meal that we all sat down and enjoyed around 4:30 or 5:00 before the onslaught of service began. Since we always had leftover lamb trimmings kicking around (we cut up most of the meat on the menu ourselves), I would often use it for the family meal. One day, Sally Darr, the chef-owner, brought in a recipe for *sfeeha*, or Middle Eastern pizza, and I tried it. Wow, it was spectacular and the staff just loved it. This is my adaptation. You can either make the Food Processor Pizza Dough (page 29) or buy the ready-made dough at the supermarket—the ground meat mixture is the star anyway. Serve with Roasted Vegetables (page 35) and a tossed green salad.

1. Place a rack in the upper third of the oven; preheat the oven to 500°F. Lightly grease two insulated or very heavy rimmed baking sheets.

2. Divide the dough into 4 balls; roll each ball into an 8-inch round, about 1/8 inch thick, on a lightly floured surface. Transfer the rounds to the baking sheets, pinching up a raised edge on each; cover loosely and let stand in a warm place while you make the filling.

3. Spread the pine nuts in a small, ungreased baking pan. Bake in the preheated oven until they just begin to brown, 3 to 4 minutes. Combine the lamb, onion, tomato, bell pepper, pine nuts, lemon juice, vinegar, tomato paste, garlic, salt, and cayenne in a medium bowl. Spoon one quarter of the lamb filling on the center of each dough round and spread to the raised edge.

4. Bake the pizzas 15 to 20 minutes, until the crust is lightly browned and the meat is cooked through.

From
the Sea

Baked Fish

with Horseradish Crust

MAKES 4 SERVINGS

3 tablespoons mayonnaise

2 tablespoons bottled
horseradish, squeezed dry

1 tablespoon Dijon mustard

1 cup fresh bread crumbs from
Bread Crumbs Four Ways
(page 23)

2 tablespoons melted butter

1 1/2 teaspoons rinsed, dried,
and finely chopped fresh
tarragon or 1/2 teaspoon
dried

2 tablespoons vegetable oil

Four 6-ounce pieces skinless
grouper or red snapper
fillet

Kosher salt and freshly milled
black pepper

Most fish is so mild tasting that it needs help in the flavor and texture department. A plain piece of sautéed or baked fish cries out for a squeeze of lemon. This horseradish topping provides both the sharp flavor and the textural crunch that make a fish fillet downright exciting. Serve with Mediterranean Orzo Pilaf (page 307) and Roasted Vegetables (page 35).

1. Position the broiler rack 6 inches from the heat source and preheat the broiler to high. Mix the mayonnaise, horseradish, and mustard. In another bowl combine the bread crumbs, butter, and tarragon. Heat the oil in a large nonstick skillet with an ovenproof handle over medium-high heat until hot. Season the fish on both sides with salt and pepper and add to the pan, skinned side up. Sauté until the bottom 1/4 to 1/2 inch of the fish is opaque, about 1 minute.

2. Turn the fish. Spread one-fourth of the horseradish mixture on top of each fillet and press one-fourth of the bread crumb mixture on top of the horseradish mixture so that the top surface of the fillet is completely coated. Broil the fillets until the crust is golden brown and the fish is just cooked through, 6 to 8 minutes.

Baked Whole Fish

with Rosemary, Olive Oil, and Lemon

MAKES 4 SERVINGS

Fish, like meat or poultry, has more flavor when it is cooked on the bone. But many people are daunted by the prospect of cooking a whole fish because they have no idea how to fillet it. In fact, if you wait to fillet your fish until after it's cooked, it's a snap—because at that point the flesh is almost ready to fall off the bone. This is one of those fun entrées that you can set up in no time at all, throw into the oven, and forget about while you read a magazine. Serve with Smashed Potatoes (page 38) and Herbed Pea Medley (page 37).

1. Remove the fish from the refrigerator 10 minutes before baking. Preheat the oven to 350°F. Remove enough leaves from the rosemary to measure about 3 tablespoons; chop them. For the marinade, combine half the chopped rosemary, 1/2 cup oil, and 2 teaspoons of the lemon zest. Rinse the fish inside and out and pat dry with paper towels. Sprinkle some salt and black pepper inside the cavity and over the surface of the fish. Stuff the cavity of each fish with 6 lemon wedges and the remaining rosemary sprigs. Arrange both fish in a shallow baking dish in one layer and pour the marinade over them, making sure they are coated all over.

2. Bake the fish in the center of the oven for 15 to 18 minutes until the meat just begins to separate from the backbone. Let it rest, covered loosely with aluminum foil, for 5 minutes before filleting.

3. Meanwhile, combine the remaining 1/4 cup oil, remaining half of the chopped rosemary, 1 teaspoon lemon zest, and the pepper flakes, if using, in a small saucepan; heat over high heat just until hot.

Hands-on time:
15 minutes

Total preparation time:
40 to 45 minutes for
a 1 1/2-pound fish;
45 to 50 minutes for
a 2-pound fish

Two 1 1/2- to 2-pound whole
  fish such as red snapper,
  gutted, fins removed, and
  scaled (get your fishmonger
  to do this for you)
8 large sprigs rinsed and dried
  fresh rosemary
3/4 cup extra virgin olive oil
3 teaspoons grated lemon zest
Kosher salt and freshly milled
  black pepper
2 whole lemons, each cut into
  8 wedges
1 teaspoon red pepper flakes,
  optional

4. To fillet the fish, peel off the top skin. Run a small sharp knife (such as a paring or boning knife) down the backbone of the fish and continue toward the belly, making sure that the knife is on top of the rib bones, until you have separated the fillet from the fish. To reach the second fillet, gently lift up the central bones, which are now exposed (they will come up in one piece), and remove the second fillet. Repeat with the second fish. Transfer a fillet to each of four plates. Divide the hot oil over the fillets and garnish each serving with one of the remaining lemon wedges.

Indian-spiced Fish Cakes

Hands-on time:
15 minutes

Total preparation time:
30 minutes

MAKES 6 SERVINGS

This recipe is meant to resuscitate leftover fish, but it's so good I imagine myself cooking up a fresh fillet for the sole purpose of turning it into these cakes. I love fish but it can be bland. Here the Indian spices and the lime-flavored herb sauce turn it into something exciting. Serve with Simple Boiled Rice (page 40) and Asian Spiced Roasted Baby Carrots (page 292).

1. Peel and quarter the potatoes and cook in boiling salted water to cover until tender, about 15 minutes; drain thoroughly and mash in a medium bowl. Meanwhile, combine the mayonnaise, mint, cilantro, 1 tablespoon lime juice, and the garlic in a blender. Blend until smooth; then transfer to a small serving bowl and refrigerate until ready to serve.

2. Stir the scallions, remaining 1 tablespoon lime juice, the chile, garam masala, ginger, cumin, coriander, and salt and pepper to taste into the mashed potato, then stir in the egg. Gently stir in the fish, keeping the chunks large. Shape the mixture into 6 patties (about 1/2 cup each); coat each patty with panko on all sides.

3. Heat 2 tablespoons of the oil in a large skillet over high heat until hot. Reduce the heat to medium, add the fish cakes, and sauté until golden brown on one side, about 5 minutes. Add another 2 tablespoons of oil to the skillet; turn the cakes and cook until brown on the other side and cakes feel firm, about 5 minutes longer. Serve the fish cakes with the herbed lime mayonnaise and lime wedges.

1 small russet or medium boiling potato (about 6 ounces)
Kosher salt
1/2 cup mayonnaise
2 tablespoons each packed rinsed, dried, and chopped fresh mint and cilantro
2 tablespoons fresh lime juice
1 garlic clove, minced (about 1 teaspoon)
4 scallions (white and light green parts), chopped (about 1/2 cup)
1 small serrano chile, chopped
1 teaspoon salt-free packaged garam masala, curry powder, or Todd's Garam Masala (page 21, add prep time)
1 teaspoon finely grated fresh ginger (use a Microplane)
3/4 teaspoon cumin seed
1/2 teaspoon ground coriander
Freshly milled black pepper
1 large egg
12 ounces cooked fish such as cod, halibut, or salmon (about 2 cups)
1 1/4 cups packaged panko, or panko from Bread Crumbs Four Ways (page 23)
4 tablespoons vegetable oil
Lime wedges

Cracker Fish

4 to 5 tablespoons extra virgin
    olive oil
2 garlic cloves, minced (about
    2 teaspoons)
1 1/2 teaspoons rinsed, dried,
    and chopped fresh oregano
    or 1/2 teaspoon dried
1 teaspoon grated lemon zest
1 cup saltine crumbs (from
    24 saltines), made by
    pulsing in a food processor
    or crushing in a zippered
    plastic bag
Four 6-ounce pieces sole,
    flounder, or scrod fillet
Lemon wedges

MAKES 4 SERVINGS

I love crunch in a recipe, particularly when the star of the dish is soft, like most white fish. Coating the fish in question with bread crumbs and then sautéing it usually provides the requisite crunch, but this time we reached for some good old-fashioned saltines.

This dish is perfect with a squeeze of lemon, but you could dress it up a bit by heating a few tablespoons of butter in a saucepan until it turns light brown (and acquires a slightly nutty taste). A drizzle of this browned butter on top of each portion of fish is a lovely final touch. Serve with Southwestern Sweet Potato Sauté (page 294) and Herbed Pea Medley (page 37).

1. Combine 2 tablespoons of the oil and the garlic, oregano, and lemon zest in a rimmed dinner plate. Spread the saltine crumbs on wax paper. Dip each fillet in the oil mixture and then coat with crumbs.

2. Heat 1 tablespoon oil in a large skillet over high heat until hot. Reduce the heat to medium-high, add the fish, and sauté until well browned, about 2 to 3 minutes. Add more oil to the pan, if necessary, turn the fish, and sauté until cooked through and brown on the remaining side, 3 to 4 minutes. Serve with lemon wedges.

Chinese-style Steamed Sole Fillets

Hands-on time:
10 minutes

Total preparation time:
40 minutes,
including
marinating time

MAKES 4 SERVINGS

Here in the West we know how to fry, bake, and poach fish. But it was the Chinese who taught us how to steam fish. Steaming keeps the flesh deliciously moist and flavorful, and it's low in fat, too. Typically, the Chinese steam whole fish, but I've applied the technique to fillets because it's quicker and easier. This recipe works using the fillets of any thin white fish. (By the way, most of the white fish labeled "sole" in the seafood display case is probably flounder. But it doesn't matter—if it's fresh, it'll taste great.) Serve with Asian Spiced Roasted Baby Carrots (page 292) and Herbed Pea Medley (page 37).

5 tablespoons soy sauce

2 tablespoons rice wine or dry sherry

1 tablespoon finely grated fresh ginger (use a Microplane)

3 teaspoons toasted sesame oil

1 teaspoon cornstarch

4 thin sole fillets (about 1 1/4 pounds)

2 tablespoons vegetable oil

1/4 pound fresh shiitake mushrooms, stems removed, caps thinly sliced

3 scallions (white and light green parts), thinly sliced (about 1/3 cup)

1/2 large jalapeño or 1 serrano chile, very thinly sliced crosswise

1. Whisk together 3 tablespoons of the soy sauce, the rice wine, ginger, 2 teaspoons of the sesame oil, and the cornstarch. Transfer the mixture to a zippered plastic bag, add the fish, and shake to coat the fish with the marinade. Refrigerate for 20 to 30 minutes.

2. Add water to a steamer following manufacturer's directions or, if using a saucepan fitted with a collapsible steamer basket, pour water within 1/4 inch of the basket. Fold a piece of aluminum foil to fit steamer basket; oil foil. Bring the water to a boil. Arrange the fillets on the oiled foil, folding if necessary to make them fit. Place in steamer; pour the marinade over the fish. Steam the fish for 3 to 6 minutes, until just cooked through.

3. Meanwhile, heat the vegetable oil in a medium skillet over high heat until hot. Reduce the heat to medium, add the mushrooms, and cook, stirring occasionally, until just tender, 3 to 5 minutes. Add the scallions and chile and cook 1 minute more. Stir in the remaining 2 tablespoons soy sauce and 1 teaspoon sesame oil. Transfer the fillets to serving plates and divide the mushroom mixture over them; serve immediately.

 *Fish Tacos*

MAKES 4 SERVINGS, 8 TACOS

I have never actually tasted a real fish taco, which I know are very popular in the Southwest, but I have imagined what they must taste like—crispy fish with zesty sauce and some sort of shredded green, all tucked into a tortilla. I gave my intrepid chili-head sous chef, Jenn Webb, the task of busting this recipe, and she managed to get it right the first time! She chose tilapia because it comes from South America, which is appropriate for this recipe. It is a mild, soft-fleshed white fish with a slightly sweet taste that is becoming more and more available in this country. Jenn decided to make the sauce with mayonnaise and yogurt to lighten it up a bit, and flavor it with chipotles (smoked jalapeños). She added vinegar to the shredded cabbage as a counterpoint to the fried fish. When she was done, even her trim chili-head fried-food-loving fiancé, Matt, liked this dish. Serve with Oven Fries (page 295) and Cole Slaw (page 38).

1. Prepare the Beer Batter, adding the cayenne and cumin, and set aside; prepare the seasoned flour as directed in the Beer Batter recipe. While the batter is resting, combine the mayonnaise, yogurt, lime juice, chipotles, and adobo sauce in a bowl and refrigerate, covered, until ready to assemble the tacos.

2. When the batter has rested, preheat the oven to 300°F. Heat 2 inches of oil in a large, deep saucepan until a deep-fat thermometer reaches 375°F. Wrap the tortillas in aluminum foil and warm them in the oven.

*Hands-on time:
30 minutes*

*Total preparation time:
45 minutes,
including resting time
for batter*

1 recipe Beer Batter (page 31)
1 teaspoon cayenne pepper
1 tablespoon ground cumin
2/3 cup low-fat mayonnaise
1/3 cup plain low-fat yogurt
2 tablespoons fresh lime juice
*2 chipotles in adobo sauce,
    chopped*
1 tablespoon adobo sauce
Vegetable oil for frying
*Eight 6- or 7-inch flour
    tortillas*
*1 pound skinless tilapia fillet,
    halved lengthwise and cut
    into 1-inch pieces*
Kosher salt
2 cups shredded cabbage
*2 tablespoons unseasoned rice
    vinegar*
*1 avocado, seeded, peeled,
    and thinly sliced*
*One 16-ounce jar store-bought
    salsa*
Pickled jalapeños, optional

3. Working with half of the fish at a time, toss the pieces in the seasoned flour, shaking off any excess, and dip them in the Beer Batter. Fry the fish, turning once or twice, until golden brown, about 2 minutes. Drain on paper towels and sprinkle with salt while hot. Repeat with remaining fish.

4. Combine the cabbage, rice vinegar, and 1/4 teaspoon salt. Remove the tortillas from the oven and place on a board. Divide the fish and avocado among the tortillas, making a mound in the center. Top with some salsa, the cabbage, the chipotle sauce, and pickled jalapeños, if using. Fold over the two sides of the tortillas to contain the filling and serve.

Sautéed Sole
with Garlicky Clam Sauce

MAKES 4 SERVINGS

Hands-on time:
25 minutes

Total preparation time:
25 minutes

I must confess that this recipe is more about the sauce than the sole, an excuse to repurpose clam broth—so deeply delicious and easily made—as a clam sauce. I soak the sole in milk to eliminate the fishy taste and start the garlic in cold oil rather than hot to get deeper flavor out of it. If you'd like, substitute mussels for clams. Serve with Butter-steamed Broccoli with Soy (page 296) and Parmigiano-Reggiano Couscous (page 41).

1 1/2 pounds sole fillets

1 1/2 cups milk for soaking the fish

1/4 cup plus 2 tablespoons extra virgin olive oil

4 garlic cloves, minced (about 4 teaspoons)

6 ounces cherry tomatoes, coarsely chopped (about 1 cup)

24 cherrystone clams, scrubbed

1 cup dry white wine

Kosher salt and freshly milled black pepper

1/3 cup Wondra or unbleached all-purpose flour

1/4 cup packed fresh basil leaves, shredded

1. Rinse the fish fillets, put them in a bowl, and cover them with the milk. Refrigerate them, covered, while you make the sauce.

2. Heat 2 tablespoons oil and the garlic in a large saucepan over medium heat until it is fragrant but not browned, 3 to 4 minutes. Add the tomatoes and cook, stirring occasionally, for 3 minutes. Add the clams and the wine; bring the mixture to a boil, cover the pan, and steam the clams until they begin to open, about 3 to 5 minutes. Transfer each clam to a bowl as it opens. (They open at different rates and you don't want to overcook the first one that opens while waiting for the last one.) Remove and discard the shells from the clams when they are cool enough to handle. Return the clams to the saucepan along with any liquid that has accumulated in the bowl. Taste the sauce and add salt and pepper, if necessary. Keep the sauce warm over very low heat.

3. Preheat the oven to 200°F. Combine the flour, 1/2 teaspoon salt, and 1/4 teaspoon pepper in a shallow bowl or pie plate. Heat another 2 tablespoons of the oil in a large skillet over high heat until hot; reduce the heat to medium. Working in batches, remove some fillets from the milk, allowing the excess to drip off. Dip them in the flour mixture to coat both sides. Put the fillets in the skillet and sauté until golden on both sides, about 4 minutes total. Transfer the fillets to a baking pan and keep them warm in the oven. Repeat the procedure with the remaining fish and the remaining 2 tablespoons oil.

4. Stir the basil into the clam sauce. Divide the fillets among 4 plates; top each portion with some of the sauce.

WHAT IS INSTANT FLOUR?

WHEN I was growing up my grandmother, Ruth Moulton, always used flour called Wondra from a round blue can to thicken her gravies. I forgot all about it until one day a few years ago I was hanging out in the kitchen at Chanterelle, a wonderful restaurant in the Tribeca section of New York City, and watching the chef, David Waltuck, make family dinner. He was dipping the salmon pieces into a very fine flour before sautéing them. I asked him if this was some kind of special flour and he replied that, yes, it was Wondra. I couldn't believe it! A three-star chef was using one of Granny's secret ingredients. Apparently the flour provides the most crispy coating to any sautéed dish. David was not the only chef to have discovered this. But what is Wondra, also known as instant flour? According to the General Mills Web site, "Instant flour is a low protein, pregelatinized wheat flour to which some malted barley flour has been added. It has been formulated to dissolve quickly in hot and cold liquids, and is most often called for to thicken gravies and sauces." Now I keep a box in my cupboard and think of Granny every time I take it out.

Salmon with Black Bean Sauce

Hands-on time:
10 minutes

Total preparation time:
20 minutes

MAKES 4 SERVINGS

Fermented black beans should be in everyone's pantry—they complement just about any protein and they can be turned into a sauce in no time at all. They are actually small black soy beans preserved in salt. You have to soak them to eliminate some of that salt, but then they are good to go. This sauce would go great not only with salmon, but on top of chicken, shrimp, tofu, or stir-fried vegetables. Serve with Butter-steamed Broccoli with Soy (page 296) and Simple Boiled Rice (page 40).

1. Preheat the oven to 400°F. Lightly grease a shallow roasting pan. Combine 1/2 cup boiling water and the chopped beans in a small bowl; set aside for 10 minutes, then drain.

2. Meanwhile, arrange the salmon in the roasting pan, skinned side down. Drizzle 2 tablespoons of the oil over the salmon and bake for 10 to 12 minutes or until cooked to your desired doneness.

3. Meanwhile, heat 2 teaspoons oil in a small saucepan over medium heat. Add the soaked and drained black beans, the ginger, and garlic; cook for 1 minute. Whisk together the broth, 1/3 cup water, the wine, cornstarch, and sugar in a bowl and add to the black bean mixture. Bring the sauce to a boil, stirring constantly, and simmer for 2 minutes. Serve each portion of salmon topped with some of the sauce and sprinkled with some of the scallions.

2 tablespoons fermented black beans, rinsed, drained, and chopped

Four 6- to 7-ounce skinless pieces center-cut salmon fillet

2 tablespoons plus 2 teaspoons vegetable oil

1 tablespoon finely grated fresh ginger (use a Microplane)

1 garlic clove, minced (about 1 teaspoon)

2/3 cup canned low-sodium chicken broth or Chicken Stock (page 32)

1 1/2 tablespoons rice wine or dry sherry

1 tablespoon cornstarch

1 teaspoon sugar

4 scallions, white and green parts, thinly sliced (about 1/2 cup)

Hands-on time:
20 minutes

Total preparation time:
20 minutes

2 tablespoons unsalted butter
1/4 cup finely chopped shallots
or onions
1 garlic clove, minced (about 1
teaspoon)
1 cup red wine
1 cup canned chicken broth or
Chicken Stock (page 32)
1 cup potato flakes
Four 5- to 6-ounce pieces
skinless center-cut salmon
fillet
Kosher salt and freshly milled
black pepper
2 tablespoons olive oil
1 1/2 teaspoons cornstarch
1 tablespoon Dijon mustard
Freshly milled black pepper

Potato-crusted Salmon
with Red Wine Sauce

MAKES 4 SERVINGS

Daniel's restaurant in New York City serves a classic wonderful dish of salmon that is wrapped in thin potato slices, sautéed, and served topped with a red wine sauce. It is more work than most home cooks would do on a weeknight, so (shush—don't tell anybody) I cheated and used instant potato flakes to come up with a quick version. Guess what, they work! The crust is crunchy, tastes like potato, and the quick red wine sauce is a nice complement. Serve with Garlic Bread (page 40) and a tossed green salad.

1. Preheat the oven to 200°F. Melt the butter in a saucepan over medium-low heat. Add the shallots and cook, stirring occasionally, until softened, about 8 minutes. Add the garlic and cook 2 minutes. Add the wine and simmer until reduced by half. Add the chicken broth and simmer until a little over 1 cup liquid is left. Set the sauce aside.

2. Meanwhile, put the potato flakes in a shallow pie plate. Season the fish with salt and pepper and coat on all sides with the flakes. Heat the oil in a large skillet (well seasoned or nonstick) over medium-high heat until hot. Cook the fish, turning to brown on all sides, until it is almost cooked through, 6 to 8 minutes total. Transfer the fish to a rimmed baking sheet and keep warm in the oven while you finish the sauce.

3. Whisk together the cornstarch and 1 tablespoon water. Return the sauce to a boil and whisk in the cornstarch mixture. Simmer for 1 minute; whisk in the mustard and pepper to taste. Serve the salmon with the sauce.

Seared Snapper
with Gazpacho Vinaigrette

MAKES 4 SERVINGS

Every cook knows that fish has to be perked up with a little acid, even if it's just a spritz of lemon or lime. This gazpacho vinaigrette addresses the problem head-on. Gazpacho is a Spanish soup with many variations, but the basic model is a cold chunky tomato vegetable soup. The dish's acidity comes from the tomatoes. I have notched up the acidity by adding sherry wine vinegar to the standard gazpacho ingredients. With the olive oil, it's transformed into a chunky vinaigrette for the sautéed snapper. I think you will find this a very refreshing quick dish. Serve with Greek Spinach Rice (page 309).

1. Set aside 1/3 cup each of the tomato, bell pepper, and cucumber. Puree the remaining tomatoes, bell pepper, and cucumber with the onion, vinegar, garlic, 1/2 teaspoon salt, and 1/8 teaspoon pepper in a blender until smooth. Set aside 3 tablespoons of the oil; add the remaining oil gradually to the vegetable mixture with the blender motor running. Transfer to a bowl and stir in the reserved chopped tomatoes, bell pepper, and cucumber along with the olives.

2. Combine the flour with 1/2 teaspoon salt and 1/4 teaspoon pepper in a pie plate. Heat half of the reserved 3 tablespoons oil in each of 2 large skillets over high heat until hot. Coat the fish on all sides with the flour, shaking off the excess. Reduce the heat to medium-high and add the fish. Cook the fish until golden, 3 to 4 minutes on each side. Transfer the fish to serving plates and spoon some of the vinaigrette over each serving.

Hands-on time:
25 minutes

Total preparation time:
30 minutes

1 beefsteak tomato (about 3/4 pound), peeled, seeded, and chopped (about 1 1/3 cups)

1 small red bell pepper, chopped (about 2/3 cup)

4-inch piece English cucumber, peeled, seeded, and chopped (about 3/4 cup)

2 tablespoons finely chopped onion, soaked in cold water for 10 minutes and drained

2 tablespoons sherry vinegar

1/2 garlic clove, minced (about 1/2 teaspoon)

Kosher salt and freshly milled black pepper

1/2 cup plus 1 tablespoon extra virgin olive oil

1/4 cup sliced pimiento-stuffed olives

1/3 cup Wondra or unbleached all-purpose flour

Four pieces red snapper or striped bass fillets (about 1 1/2 pounds total), skinned

Sam's Baked Shrimp
with Garlic Crumbs

MAKES 4 SERVINGS

1 pound large shrimp, shelled
   and deveined
4 tablespoons extra virgin
   olive oil
1 tablespoon fresh lemon juice
Kosher salt
1/2 teaspoon red pepper
   flakes
2 garlic cloves, minced
6 scallions (white and light
   green parts), thinly sliced
   (about 3/4 cup)
1 cup fresh bread crumbs from
   Bread Crumbs Four Ways
   (page 23)
1 tablespoon rinsed, dried,
   and shredded fresh basil
Freshly milled black pepper

This is one of my son Sam's favorite dishes, but I don't make it very often because it calls for large shrimp, and those monsters are expensive. On those occasions when you've got more money than time, however, you'll love this recipe because it takes less time to peel and devein a portion's worth of large shrimp than it does smaller shrimp. Of course, when you have more time than money, go for medium-sized shrimp. Serve with Roasted Peppers (page 30) and Bean Salad (page 39).

1. Preheat the oven to 400°F. To butterfly the shrimp, arrange them in one layer on a cutting board. Starting at the back side (the larger curved side) cut each shrimp until it is almost separated in two horizontally but still attached at the smaller curved side. Gently toss the prepared shrimp with 1 tablespoon of the oil, the lemon juice, and 1/2 teaspoon salt.

2. Heat the remaining oil in a large skillet over medium-high heat. Add the pepper flakes and cook for 10 seconds. Add the garlic and cook for 30 seconds. Stir in the scallions and cook until they are slightly softened, about 10 seconds. Remove from the heat and add the bread crumbs, basil, and salt and pepper to taste.

3. Arrange the shrimp in one layer in a shallow baking pan, cut side up (so they look like an open book). Put a mound of the crumbs on top of each one and bake them on the top shelf of the oven for 7 minutes or until they are just cooked and the crumbs are golden.

Spicy New Orleans Shrimp

Hands-on time:
15 minutes

Total preparation time:
25 minutes

MAKES 4 SERVINGS

Everyone in New Orleans cooks "barbecue" shrimp and everyone believes his or her version is the one true and authentic recipe. Me, I'm a New Yorker and I'm not looking for a fight. So I call my version Spicy New Orleans Shrimp. It has most of the ingredients of traditional "barbecue" shrimp. It is also very tasty and ridiculously easy to make. Serve with Simple Boiled Rice (page 40) and Cole Slaw (page 38).

1 1/2 pounds medium shrimp, shelled and deveined

1 1/2 tablespoons packaged Creole or Cajun spice mix or Creole Spice Mix (page 20, add prep time)

3 tablespoons unsalted butter

1 tablespoon vegetable oil

4 scallions (white and light green parts), sliced (about 1/2 cup)

2 large garlic cloves, minced (about 1 tablespoon)

1/3 cup beer

2 tablespoons Worcestershire sauce

1 tablespoon fresh lemon juice

1. Toss the shrimp with half of the Creole Spice Mix and refrigerate, covered, for 15 minutes while you prepare the remaining ingredients.

2. Heat 1 tablespoon of the butter and half the oil in a large skillet over medium-high heat until hot but not browned. Add half the shrimp and sauté, stirring constantly, for 2 minutes; remove the shrimp to a bowl. Repeat with another tablespoon of the butter, the remaining oil, and shrimp.

3. Return the first batch of shrimp to the skillet along with the scallions and garlic; cook for 2 more minutes. Add the beer, remaining tablespoon butter, Worcestershire sauce, and lemon juice and simmer gently until reduced slightly and the shrimp are just cooked through, 2 to 3 minutes.

2 tablespoons vegetable oil

2 plum tomatoes, chopped
    (about 3/4 cup)

2 large shallots, finely
    chopped (about 1/4 cup)

1 tablespoon finely grated
    fresh ginger (use a
    Microplane)

2 kaffir lime leaves, shredded,
    optional

1 stalk lemongrass, white part
    only, finely chopped,
    optional

2 garlic cloves, minced (about
    2 teaspoons)

2 cups unsweetened canned
    coconut milk

1/4 cup red or green curry
    paste

3 pounds (about 60) cultivated
    mussels, scrubbed

3 scallions (white and light
    green parts), thinly sliced
    (about 1/3 cup)

2 tablespoons rinsed, dried,
    and finely chopped fresh
    cilantro or basil

1 to 2 tablespoons fresh lime
    juice

Kosher salt and freshly milled
    black pepper

Steamed Mussels
in Curried Coconut Broth

MAKES 4 SERVINGS

This is about as exotic as any recipe in this book. It calls for a few ingredients that you might have to search for: kaffir lime leaves, lemongrass, and curry paste. You can find all of them in Asian markets and in some supermarkets. But if you don't live near a convenient Asian market, use two teaspoons freshly grated lemon or lime rind in place of the kaffir lime leaves and lemongrass, and use one small minced chile in place of the curry paste. But don't sweat it. This recipe is really about the delicious broth given off by the mussels when they're steamed. Everything else is just commentary. Serve with toasted country bread or Simple Boiled Rice (page 40).

1. Heat the oil in a large saucepan over medium heat. Add the tomatoes, shallots, ginger, lime leaves and lemongrass, if using, and the garlic and cook over medium-low heat until softened, about 5 minutes

2. Add the coconut milk and curry paste and bring to a simmer. Add the mussels, cover tightly, and steam over medium heat, transferring them with tongs to a bowl as they open, about 6 minutes total. Discard any mussels that do not open.

3. Stir the scallions and cilantro into the coconut mixture; add lime juice, salt, and pepper to taste. Transfer the mussels to bowls and ladle the sauce over them.

MOST of the mussels we find in restaurants, fish stores, and super-markets are blue mussels from North Atlantic waters. They probably came from Prince Edward Island, Newfoundland, Nova Scotia, or Maine. You can tell right away whether they are wild or cultivated.

Wild mussels have larger, rougher-looking shells, often with beards (a hairy string from the side of the shell) and barnacles attached. Cultivated mussels have small, smooth, dark shells and negligible beards, if any at all. The wild mussels are stronger in flavor, almost gamey. They also contain more grit than the cultivated. I prefer the more delicate taste and tender texture of the cultivated.

Store your mussels in a bowl in the fridge with a damp towel on top and try to cook them within a few days, although they will last for up to a week. If they are the wild variety, you need to scrub them, knock off any barnacles, and pull off the beards. If they are cultivated, wash them and pull off any beards. Do not soak mussels in fresh water or you will kill them. Don't clean them until right before you throw them in the pot to cook. If the shell is open, give the mussel a little tap on the counter. It should close within 30 seconds or so if it is alive. If it doesn't close, toss it. Likewise, if a mussel doesn't open when you cook it, toss it.

WILD VS. CULTIVATED MUSSELS

Hands-on time:
20 minutes

Total preparation time:
25 minutes

*8 small soft-shell crabs,
cleaned (see sidebar)*
2 cups milk
*1 recipe Mexican Tomatillo
Salsa (page 318)*
*1/3 cup Wondra or unbleached
all-purpose flour*
*Kosher salt and freshly milled
black pepper*
*2 to 4 tablespoons vegetable
oil*
1 Hass avocado

Sautéed Soft-shell Crabs
with Mexican Tomatillo Salsa

MAKES 4 SERVINGS

One of the ingredients I look forward to the most when spring rolls around is soft-shell crabs. I first tasted them at the New York World's Fair in 1964 and fell in love immediately, even though I didn't particularly care for fish of any kind at the time. They were probably deep fried, which meant that the delicious contrast of crunchy shell to sweet crabmeat was even more pronounced than if the crab had been sautéed. Years later when I was working as chef tournant at the three-star La Tulipe in New York City, I learned the proper and more elegant way to prepare them: *à la meunière* or "in the style of the miller's wife," which means dipped in flour and sautéed. We served them very dramatically with butter that had been browned in the kitchen and poured over the crabs at the last minute at the dinner table so that it foamed up.

I have gone the Southwestern route here with Mexican Tomatillo Salsa (page 000) and chopped avocado because the salsa provides a necessary acidic touch and the avocado, contrast of texture. Sally Darr, La Tulipe's chef-owner, taught me to look for crabs with the softest shells and liveliest attitude. It is best if you clean them yourself so you know they are very fresh. Serve with Southwestern Sweet Potato Sauté (page 294) and a tossed green salad.

1. Combine the crabs and milk in a baking dish or bowl and set aside for 15 minutes. (The milk will get rid of any fishy taste.) Meanwhile, prepare the salsa, preheat the oven to 200°F, and combine the flour with 1/2 teaspoon salt and 1/4 teaspoon pepper in a pie plate or large soup plate.

2. Remove half the crabs from the milk and coat them with the flour mixture, shaking off any excess. Heat 2 tablespoons of the oil in a large skillet over high heat until hot; reduce the heat to medium-high and add the crabs to the skillet, belly side down. Sauté until golden, 3 to 5 minutes; turn and sauté until golden on the remaining side, 3 to 5 minutes longer. Transfer the crabs to a rimmed baking sheet and keep warm in the oven. Repeat with remaining crabs, adding more oil. Meanwhile, halve, seed, and peel the avocado and cut it into cubes.

3. To serve, arrange 2 crabs on each plate. Top with a mound of cubed avocado and some of the salsa.

CLEANING SOFT-SHELL CRABS

FIRST, lay the live crab down flat on a cutting board with the head facing up. Cut off the top part of the crab—the part with the eyes. (I know this sounds brutal, but you want to put it out of its misery fast.) Next, turn it over and pull off the "apron," the little flap on the underside. (In female crabs it is rounded and in males it is pointy—some things don't change.) Last, turn it over and lift up either side of the shell, one side at a time, to expose and pull out the spongy lungs.

Seared Scallops

with Shredded Zucchini and Lemon Cream

Hands-on time:
20 minutes

Total preparation time:
20 minutes

MAKES 4 SERVINGS

My thinking here was to pair scallops and zucchini, both of which are sweet and delicate, and see if they made a happy match. I think they do team up nicely, and so does my husband, who usually finds zucchini too bland. The key is salting and squeezing the zucchini, which eliminates excess liquid and concentrates its flavor.

When buying the scallops, try to get the "dry" or "day boat" variety. They'll be fresher than "wet" scallops. Soaked in a liquid preservative, "wet" scallops are impossible to sauté; they just weep. Serve with Parmigiano-Reggiano Couscous (page 41).

*2 medium zucchini (about
 1 pound), shredded,
 preferably in a food
 processor
1 teaspoon kosher salt
3 tablespoons vegetable oil
1/3 cup Wondra or unbleached
 all-purpose flour
Freshly milled black pepper
1 pound bay scallops, rinsed
 and patted dry
4 scallions (white and light
 green parts), finely
 chopped (about 1/2 cup)
1 cup chicken stock
1/2 cup heavy cream
2 teaspoons fresh lemon juice
1 teaspoon freshly grated
 lemon zest*

1. Toss the zucchini in a colander with 3/4 teaspoon salt and let drain for 10 minutes. Squeeze the zucchini by small handfuls to remove the excess water.

2. Meanwhile, combine the flour, 1/2 teaspoon salt, and 1/4 teaspoon pepper in a pie plate or shallow bowl. Heat 2 tablespoon of the oil in a large skillet over high heat until hot; reduce the heat to medium-high. Toss the scallops in the flour, shaking off the excess, and add the scallops to the skillet. Sauté until golden on both sides, about 4 minutes total.

3. Transfer the scallops with a slotted spoon or tongs to a bowl and cover with aluminum foil. Add the remaining tablespoon of oil, the scallions, and zucchini to the skillet and sauté for 2 minutes. Transfer with a slotted spoon to the bowl with the scallops. Add the chicken stock, cream, lemon juice, and zest to the skillet and simmer for 4 minutes or until thickened slightly. Add the scallops, zucchini, and any juices from the bowl and cook until just heated through.

Vegetable Plates

Exotic Mushroom Pot Pie

V

MAKES 6 SERVINGS

One 14- or 14 1/2-ounce can
vegetable broth

1 ounce dried porcini
mushrooms

1 sheet (about 9 1/4 X 9 3/4
inches) frozen puff pastry
(half of a 17.3-ounce
package), defrosted enough
to unfold

2 medium leeks (white part
only)

4 tablespoons (1/2 stick)
unsalted butter

2 pounds assorted fresh
mushrooms such as button,
crimini, shiitake, oyster,
chanterelle, or morel,
cleaned, quartered if large,
shiitake stems discarded

3/4 teaspoon rinsed and dried
fresh thyme or 1/4
teaspoon dried

1/2 cup white wine

2 tablespoons unbleached all-
purpose flour

Kosher salt and freshly milled
black pepper

My husband as a kid sometimes used to eat three pot pies at a sitting and call it lunch. Although he's capable of eating less today, he still loves his pot pie. I understand that it is not really the chicken or beef or turkey that makes him happy—it is the gravy and crust. My version features mushroom gravy and puff pastry crust. You can find puff pastry in the frozen food section of the supermarket. Look for the brand with the most butter—as opposed to shortening—because that's the one that will taste the best.

Strictly speaking, this isn't really a pie. I cook the crust and the filling separately to keep the crust crisp. Then I place a square of the crust on top of the cooked mushroom mixture like a little hat. The porcini soaking liquid is what gives the gravy its deep flavor. If you cannot find porcini, use any dried mushroom you see at the store. Serve with Herbed Pea Medley (page 37) and Grated Carrot Salad (page 293).

1. Preheat the oven to 375°F. Bring the broth to a boil in a small saucepan over high heat. Remove from the heat, add the dried porcini mushrooms, and set aside to soak for 15 minutes or until they have softened.

2. Unfold the puff pastry sheet onto a rimmed baking sheet; cut it into 3 strips at the folds and cut each strip crosswise in half to make a total of 6 rectangles; separate them slightly on the baking sheet. Bake the puff pastry until crisp and golden, 12 to 15 minutes.

3. Meanwhile, quarter the leeks lengthwise and cut into 1/2-inch lengths. Soak according to step 1 on page 53. Melt the butter in a large skillet over medium-low heat. Add the leeks and cook, stirring occasionally, until softened, about 8 minutes. Add the fresh mushrooms and thyme; cook over medium heat until all the liquid the mushrooms release has evaporated, 15 minutes.

4. Lift the porcini mushrooms out of the soaking liquid gently to let any sand sink to the bottom of the pan. Pour the liquid through a coffee filter or dampened paper towel in a fine strainer and reserve. Rinse the porcini thoroughly to remove any remaining sand. Stir them into the fresh mushroom mixture along with the wine; cook until the liquid has reduced by half, 3 to 4 minutes.

5. Whisk the flour into the reserved mushroom soaking liquid. Whisk the mixture into the mushrooms; bring to a boil, whisking, and simmer 3 minutes longer. Add salt and pepper to taste. Divide among 6 soup plates. Top each portion of mushrooms with a puff-pastry rectangle and serve.

Giant Stuffed Mushrooms

V

MAKES 4 SERVINGS

4 portobello mushrooms (4 to
    5 ounces each), cleaned,
    stems removed and
    reserved, and gills scraped
    out and discarded (see
    sidebar)
2 tablespoons olive oil
1 small onion, chopped (about
    1/2 cup)
1/2 pound green beans,
    trimmed and sliced into
    1/2-inch pieces
1 recipe Parsley Pesto (page
    320)
1 plain English muffin, finely
    chopped
Kosher salt and freshly milled
    black pepper
4 ounces Muenster cheese, cut
    into 4 slices

When I was growing up, one of the more exotic items in my
mom's culinary repertoire was stuffed mushrooms. She would
make them with cultivated white mushrooms, which were
considered very elegant at the time, and stuff them simply with
chopped-up mushrooms, onions, and bread crumbs. She usually
served them as a side dish, which seemed a little over the top
to me.

They were substantial, which is why I thought to do a large
version, using portobellos, here in the vegetarian chapter.
Portobello mushrooms are one of the meatiest mushrooms, with a
great taste as well. I used three of my mom's ingredients for the
stuffing—onion, mushrooms, and bread—and then added some
green beans, pesto, and cheese. You can use store-bought pesto if
you want to speed up the process, but this is a pretty quick recipe
anyway. Serve with a tossed green salad and Sautéed Beets with
Balsamic Vinegar (page 305).

1. Discard a thin slice from the root end of the mushroom stems; chop
the remaining stems. Heat 1 tablespoon of the oil in a large skillet over
high heat until hot. Reduce the heat to medium; add the onion and cook,
stirring occasionally, until softened, about 5 minutes. Add the mushroom
stems and green beans and cook, stirring occasionally, until both are just
tender, about 8 minutes. Transfer the bean mixture to a small bowl;
reserve the skillet. Stir the pesto, English muffin, and salt and pepper to
taste into the bean mixture.

2. Heat the remaining tablespoon of oil in the same skillet until hot. Reduce the heat to medium and add the mushroom caps, open side down. Cook, covered, 5 minutes. Turn the caps over and divide the bean mixture among them; cook, covered, 5 minutes. Top each mushroom with a slice of cheese, remove from the heat, and set aside, covered, just until the cheese melts, about 1 minute. Serve immediately.

IT IS a good idea to remove the gills from the cap of a portobello mushroom because the dark gills share their color with everything they touch and will discolor (turn black) any stuffings, sauces, and salad dressings that accompany the mushrooms in the recipe. Also, the gills sometimes hide a little sand from the substrate on which the mushrooms were grown; scooping them out prevents any grittiness in the finished dish. The best way to remove them is to scrape them out with a small spoon.

PORTOBELLO GILLS

Hands-on time:
10 minutes

Total preparation time:
50 minutes,
including
marinating time

1/2 cup soy sauce

1/3 cup rice wine or dry sherry

2 tablespoons sugar

1 1/2 tablespoons finely grated fresh ginger (use a Microplane)

1 tablespoon toasted sesame oil

1 large sweet potato (about 12 ounces)

2 small Asian eggplants (about 10 ounces), sliced crosswise 1/3 inch thick

16 large shiitake mushrooms, stems discarded and caps quartered, or 32 smaller shiitake caps, stems discarded and caps halved

1 recipe Sesame Miso Sauce (page 323)

Grilled Shiitake, Sweet Potato, and Eggplant Kabobs

V

MAKES 4 SERVINGS

Shiitake mushrooms, sweet potatoes, and eggplant are all very "meaty" vegetables. Similarly, there's a creaminess to Sesame Miso Sauce, although it contains no cream. Put them together and you've got a very filling dish. Tasty, too, of course. Grilling these vegetables as kabobs brings out their natural sugars. (You can broil them if you don't have a grill or grill pan.) Serve with Simple Boiled Rice (page 40) and Herbed Pea Medley (page 37).

1. Combine the soy sauce, wine, 3 tablespoons water, the sugar, ginger, and sesame oil in a small saucepan; heat over medium heat, stirring until the sugar is dissolved. Let cool slightly.

2. Peel the sweet potato and cut crosswise into 1/3-inch-thick slices. Cut the slices into quarters or halves so that they are roughly the same size as the eggplant slices. Steam the sweet potato slices in a steamer set over boiling water for 6 to 7 minutes or until they are just al dente. Alternate the sweet potato, eggplant, and mushrooms on eight 8-inch metal skewers. Place the skewers in one layer in a shallow baking pan. Pour the marinade over them and marinate at room temperature, turning a few times, for 30 minutes.

3. Meanwhile, prepare the Sesame Miso Sauce.

4. Preheat the grill or a grill pan. Grill the kabobs, turning frequently, 4 to 5 minutes or until the vegetables are tender and slightly golden. Serve with the Sesame Miso Sauce on the side.

Baked Eggplant, Tomato, and Feta Stacks

𝒱

MAKES 4 SERVINGS

Hands-on time:
20 minutes

Total preparation time:
20 minutes

Eggplants are great, but when it comes to soaking up oil, they're more absorbent than sponges. It was my mother who taught me a far lighter—but no less flavorful—way to cook them. Just slice them, brush them with vinaigrette, and bake them in the oven.

It is best to make this recipe in August and September, when beefsteak tomatoes are at their peak. But if you want to prepare it off season, plum or Roma tomatoes are your best bet. Feel free to substitute your favorite cheese for the feta. Monterey Jack, aged Cheddar, or even blue cheese—whatever melts—will work nicely in this dish. Serve with a tossed green salad and Garlic Bread (page 40).

1 medium eggplant (about 1 pound)
2 medium beefsteak tomatoes (about 3/4 pound)
3 tablespoons red wine vinegar
2 teaspoons rinsed, dried, and finely chopped fresh rosemary
Kosher salt and freshly milled black pepper
1/3 cup extra virgin olive oil
6 ounces feta or ricotta salata cheese, cut into 12 slices
8 ounces mozzarella, cut into 12 slices

1. Preheat the broiler to high. Cut the eggplant crosswise into twelve 1/3-inch slices, discarding a thin slice from the top and bottom. Cut each tomato crosswise into four 1/3-inch slices (8 slices total), discarding a thin slice from the top and bottom.

2. Whisk together the vinegar, rosemary, and salt and pepper to taste; slowly whisk in the olive oil. Brush the eggplant and tomato slices generously on both sides with the dressing. Arrange the eggplant on a rimmed baking sheet 4 inches from the heat source and broil 5 minutes. Turn and broil until browned on the other side, 4 to 5 minutes.

3. Remove the eggplant and reduce the oven to 375°F. Arrange 4 stacks on the baking sheet, starting with an eggplant slice, then a slice of tomato, a slice of feta, and a slice of mozzarella. Repeat, then top each stack with a third slice of eggplant, feta, and mozzarella. Return the stacks to the oven and bake them for 10 to 12 minutes, or just until the cheese melts. Serve immediately.

Corn and Jalapeño Cakes
with Goat Cheese

𝒱

MAKES 4 SERVINGS

1 1/2 cups fresh or defrosted
frozen corn kernels
1 large beefsteak tomato, cut
into 8 slices
Kosher salt
2/3 cup yellow cornmeal
3 tablespoons unbleached all-
purpose flour
1/4 teaspoon baking soda
1/2 cup buttermilk or sour
cream
1 large egg
1 to 2 large jalapeños,
stemmed, seeded, and
chopped
1/3 cup vegetable oil
4 ounces soft goat cheese, cut
into 8 slices
2 scallions (white and light
green parts), chopped
(about 1/4 cup)

When I made the first batch of these corn cakes and topped them off with a slice of tomato and goat cheese, they were so substantial they reminded me of a burger. The fresher the corn, the tastier these cakes will be, because the minute you pick an ear of corn its sugar starts to turn to starch. The best scenario would be to put a pot of water on to boil, pick and husk the corn from the cornfield in the backyard, and get it right into the pot. Most of us do not have a cornfield in the backyard, but at least try to get your corn in the pot the same day you buy it. If you are not a fan of goat cheese, any good melting cheese will do, such as mozzarella, Swiss, or even Cheddar. I love all of those cheeses with corn and tomatoes. Serve with Cole Slaw (page 38).

1. Preheat the oven to 375°F. If using frozen corn, drain it and pat dry. Sprinkle the tomato slices with 1/4 teaspoon salt and set aside in a colander.

2. Whisk together the cornmeal, flour, 1/4 teaspoon salt, and the baking soda in a bowl. Whisk together the buttermilk and egg in another bowl, then add to the dry ingredients and stir until just combined (do not overmix). Stir in the corn and desired amount of chopped jalapeños.

3. Heat half the oil in a large skillet over medium heat. Drop enough batter into the skillet to form four 3 1/2-inch pancakes. Cook for about 2 minutes, turning over once, until lightly browned on both sides, about 4 minutes total. Transfer with a spatula to paper towels to drain. Repeat with the remaining oil and batter.

4. Arrange all of the pancakes in one layer on a rimmed baking sheet. Pat the tomato slices dry with paper towels and place one on each corn cake. Top each with a slice of cheese and bake for 10 minutes or just until the cheese has melted. Divide the pancakes among 4 plates and top each portion with some of the scallions.

Cauliflower "Steak" with Sautéed Peppers and Mediterranean Salsa Verde

V

MAKES 4 SERVINGS

Forget what you think you know about cauliflower—cooking it this way brings out the natural sugars and will turn you into a fan. (This dish was inspired by a recipe that ran in the Rome issue of *Gourmet* in October 2003.) Once you've sautéed the cauliflower and finished it off in the oven, you can top it off with almost anything. I've chosen sautéed peppers and salsa verde, but artichoke hearts, cheese, or toasted bread crumbs would all work nicely as well. Serve with Mediterranean Orzo Pilaf (page 307) and sliced tomatoes.

1. Preheat the oven to 350°F. Trim the cauliflower stalk flush with the base of the crown, being careful that all florets remain attached. Discard the stalk and any leaves. Put the cauliflower crown, stalk side down, on a cutting board. Cut a 1-inch slice from 2 opposite sides of the crown and reserve for another use. Then cut the crown lengthwise into four steaks 3/4 to 1 inch wide, each still attached to a portion of the stalk. Season the cauliflower slices with salt and pepper on both sides.

2. Heat 2 tablespoons of the oil in a large skillet over high heat until hot. Add the cauliflower slices in a single layer; reduce the heat to medium-high and cook, turning once, until both sides are well caramelized, about 6 minutes a side. Meanwhile, prepare the Mediterranean Salsa Verde, if using, eliminating the anchovy.

Hands-on time:
25 minutes with Mediterranean Salsa Verde,
15 minutes with bottled sauce

Total preparation time:
45 minutes with Mediterranean Salsa Verde,
35 minutes with bottled sauce

1 small head cauliflower (about 1 3/4 pounds)
Kosher salt and freshly milled black pepper
4 tablespoons extra virgin olive oil
1 cup bottled salsa verde or pesto or 1 recipe Mediterranean Salsa Verde (page 317, add prep time)
1 medium red bell pepper, sliced (about 1 cup)
1 medium green bell pepper, sliced (about 1 cup)

3. Transfer the browned cauliflower to a rimmed baking sheet and bake 12 to 15 minutes or until the slices are just tender. While the cauliflower is baking, add the remaining 2 tablespoons oil and the bell peppers to the skillet in which the cauliflower was cooked; cook over medium heat, stirring occasionally, about 8 minutes or until the peppers are just tender. Add salt and pepper to taste.

4. To serve, divide the cauliflower among 4 plates, top with some of the peppers, and drizzle with the salsa verde.

Stuffed Smashed Potato Cakes

V

MAKES 4 SERVINGS

1 1/4 pounds small red
    potatoes, scrubbed
Kosher salt
Green Chutney (recipe
    follows)
1/4 to 1/2 cup milk
4 tablespoons unsalted butter
2 tablespoons vegetable oil
4 scallions (white and light
    green parts), chopped
    (about 1/2 cup)
1 garlic clove, minced (about
    1 teaspoon)
1 teaspoon finely grated fresh
    ginger (use a Microplane)
1/2 teaspoon salt-free
    packaged garam masala,
    curry powder, or Todd's
    Garam Masala (page 21,
    add prep time)
1/2 cup 1/2-inch cauliflower
    flowerets
1/2 cup frozen green peas
1/3 cup Wondra or unbleached
    all-purpose flour
Freshly milled black pepper

We make smashed potatoes (by smashed I mean coarsely mashed, unpeeled, cooked boiling potatoes) in my house about once a week. My son Sam has become quite a pro. We always make a double batch so I can turn them into smashed potato cakes on another day. When they are cool they can be formed into patties (with a little gentle care), dipped in seasoned flour, and sautéed until golden on both sides. It occurred to me they might make a good stuffed potato pancake for the vegetarian chapter, and I thought of stuffing them with a curried cauliflower-pea mixture, which is one of the typical fillings for samosas or Indian turnovers. Topped off with the Green Chutney (adapted from a recipe in *Gourmet*), these potato pancakes make a very tasty entrée indeed. Serve with Grated Carrot Salad (page 293).

1. Combine the potatoes and salted water to cover by 2 inches in a large saucepan. Bring the water to a boil over high heat; reduce the heat to low and simmer the potatoes for 15 to 18 minutes or until tender. Meanwhile, make the chutney.

2. Drain the potatoes and return them to the saucepan. Add 1/4 cup milk, 2 tablespoons butter, and salt to taste; smash with a potato masher until mashed enough to hold together. Add additional milk until the desired consistency is reached. The potatoes should be firm enough to hold their shape when formed into patties. Spread the potato mixture in a shallow baking pan, cover, and place in the freezer for 10 minutes to cool quickly.

3. While the potatoes are cooling, heat the oil in a medium skillet over high heat until hot; reduce the heat to medium and add the scallions, garlic, ginger, and garam masala. Cook for 2 minutes, stirring. Add the cauliflower, 1/3 cup water, and 1/8 teaspoon salt. Cover and cook 5 minutes or until the cauliflower is just tender. Add the peas and cook, uncovered, until the water has evaporated.

4. Divide the cooled potato mixture into 8 equal balls. Shape each into a 1/2-inch-thick cake. Divide the cauliflower mixture among 4 of the cakes. Top each with 1 teaspoon Green Chutney and one of the remaining potato cakes, pressing the potatoes together to enclose the filling.

5. Combine the flour, 1/2 teaspoon salt, and 1/4 teaspoon pepper on a plate. Coat the filled potato cakes with the flour mixture. Heat the remaining butter in a medium skillet over medium-low heat until the foam starts to subside. Add the potato cakes and cook until golden, about 5 minutes a side. Serve each cake topped with some of the remaining chutney.

Green Chutney

In a food processor fitted with the chopping blade, combine 2 cups firmly packed rinsed and dried fresh cilantro sprigs, 1/4 cup sweetened flaked coconut, 3 coarsely chopped scallions (white and green parts), 3 tablespoons vegetable oil, 2 seeded and chopped fresh jalapeño peppers, 2 tablespoons fresh lime juice, and a 1-inch piece of fresh ginger, peeled and very thinly sliced. Pulse until the mixture is coarsely pureed. Add kosher salt and freshly milled black pepper to taste. Transfer to a covered container and refrigerate until ready to use.

Indian Egg Curry

V

MAKES 4 SERVINGS

6 large eggs

1/4 cup vegetable oil

1 1/2 teaspoons cumin seeds

1 large jalapeño or 2 green
serrano chiles, thinly sliced
lengthwise

1/2-inch-piece fresh ginger,
peeled and finely chopped

2 large red onions, finely
chopped (about 3 cups)

1/2 teaspoon turmeric

1/4 teaspoon cayenne or to
taste

3/4 pound ripe plum tomatoes,
finely chopped

Kosher salt and freshly milled
black pepper

1/4 cup rinsed, dried, and
chopped fresh cilantro

This recipe was sent to me by Aparna Subramanian of San Diego for use on my Web site. She said that her nine-month-old son, Rohan, enjoyed watching my show with her every day. What is so unusual about this recipe is that you essentially make a spicy tomato sauce and then just warm some hard-cooked eggs in it. I have included a recipe for cooking the eggs that is my shortened version of Julia Child's method. Since you don't actually boil the eggs, the white comes out much more tender than the usual boiled egg white. The eggs get plunged in an ice bath after they are cooked, which is key; the ice bath prevents that green line from forming between the yolk and the white. You can "boil" the eggs and cook the sauce ahead of time and then just warm the eggs in the sauce right before dinner. Serve with Simple Boiled Rice (page 40) and Grated Carrot Salad (page 293).

1. Place the eggs in a large saucepan with enough cold water to cover by 1 inch. Bring to a boil over high heat. Remove from the heat, cover, and set aside for 15 minutes. Transfer the eggs to a bowl of half ice and half water. Cool completely, then peel under cold running water and cut in half lengthwise.

2. Heat the oil in a medium skillet over high heat until hot. Reduce the heat to medium; add the cumin seeds and heat 30 seconds. Add chiles to taste and the ginger; cook for 1 minute. Stir in the onions, turmeric, and cayenne; cook, stirring occasionally, until the onions soften, about 5 minutes.

3. Add the tomatoes and 1/2 cup water to the sauce and cook until soft, about 5 minutes. Taste and add salt and pepper. Place the eggs, cut side up, in the sauce and heat until the sauce bubbles and the eggs are hot. Sprinkle with cilantro and serve.

Green Bean Casserole Moderne

V

MAKES 4 TO 6 SERVINGS

Kosher salt
1 large white onion, sliced
(about 2 cups)
1 tablespoon vegetable oil
Freshly milled black pepper
8 ounces haricots verts or
green beans, trimmed
3 tablespoons unsalted butter
2 tablespoons chopped
shallots
1 garlic clove, minced (about 1
teaspoon)
12 ounces mixed shiitake and
white mushrooms or any
assortment of mushrooms,
cleaned
2 teaspoons rinsed and dried
fresh thyme or 2/3
teaspoon dried
3 tablespoons unbleached all-
purpose flour
2 cups whole milk, heated
4 ounces sharp Cheddar
cheese, grated (about
1 cup)

All right, I was trying to update that sentimental favorite of yesteryear, the Green Bean Casserole—but with fresh ingredients in place of the canned green beans, canned mushroom soup, and canned crispy onions that made the original so, uh, convenient. The result is a dish so hearty it qualifies as an entrée, which is why it lives here in the vegetarian chapter. I prefer the thin French green beans called *haricots verts* to the husky variety we grow here, but our native fatties would work just fine, as would any variety of mushroom. Serve with Cole Slaw (page 38) and Sautéed Beets with Balsamic Vinegar (page 305).

1. Bring a large pot of salted water to a boil. Preheat the broiler to high. Grease a shallow 2-quart baking dish.

2. Toss the onion in a bowl with the oil, 1/4 teaspoon salt, and 1/8 teaspoon pepper. Spread the onion on a baking sheet and place under the broiler, about 5 inches from the heat source. Broil until the edges begin to brown, about 8 minutes. Set onion aside. Reduce the oven to 375°F.

3. Add the haricots verts to the boiling water and cook 2 minutes; drain immediately and pat dry.

4. Melt the butter in a large skillet over medium-low heat. Add the shallots and garlic and cook for 2 minutes. Discard the shiitake stems; slice the shiitake caps and white mushrooms. Turn the heat up to medium; add all the mushrooms and the thyme and cook, stirring occasionally, until most of the liquid the mushrooms release has evaporated. Sprinkle the flour over the mushrooms and cook, stirring, 2 minutes.

5. Add the milk gradually, whisking constantly. Bring the mixture to a boil and simmer for 3 minutes. Stir in the green beans and half the cheese; season with salt and pepper to taste.

6. Transfer the mixture to the baking dish. Top with the remaining cheese and the broiled onion rings and bake until hot and bubbling, about 25 minutes.

Sautéed Falafel

𝒱

MAKES 4 SERVINGS

4 to 5 tablespoons olive oil

1 small onion, chopped (about
1/2 cup)

2 garlic cloves, minced (about
2 teaspoons)

3/4 teaspoon ground cumin

1/2 teaspoon ground coriander

1/4 teaspoon cayenne pepper

One 15 1/2-ounce can
chickpeas, drained and
rinsed (about 1 1/3 cups)

Kosher salt and freshly milled
black pepper

1 large egg, lightly beaten

3 tablespoons unbleached all-
purpose flour

1/2 teaspoon baking soda

3/4 cup packaged panko or
dried bread crumbs or from
Bread Crumbs Four Ways
(page 23, add prep time)

1 recipe Tahini Sauce (page
324)

Two 6-inch pitas with pockets,
halved

Falafel are a favorite of connoisseurs of street food from Jerusalem to New York City. Made with ground dried chickpeas or fava beans, they're hot, peppery, meaty, inexpensive, and satisfying—a handy little meal in a pita pocket. Given that we're starting with canned beans instead of dried beans and that we sauté the falafel rather than deep-fry it, this version is both quicker to make and less caloric than the standard recipe . . . but no less lovable.

1. Heat 2 tablespoons of the oil over high heat until hot. Reduce the heat to medium, add the onion, and cook, stirring occasionally, until softened, about 5 minutes. Add the garlic, cumin, coriander, and cayenne and cook for 1 minute; transfer to a medium bowl. Pulse 1/2 cup of the chickpeas in a food processor fitted with the chopping blade until coarsely chopped; add to the onion mixture. Process the remaining chickpeas until they are very finely ground; stir into the onion mixture. Add salt and pepper to taste. Then stir in the egg, flour, and baking soda.

2. Shape the mixture into four 1/2-inch-thick patties and coat on both sides with panko crumbs. Heat 1 tablespoon of the remaining oil in a large skillet over high heat until hot; reduce the heat to medium. Add the patties and cook until crisp and golden on both sides, 6 to 8 minutes per side, adding more oil as needed.

3. Meanwhile, prepare the Tahini Sauce. To serve, tuck a falafel into each of the pita halves with some shredded romaine and carrot; drizzle with some of the Tahini Sauce.

1/4 head romaine lettuce heart, rinsed, dried, and shredded (about 1/2 cup)

1 medium carrot, shredded (about 1/2 cup)

Zucchini Cakes
with Mediterranean Salad Topping

V

MAKES 4 SERVINGS, 16 TO 20 PANCAKES

Two 6- to 7-inch zucchini (about 1 pound)
One medium baking potato (about 8 ounces), peeled
1 medium onion, quartered
Kosher salt
2 cups packed rinsed and dried fresh flat-leaf parsley leaves
1 cup cherry or grape tomatoes, halved
1/3 cup pitted, brine-cured olives such as kalamata, halved
5 tablespoons extra virgin olive oil
2 tablespoons red wine vinegar
4 ounces ricotta salata or feta cheese, crumbled (about 2/3 cup)
1/3 to 1/2 cup packaged dried bread crumbs or from Bread Crumbs Four Ways (page 23, add prep time)
1 large egg, lightly beaten
1 tablespoon rinsed, dried, and chopped fresh dill
2 garlic cloves, minced (about 2 teaspoons)
1/2 teaspoon grated lemon zest
1 cup packaged croutons or from Croutons Four Ways (page 26, add prep time)

Zucchini in its natural state is watery and bland. If you salt it, though, you will draw out most of its water—and reveal the wonderfully sweet flavor of this modest little squash. Eat these zucchini cakes with a topping of Mediterranean salad and you've got a light and tasty dish for a summer's day. By the way, if you have never before eaten parsley this way—as a salad, not a garnish—please give it a try. It's very refreshing. Of course, if you can't stand parsley, just substitute the lettuce of your choice.

1. Preheat oven to 200°F. Using the grating disk of a food processor or the coarse side of a four-sided grater, grate the zucchini, potato, and onion. Add 3/4 teaspoon salt and stir until the vegetables are well mixed; transfer to a colander placed over a bowl and set aside to drain while making the salad.

2. Combine the parsley, tomatoes, and olives in a salad bowl; cover and refrigerate until ready to serve. Shake together 2 tablespoons of the olive oil, the vinegar, and 1/4 teaspoon salt in a small jar; set aside.

3. Using your hands, gently but firmly squeeze the zucchini mixture to get out as much moisture as possible. Transfer the mixture to a dry bowl and stir in the ricotta salata, 1/3 cup bread crumbs, the egg, dill, garlic, and lemon zest. Add more bread crumbs if necessary to absorb any remaining moisture from the zucchini mixture.

4. Heat 1 tablespoon of the remaining oil in a large nonstick skillet over low heat until hot. Add the zucchini mixture by heaping tablespoons and press with a spatula to make a flat 2 1/2-inch round. Cook until lightly browned, about 4 minutes. Turn the pancakes and cook, uncovered, until browned on the other side and the vegetables are tender, about 4 minutes. Transfer to a platter or cookie sheet and keep warm in the oven. Repeat with the remaining zucchini mixture, adding oil to the skillet as needed.

5. To serve, shake the oil and vinegar mixture and pour over the salad; top with croutons and toss to combine. Divide the pancakes among 4 dinner plates; top with the salad and serve.

Moroccan Vegetable Stew

V

MAKES 8 SERVINGS

2 tablespoons extra virgin olive
oil
1 medium onion, chopped
(about 1 cup)
4 garlic cloves, minced (about
4 teaspoons)
2 teaspoons finely grated fresh
ginger (use a Microplane)
1 cinnamon stick
1 teaspoon ground cumin
1/2 teaspoon allspice
6 medium parsnips (about 1 3/4
pounds), peeled and sliced
1/2 inch thick
2 large sweet potatoes (about
1 1/2 pounds), peeled and
cut into 1/2-inch chunks
One 15 1/2-ounce can chopped
tomatoes
One 14- or 14 1/2-ounce can
vegetable broth
1 recipe Harissa (page 322)
One 15-ounce can chickpeas,
rinsed and drained
2 small zucchini (12 to 14 ounces),
cut into 1/2-inch chunks
One 5-ounce package rinsed
baby spinach
1/2 cup golden raisins
Kosher salt and freshly milled
black pepper
Rinsed and dried chopped fresh
cilantro or mint

So many meaty vegetables go into this vegetable stew that my caveman husband did not think to utter his usual bon mot in these situations, namely, "Where's the beef?" Indeed, this is a very satisfying stew, flavored in the Moroccan style with "sweet spices" as well as cumin and ginger. The classic accompaniment would be couscous. Here in the twenty-first century a fast-cooking couscous—five minutes!—is available in the supermarket.

My favorite part of this dish is the garnish, the Tunisian chili paste called harissa. You can make your own using the recipe in the Sauces chapter (page 322) or simply top the stew with your favorite hot sauce. It is this last touch that really completes the stew. Serve with Parmigiano-Reggiano Couscous (page 41).

1. Heat the oil in a Dutch oven or large saucepan over high heat until hot. Reduce the heat to medium; add the onion and cook, stirring occasionally, until softened, about 5 minutes. Add the garlic and cook 1 minute longer. Add the ginger, cinnamon stick, cumin, and allspice and cook 2 minutes. Add the parsnips, sweet potatoes, tomatoes, and broth; bring to a boil over high heat. Reduce the heat to low and simmer 10 minutes.

2. Meanwhile, prepare the harissa. Add the chickpeas and zucchini to the stew; simmer 5 minutes longer. Add the spinach and raisins and simmer just until the spinach has wilted. Add salt and pepper to taste. Remove the cinnamon stick.

3. Ladle the stew into bowls and top each portion with some of the harissa and cilantro.

A RAISIN is simply a dried grape, and about half of the world's raisin supply comes from California. Shortly after I started working on Food Network's *Cooking Live,* someone called in and asked what the difference was between golden and black raisins. I said I wasn't sure but I thought they came from different-colored grapes. That was the last time I guessed at any answer; I was wrong. The most common grapes used for raisins in this country are Thompson seedless, and the raisin's final color is not related to the color of the grape, which is light green. Black raisins are sun dried for several weeks, thereby producing their shriveled appearance and dark color. Golden raisins are treated with sulfur dioxide to preserve their color and dried with artificial heat, producing a moister, plumper product. Currants are made from the tiny seedless Black Corinth (also known as Zante) grape.

WHAT IS THE DIFFERENCE BETWEEN GOLDEN AND BLACK RAISINS?

Shop
and Serve

Crispy Polenta Slices
with Gorgonzola and Leeks

V

MAKES 4 SERVINGS

3 medium leeks (white and
   light green parts)
2 tablespoons olive oil
One 16- or 17-ounce package
   prepared polenta, cut into
   12 slices
4 ounces gorgonzola,
   crumbled (about 2/3 cup)
1/2 cup heavy cream
Kosher salt and freshly milled
   black pepper
1/3 cup roasted chopped
   walnuts (see page 89)

Here's a midweek meatless entrée that is decadently delicious and ridiculously easy to make. Your head start is provided by pre-cooked polenta, which is becoming available in most super-markets. Slice the polenta and crisp it up in a sauté pan. Top it off with the creamy leek sauce given here, the Sautéed Cherry Tomato Sauce (page 319) with a little grated cheese, or the Porcini Mushroom Sauce (page 263). Serve with marinated Roasted Peppers (page 30) and a tossed green salad.

1. Quarter the leeks lengthwise and cut them into 1-inch lengths. Soak according to step 1 on page 53. Heat 1 tablespoon of the oil in a large skillet over high heat until hot. Reduce the heat to medium-low; add the leeks and cook, stirring occasionally, until softened, about 5 minutes. Set aside.

2. Meanwhile, heat the remaining tablespoon of oil in a large nonstick skillet over medium-high heat until hot. Add the polenta slices, in batches if necessary. Sauté until they are crispy and browned on both sides and heated through, 8 to 10 minutes.

3. Add the gorgonzola and cream to the leeks and cook the mixture until it is just heated through. Add salt and pepper to taste. Transfer 3 polenta slices to each of 4 warm serving plates. Top each portion with one fourth of the leek mixture and some of the nuts.

Salad Bar Gazpacho

V

MAKES 4 SERVINGS

The only really time-consuming part of making gazpacho is chopping, slicing, and dicing the vegetables. You can save that time by buying prechopped vegetables—as well as salad dressing and croutons—from the salad bar at your supermarket. Add a can of tomato-vegetable juice from the chilled drink case, and you'll find that assembling a refreshing gazpacho soup takes no time at all. If you're feeling slightly more ambitious—not to say hungrier—you might sashay down to the deli counter and purchase some cooked shrimp or chicken. Put these in your gazpacho and you've got a very satisfying warm-weather meal. Serve with Garlic Bread (page 40).

1. Combine the tomato-vegetable juice with 1/2 cup each of the cucumber and green pepper, the vinaigrette, sherry vinegar, and garlic in a food processor or blender. Blend until the vegetables are pureed. Taste and add salt and pepper to taste.

2. Divide the gazpacho among 4 chilled soup plates and top with the remaining chopped cucumber and pepper, the shrimp, tomatoes, croutons, and onion.

Two 11 1/2-ounce cans tomato-vegetable juice, chilled

1 1/2 cups chopped cucumber (from the salad bar)

1 1/2 cups chopped green pepper (from the salad bar)

1/4 cup bottled balsamic vinaigrette or All-Purpose Vinaigrette (page 28, add prep time) made with balsamic vinegar

2 teaspoons sherry vinegar

1 garlic clove, quartered

Kosher salt and freshly milled black pepper

3/4 pound cooked shrimp, halved and tails removed, or cubed cooked chicken

1 cup chopped fresh tomatoes or halved cherry tomatoes (from the salad bar)

1 cup garlic-flavored croutons (from the salad bar)

1/4 cup chopped onion or scallions (from the salad bar)

Ratatouille Pizza

_V_

MAKES 2 SERVINGS

Hands-on time:
15 minutes

Total preparation time:
30 minutes plus
thawing or rising time

Store-bought pizza dough, which you can find in the freezer section of your supermarket, is a wonderful shortcut ingredient. If you live in an area with many pizza parlors, you can purchase prepared pizza dough from them as well. Just top the dough with any vegetable and cheese, and ten minutes later you have dinner. I have topped it with the kind of vegetables that are found in ratatouille, a mixed-vegetable stew from the south of France. Brie isn't from that area, but it sure does taste good with the vegetables. You could use soft goat cheese, mozzarella, Cheddar, or Monterey Jack in its place, if you prefer. Serve with a tossed green salad or Bean Salad (page 39).

One 1-pound package defrosted frozen pizza dough or 1 recipe Food Processor Pizza Dough (page 29, add prep time)

3/4 pound mixed roasted vegetables, such as peppers, onion, zucchini, and eggplant (from the deli)

1/4 cup pitted Niçoise olives, quartered

One 4-ounce wedge Brie cheese, cut into 1/2-inch pieces

1. Preheat the oven to 500°F. Position one of the oven shelves as low as it can go in the oven. Grease a 12-inch pizza pan. Roll or press the dough into a 12-inch round on the pan. If you don't have a pizza pan, you can use a rimmed baking sheet and shape the dough into a rectangle.

2. Cut the vegetables into bite-size pieces, if desired, and arrange on the pizza dough along with the olives. Top with the cheese. Bake the pizza on the lowest shelf of the oven until the crust is golden, the vegetables are hot through, and the cheese has melted, 10 to 15 minutes. Cut into wedges and serve.

Hands-on time:
10 minutes

Total preparation time:
30 minutes plus
thawing
or rising time

One 1-pound package
defrosted frozen pizza
dough or 1 recipe Food
Processor Pizza Dough
(page 29, add prep time)
One 10-ounce package frozen
chopped spinach, thawed
2/3 cup whole-milk ricotta
cheese
1 teaspoon dried basil
1/2 teaspoon dried oregano
Kosher salt and freshly milled
black pepper
8 ounces provolone cheese,
sliced
1 tablespoon extra virgin olive
oil

Spinach and Ricotta Calzones

V

MAKES 4 SERVINGS

Calzone is just stuffed pizza dough, and as with pizza toppings, the stuffing possibilities are endless. I have opted for spinach, mozzarella, and ricotta, but you could use any leftover vegetables, meats, and cheeses you had in the fridge. You could even just pull out a bunch of leftovers and let each person design his or her own calzone. Once stuffed, they take only fifteen to twenty minutes in the oven. Serve with Radish and Orange Salad with Peppery Orange Dressing (page 303).

1. Divide the pizza dough into 4 balls. Roll each ball to an 8-inch round and set aside to rise slightly while you make the filling.

2. Preheat the oven to 400°F. Squeeze as much moisture out of the spinach as possible; the spinach should measure about 1/2 cup. Combine the spinach, ricotta, basil, oregano, and salt and pepper to taste.

3. Break the cheese slices into pieces and arrange half of it to cover one half of each dough round, leaving a 1/2-inch border. Place the spinach filling on the cheese and top with the remaining cheese. Moisten the edge of each round with water and fold the unfilled half of the dough over the filling; press with the tines of a fork to seal. Pierce each calzone once with the fork to allow steam to escape during baking.

4. Brush the calzones on all sides with the olive oil and place on a rimmed baking sheet. Bake 15 to 20 minutes or until puffed and golden. Serve hot.

Meatless Moussaka

Hands-on time:
10 minutes

Total preparation time:
40 minutes

V

MAKES 4 SERVINGS

Moussaka has probably been around since before the Parthenon was built. It is a classic rustic Greek dish consisting of layers of ground lamb and eggplant that are topped with a custard and baked. It is absolutely delicious to eat, but very labor-intensive to make. I have removed the lamb, added spinach, and streamlined the dish significantly to turn it into a quick vegetarian weeknight entrée.

1. Preheat the oven to 400°F. Lightly grease a shallow 2-quart baking dish or pan. Combine the tomatoes and flour in a small saucepan. Bring the mixture to a boil over medium heat, stirring constantly.

2. Reserve the 6 best-shaped eggplant cutlets; arrange the rest in the baking dish. Squeeze the spinach to remove as much liquid as possible; season the spinach with salt and pepper to taste and spread it over the eggplant. Pour the tomato mixture over the spinach and top it with the reserved eggplant cutlets. Stir together the yogurt and feta in a small bowl and dollop it over the top.

3. Bake the moussaka until bubbly and lightly browned on top, about 30 minutes. Cut into quarters to serve.

One 14 1/2-ounce can diced tomatoes with garlic and onion

2 tablespoons unbleached all-purpose flour

One 10-ounce package frozen breaded eggplant cutlets

One 10-ounce package defrosted frozen chopped spinach

Kosher salt and freshly milled black pepper

2/3 cup plain whole-milk Greek yogurt or drained regular plain whole-milk yogurt (see Note, page 97)

One 4-ounce container crumbled feta cheese with basil, black olives, and sun-dried tomatoes

Nacho Pie

V

MAKES 6 SERVINGS

1 tablespoon vegetable oil

1 1/2 cups sliced green bell
peppers (from the salad
bar)

1 1/2 cups sliced onions (from
the salad bar)

One 16-ounce jar chipotle
salsa

One 10-ounce package frozen
corn

1 cup black beans (from the
salad bar)

One 11 1/2-ounce can tomato-
vegetable juice

One 5-ounce bag tortilla chips,
coarsely crushed

8 ounces pepper Jack cheese,
coarsely grated (about 2
cups)

Everyone loves nachos, but we wondered how to transform this all-American barroom staple made of tacos and melted cheese into a respectable (and less fattening) dinner entrée. Here's how: Use the nachos as a pie crust and cut back on the cheese in favor of bell peppers, corn, onions, and black beans. In fact, almost any vegetable from the salad bar would work nicely in this recipe—mushrooms, broccoli, carrots, whatever. Just decide what you are in the mood for and sauté your choices in oil until they are crisp-tender. You can crush the tortilla chips by putting them in a zippered plastic bag and rolling over them with a rolling pin or wine bottle. Serve with a tossed green salad.

1. Preheat the oven to 375°F. Lightly grease a shallow 2 1/2-quart baking dish. Heat the oil in a large skillet over high heat until hot. Reduce the heat to medium; add the peppers and onions and cook, stirring occasionally, until softened, about 5 minutes. Add the salsa, corn, beans, and juice. Bring the mixture to a boil.

2. Arrange half of the crushed chips in the bottom of the baking dish. Stir half of the cheese into the vegetable mixture and spoon over the chips. Top with the remaining chips and cheese. Bake until the edges begin to bubble, about 30 minutes.

Sautéed Scallops and Asparagus

with Parsley Pesto

MAKES 4 SERVINGS

Hands-on time:
15 minutes

Total preparation time:
15 minutes

Here's a chance for the fainthearted among us to mop up the wonderful sauce served over escargots (a.k.a. snails) without actually having to eat any of them. In this recipe the olive oil and white wine in which the scallops are cooked, combined with the garlic and parsley in the pesto, recall that escargot sauce. If you can't find grilled asparagus at your supermarket deli counter, use fresh asparagus instead and cook it with the scallops. Serve with buttered noodles or Simple Boiled Rice (page 40).

3 tablespoons extra virgin olive oil
1 pound sea scallops, rinsed and dried
Kosher salt and freshly milled black pepper
1/2 cup sliced onion (from the salad bar)
1/2 pound (scant 2 cups) grilled or roasted asparagus (from the deli), halved diagonally
1/2 cup white wine
1/3 cup bottled pesto or Parsley Pesto (page 320, add prep time)
1 lemon, cut into 8 wedges

1. Heat the oil in a large skillet over high heat until hot. Season the scallops with salt and pepper and add to the skillet. Sauté, turning once, until they are brown on both sides, about 3 minutes total; transfer the scallops to a bowl using tongs. Reduce the heat to medium; add the onion and cook, stirring occasionally, until softened, about 5 minutes. Stir in the asparagus and cook 1 minute longer.

2. Add the wine to the skillet and reduce by two-thirds. Then stir in the pesto and 2 tablespoons of water. Bring the mixture to a boil, stirring to incorporate browned bits from the pan. Add the scallops along with any liquid in the bowl and cook just until the scallops are hot, 1/2 to 1 minute. Taste and add salt and pepper, if desired. Serve with lemon wedges.

2 pounds chicken wings,
    cut in half
Hot sauce
1/2 teaspoon kosher salt
3 ounces blue cheese,
    crumbled (about 1/2 cup)

Easy Buffalo Chicken Wings

MAKES 4 SERVINGS

If you are a fan of Buffalo Chicken Wings you will not be disappointed by these, even though they are a much-simplified version of the original, which involves deep frying, sauces, and celery stalks. You will be happy for the shortcut because it means you can whip them up in five minutes on a school night. Serve with Cole Slaw (page 38) and Oven Fries (page 295).

1. Preheat the oven to 450°F. Generously oil a rimmed baking sheet. Toss the wings with hot sauce (1 to 4 tablespoons, depending upon your taste) in a medium bowl and arrange them on the baking sheet. Drizzle with any hot sauce remaining in the bowl and sprinkle with the salt.

2. Roast the wings until they are brown and cooked through, 20 to 25 minutes. Sprinkle with the blue cheese and return to the oven just until the cheese melts, about 4 minutes.

Cheatin' Jambalaya

Hands-on time:
15 minutes

Total preparation time:
15 minutes

MAKES 4 TO 6 SERVINGS

In its authentic form this Cajun specialty is so wonderful that Hank Williams wrote a love song to it half a century ago. My version is much simpler than the classic. It does indeed boast many of the elements of the traditional jambalaya, but it's mainly a great way to use leftover rice—especially the kind left over from Chinese takeout. Of course, this recipe is equally delicious using freshly cooked Simple Boiled Rice (page 40).

1. If the onion, bell pepper, and celery are in large pieces, cut them into 1-inch pieces. Cut the ham into 1-inch pieces. Heat the oil in a large skillet over high heat until hot. Reduce the heat to medium; add the vegetables and ham to the skillet and cook, stirring occasionally, until the vegetables soften, about 5 minutes.

2. Stir in the flour and seasoning until vegetables are completely coated. Add the chicken broth. Bring to a boil and cook, stirring, for 1 minute. Stir in the rice and corn; cook until hot. Transfer to a serving platter and garnish with pickled okra, if desired.

1 cup sliced onion (from the salad bar)
1 cup sliced red bell pepper (from the salad bar)
1 cup sliced green bell pepper (from the salad bar)
1 cup sliced celery (from the salad bar)
1-pound slice fully cooked ham (about 1 1/4 pounds if it has fat and bone)
1 tablespoon olive oil
1 tablespoon unbleached all-purpose flour
1 tablespoon packaged Creole or Cajun spice mix or Creole Spice Mix (page 20, add prep time)
1 cup canned chicken broth or Chicken Stock (page 32)
2 cups cooked long-grain white rice
One 10-ounce package frozen corn
1/2 16-ounce jar hot pickled okra, optional garnish (see Sources, page 346)

Green Posole with Chicken

Hands-on time:
25 minutes

Total preparation time:
30 minutes

MAKES 4 TO 6 SERVINGS

Posole is a hearty soup from the Jalisco region of Mexico that is traditionally made with pork and hominy. Hominy is dried corn kernels from which the hulls and germs have been removed. (In its ground form hominy is called grits.) Dried hominy takes several hours to cook, so I have opted for the canned version in the interest of time. I have also developed a lighter version with shredded chicken and tomatillo salsa (hence green posole). This dish is ridiculously easy to make and quite satisfying with all the additional garnishes. Serve with Southwestern Sweet Potato Sauté (page 294) and Cole Slaw (page 38).

1. Heat the oil in a large saucepan over high heat until hot. Reduce the heat to medium, add the onion, and cook, stirring occasionally, until softened, about 5 minutes. Add the salsa and cook, stirring, for 5 minutes.

2. Add the chicken broth and simmer, partially covered, for 10 minutes. Add the chicken and hominy and simmer until heated through. Add salt and pepper to taste. To serve, ladle into bowls and let everyone garnish their own portion.

2 tablespoons vegetable oil
1 medium onion, finely chopped (about 1 cup)
1 cup bottled green salsa or 1 recipe Mexican Tomatillo Salsa (page 318, add prep time)
4 cups canned chicken broth or Chicken Stock (page 32)
1 rotisserie chicken, skin and bones discarded and meat shredded
Two 15-ounce cans white hominy, rinsed and drained
Kosher salt and freshly milled black pepper
Accompaniments: finely chopped onion, chopped avocado, sliced radishes, chopped cucumbers, shredded napa cabbage, and tortilla chips

Tortellini Pepperoni Spinach Soup

24 slices pepperoni (about
1 3/4 inch in diameter)
1 medium onion, chopped
(about 1 cup)
One 48-ounce can chicken
broth or 6 cups Chicken
Stock (page 32)
One 9-ounce package
refrigerated three-cheese
or other flavor tortellini
One 5-ounce bag rinsed baby
spinach
Parmigiano-Reggiano cheese,
optional
Freshly milled black pepper,
optional

MAKES 4 SERVINGS

This is a ridiculously simple dinner. If you use the prerinsed spinach (I prefer the baby spinach variety), it is really a snap. You can finish it off with some freshly grated Parmigiano-Reggiano cheese and freshly milled black pepper; round out the meal with Garlic Bread (page 40) and a tossed green salad.

1. Heat the pepperoni in a heavy 3-quart or larger saucepan over medium-high heat until it releases a little fat. Reduce the heat to medium; add the onion and cook, stirring occasionally, until softened, about 5 minutes.

2. Add the broth and tortellini; cook until tender. Stir in the spinach; cook just until it is wilted; serve with Parmigiano-Reggiano and pepper, if desired.

Roast Beef and Broccoli Slaw
with Blue Cheese Dressing

Hands-on time:
10 minutes

Total preparation time:
10 minutes

MAKES 4 SERVINGS

Broccoli slaw is one of those great new ready-made salads you can find in the produce section of most supermarkets. It is a nice alternative to cabbage-based cole slaw—although you can certainly stick with the regular old mix if you don't care for broccoli. This is a great recipe for using up any leftover roast beef. (Of course, if you don't have any, your friendly deli clerk can slice you some to order.) Finally, if you really want to speed up the prep for this salad, use your favorite bottled blue cheese dressing instead of making it from scratch. Serve with Garlic Bread (page 40).

1/2 cup chopped walnuts
Bottled blue cheese dressing or Blue Cheese Dressing (recipe follows, add prep time)
1 pound thinly sliced roast beef, cut into ribbons
One 10-ounce package broccoli slaw
1 cup sliced red bell pepper (from the salad bar)
Kosher salt and freshly milled black pepper

1. Preheat the oven to 350°F. Toast the walnuts in a pie plate in the center of the oven for about 10 minutes. While the nuts are toasting, make the Blue Cheese Dressing, if using homemade.

2. Toss together the roast beef, broccoli slaw, bell pepper, dressing to taste, and the walnuts in a large bowl. Taste and add salt and black pepper, if desired.

Blue Cheese Dressing:
In a blender or mini food processor pulse together 1/2 cup buttermilk, 1/4 cup low-fat mayonnaise, 1/4 cup crumbled blue cheese (about 1 1/2 ounces), and 2 scallions (white part only) until combined but still chunky. Add kosher salt and freshly milled black pepper to taste. Thin with water if desired. Makes about 3/4 cup.

*Just
Open the
Pantry*

Ramen Noodles and Asian Vegetables
with Peanut Sauce

V

MAKES 4 TO 6 SERVINGS

2 tablespoons vegetable oil

1 medium onion, sliced (about 1 cup)

One 15-ounce can cut baby corn, drained

One 10-ounce bag Asian stir-fry vegetables

One 8-ounce can sliced water chestnuts, drained

Two 3-ounce packages ramen noodles (any flavor)

1 cup bottled peanut sauce or Peanut Sauce (page 325, add prep time)

Kosher salt and freshly milled black pepper

1 cup wasabi peas

Who says that ramen noodles need to be prepared using nothing but that little flavor packet that comes in the box? Given that they boil up nice and tender in just three minutes, I figured it might make sense to combine them with other ingredients for a speedy supper. I stayed in the Asian mode, adding Asian stir-fry vegetables from the freezer, a can of baby corn, wasabi peas, and bottled peanut sauce (although you could make my homemade version, page 325). If you want to add more protein, the shelled and deveined shrimp from your freezer or a rotisserie chicken from a deli are good choices. Serve with Grated Carrot Salad (page 293).

1. Heat the oil in a large skillet over high heat until hot. Reduce the heat to medium; add the onion and cook, stirring occasionally, until softened, about 5 minutes.

2. Add 3 cups water, the corn, stir-fry vegetables, water chestnuts, and the noodles without their seasoning packets (reserve the seasoning for another use). Bring the mixture to a boil over high heat; reduce the heat to medium-low and cook, covered, 2 minutes. Using tongs, turn the noodles over so all are moistened and cook 1 minute longer.

3. Stir the Peanut Sauce into the mixture, separating the noodles and mixing them with the vegetables. Add salt and pepper to taste. Divide among 4 to 6 warmed soup plates and top with wasabi peas.

Fried Rice

Hands-on time:
15 minutes

Total preparation time:
15 minutes

MAKES 4 SERVINGS

If you order Chinese takeout (and who doesn't?), chances are you often have cooked white rice on your hands. I can't think of any better use for it than to transform it into fried rice. The kids love it. I have suggested using frozen shrimp and vegetables, but any leftover protein and vegetables would work. Serve with Butter-steamed Broccoli with Soy (page 296).

1. Heat 1 tablespoon of the oil in a large nonstick skillet over medium-high heat until hot. Reduce the heat to medium. Combine the eggs with 1/8 teaspoon salt and 1/8 teaspoon pepper and pour into the skillet. Cook, stirring, until scrambled, about 1 minute. Break into small pieces and transfer to a bowl.

2. Add another tablespoon of oil, the onion, and garlic to the pan; cook, stirring, 2 minutes. Add the shrimp and peas; cook until the shrimp are cooked through, about 3 minutes. Transfer the mixture to the bowl with the eggs.

3. Heat the remaining tablespoon oil in the same skillet over medium-high heat until hot. Add the rice and cook, stirring occasionally, until slightly crispy.

4. Stir together the soy sauce, rice wine, ginger, and sesame oil; add to the rice in the skillet along with the shrimp, peas, and egg. Cook just until the egg is heated through and serve.

3 tablespoons vegetable oil
2 large eggs, lightly beaten
Kosher salt and freshly milled black pepper
1 medium onion, chopped (about 1 cup)
2 garlic cloves, minced (about 2 teaspoons)
2 cups frozen shelled and deveined shrimp, halved
One 10-ounce package frozen green peas
3 cups leftover cooked long-grain white rice or Simple Boiled Rice (page 40)
1/4 cup soy sauce
3 tablespoons rice wine or dry sherry
2 tablespoons finely chopped crystallized ginger
4 teaspoons toasted sesame oil

$\mathcal{E}$damame and Bulgur Salad

$\mathcal{V}$

MAKES 4 TO 6 SERVINGS

One 16-ounce package frozen
    shelled edamame
Kosher salt and freshly milled
    black pepper
1 cup medium bulgur
2/3 cup bottled sesame soy
    dressing or Sesame Soy
    Dressing (recipe follows)
3 medium carrots, coarsely
    shredded (preferably using
    a food processor; about
    1 1/2 cups)
One 6 1/2-ounce jar pimientos,
    drained and sliced
1 tablespoon soy sauce
1/2 cup chow mein noodles

A great alternative to peas or lima beans, Japanese edamame—
fresh soybeans—are now available in the frozen food section of
your supermarket, already removed from their pods and blanched.
I've combined them in this recipe with bulgur—parboiled cracked
whole wheat—in order to make this salad substantial enough for
a meal. (Sometimes bulgur is mislabeled tabbouli on the
supermarket shelf, because tabbouli salad—cracked wheat with
parsley and vegetables—is usually what bulgur is used for.) As
alternatives to bulgur, you'll find that soba or buckwheat noodles
or even cooked spaghetti also work nicely with the edamame. I
rounded out this dish with a few Asian ingredients for crunch—
bean sprouts and chow mein noodles—and a tasty little sesame
soy dressing I discovered at the store. (A recipe for a homemade
version follows if you would rather make your own.)

1. Combine 1 1/2 cups water, the edamame, 1/4 teaspoon salt, and 1/4
teaspoon pepper in a medium saucepan. Bring to a boil over high heat;
reduce the heat to low and simmer, covered, 5 minutes. Stir in the bulgur
and 1/3 cup of the dressing; set aside, covered, 15 minutes. Stir in the
carrots, pimientos, and soy sauce. Add salt and pepper to taste.

2. If serving warm, stir in the remaining 1/3 cup dressing. To serve cold,
refrigerate the bulgur mixture and remaining dressing separately and
combine just before serving. Top each serving with some of the noodles.

Sesame Soy Dressing:
Whisk together 6 tablespoons vegetable oil, 2 1/2 tablespoons rice vinegar,
1 1/2 tablespoons soy sauce, and 2 teaspoons toasted sesame oil.

Creamy Baked Polenta

V

MAKES 4 SERVINGS

Hands-on time:
5 minutes

Total preparation time:
55 minutes

The cornmeal mush known as *polenta,* one of the national dishes of Italy, emerged in its original form as the field ration of the Roman soldier. Although *pulmentum* was made of millet or spelt (cornmeal was unknown to the ancient Romans), it boasted the same versatility that we love in polenta today—you can cook it up and serve it immediately while it's still creamy, or let it set up like a cake that can be sliced and sautéed.

Cooking polenta on the stove requires a lot of hands-on time— and not a little care. It is hot and sticky and bubbles up and out in a Vesuvius-like way. Here I cook polenta in the oven, which drastically decreases the hands-on time. This recipe can do double duty as a great weeknight side dish or a vegetarian main dish topped with Porcini Mushroom Sauce (page 263) or some chopped canned tomatoes sautéed with onions and garlic, and a few bottled artichokes added at the end. A green salad would be a nice addition if you turn it into an entrée.

1 cup yellow cornmeal or regular (not instant) coarse polenta
3 tablespoons unsalted butter, thinly sliced
1 teaspoon kosher salt
1/2 teaspoon freshly milled black pepper
2 ounces provolone cheese, grated (about 1/2 cup)
2 ounces Parmigiano-Reggiano cheese, finely grated (about 2/3 cup; see grating information, page 10)

1. Preheat the oven to 350°F. Combine 4 cups water, the cornmeal, butter, salt, and pepper in a 1 1/2-quart baking dish. Bake, uncovered, on the top shelf of the oven for 40 minutes.

2. Remove the polenta from the oven, give it a stir, and bake for another 10 minutes. Remove it from the oven; stir in the provolone and salt and pepper to taste; let stand 5 minutes before serving. Serve topped with Parmigiano-Reggiano.

Hands-on time:
10 minutes

Total preparation time:
20 minutes

Kosher salt

1 pound linguine

2 tablespoons extra virgin
olive oil

1 medium onion, finely
chopped (about 1 cup)

3 garlic cloves, minced (about
1 tablespoon)

1/2 teaspoon rubbed sage

1 ounce sun-dried tomatoes
(about 6 halves), sliced
crosswise into 1/4-inch
strips (scant 1/4 cup)

1/2 cup white wine

One 19-ounce can white beans
such as cannellini, navy, or
Great Northern, drained
and rinsed

One 14- or 14 1/2-ounce can
vegetable or chicken broth,
or 1 3/4 cups Chicken Stock
(page 32)

1/2 cup pitted, brine-cured
olives such as kalamata,
chopped

Freshly milled black pepper

1 1/2 ounces grated
Parmigiano-Reggiano,
finely grated (about 1/2 cup;
see grating information,
page 10), optional

Linguine with White Bean, Sun-dried Tomato, and Olive Sauce

𝒱

MAKES 4 SERVINGS

Mashing up white beans instantly produces a creamy pasta sauce—without cream—that's capable of binding together all the ingredients in a dish. Here I've "beefed up" the sauce with sun-dried tomatoes and olives from the pantry. Of course, you could add any number of other handy pantry items—marinated artichoke hearts, canned tuna, frozen shrimp—or just toss in some leftover vegetables from the fridge. Serve with an arugula salad and Garlic Bread (page 40).

1. Bring a large pot of salted water to a boil over high heat. Cook the linguine in the boiling water until al dente, 8 to 10 minutes; drain, reserving 1 1/2 cups cooking liquid.

2. While the water comes to a boil and the pasta cooks, heat the oil in a large skillet over high heat until hot. Reduce the heat to medium; add the onion and cook, stirring occasionally, until softened, about 5 minutes. Add the garlic and sage and cook 1 minute. Add the tomatoes and wine and simmer until reduced by half, about 4 minutes. Add the white beans and broth and simmer for 5 minutes. Coarsely mash the sauce with a potato masher or fork.

3. Add some of the reserved cooking liquid to the sauce, as necessary, to reach a creamy consistency; add the olives and salt and pepper to taste. Toss the sauce with the linguine and serve. Top with grated Parmigiano-Reggiano, if desired.

Tuna Salad
with Radiatore and Giardiniera

MAKES 4 SERVINGS

Hands-on time:
15 minutes

Total preparation time:
15 minutes

Giardiniera salad, a delicious mixture of pickled Italian vegetables, gives this pasta salad its crunch and tartness, and its marinade doubles as the base of the dressing. I recommend using tuna packed in oil, because it has so much more flavor and moisture than tuna packed in water—although you can certainly use the tuna in water if you want to cut back on some calories. Serve with grilled bread.

Kosher salt
4 ounces radiatore or other small-shaped pasta
1 cup bottled giardiniera salad
2 teaspoons Dijon mustard
1/2 teaspoon sugar
1/4 teaspoon freshly milled black pepper
1/4 cup plus 2 tablespoons vegetable oil
Two 6-ounce cans solid white tuna packed in oil, drained and flaked
1/3 cup pitted, brine-cured olives such as kalamata
1 tablespoon drained, bottled capers

1. Bring a large pot of salted water to a boil over high heat. Cook the radiatore in the boiling water until al dente, 8 to 10 minutes; drain, reserving 1 1/2 cups cooking liquid.

2. Meanwhile, drain and reserve the marinade from the giardiniera salad and cut any large vegetables into 3/4-inch pieces. Whisk together 2 tablespoons of the marinade with the mustard, sugar, and pepper in a large bowl; gradually whisk in the oil.

3. Add the pasta, giardiniera salad, tuna, olives, and capers to the dressing and toss until well coated.

WHAT ARE CAPERS?

CAPERS are the preserved flower buds of a prickly shrub of the Capparidaceae family. Native to the Mediterranean and Asia, they range in size from the tiny nonpareils of France to plump capers larger than 1/4 inch. You can purchase capers either pickled in a vinegar brine or salted. Salted capers need to be rinsed to reduce the saltiness. Capers of all kinds add a delicious crunch and saltiness to any dish, like tiny little pickles. Some people prefer the small French capers, but I like them all.

Porcini Mushroom Sauce

Hands-on time:
15 minutes

Total preparation time:
30 minutes

V

MAKES ABOUT 2 CUPS

Dried porcini mushrooms don't become soft and edible until you soak them in the liquid of your choice. In the process, the liquid itself becomes a delicious instant sauce. It is one of those rare situations in which, so to speak, the bath water is just as important as the baby. I have suggested several different soaking liquids (alcohol always adds flavor) for this recipe, but you could also use chicken or vegetable broth or even water. This sauce goes with just about any pantry item: pasta, rice pilaf, risotto, or Creamy Baked Polenta (page 259).

*1/2 cup dry Madeira, dry
   Marsala, or dry sherry*
*1 1/2 ounces dried porcini
   mushrooms*
2 tablespoons unsalted butter
*2 large shallots or 1/2 small
   onion, finely chopped
   (about 1/4 cup)*
*3 tablespoons unbleached all-
   purpose flour*
*One 14- or 14 1/2-ounce can
   chicken broth or 1 3/4 cups
   Chicken Stock (page 32),
   heated*
*4 canned Italian plum
   tomatoes, finely chopped*
*Kosher salt and freshly milled
   black pepper*

1. Bring the Madeira and 1/2 cup water to a boil in a small saucepan over high heat. Remove from the heat, add the mushrooms, and set aside to soak for 15 minutes or until they have softened. Lift the mushrooms out of the soaking liquid gently to let any sand sink to the bottom of the pan. Pour the liquid through a coffee filter or dampened paper towel in a fine strainer and reserve. Rinse the porcini thoroughly to remove any remaining sand, then finely chop them.

2. While the mushrooms are soaking, melt the butter in a medium skillet over medium-low heat. Add the shallots and cook, stirring occasionally, until softened, about 5 minutes. Add the flour and cook, stirring, 2 minutes. Add the broth and tomatoes and bring to a boil. Reduce the heat to low and simmer 3 minutes. Add the mushroom soaking liquid and mushrooms and simmer until reduced to 3 cups, about 5 minutes. Season with salt and pepper to taste.

3 tablespoons vegetable oil
1 small onion, chopped (about 1/2 cup)
One 7 1/2-ounce can red salmon, drained
One 4 1/2-ounce can chopped mild green chiles, drained
1/2 cup crumbled tortilla chips
1 tablespoon mayonnaise
1/2 teaspoon ground cumin
1/4 cup Wondra or unbleached all-purpose flour
One 10-ounce package frozen corn kernels
Kosher salt
1 cup bottled salsa

Quick Salmon Cakes
with Corn Salsa

MAKES 4 SERVINGS

Canned salmon has come a long way in terms of quality, and when combined with chiles, crushed tortilla chips, and cumin, moistened with mayonnaise, and topped with corn salsa, you almost wouldn't know that it was canned.

I've long been a fan of frozen corn, at least when fresh was out of season. As soon as you pick corn, its sugar begins to turn to starch and it is not as tasty. (The same goes for peas.) Frozen corn (and peas) is picked when ripe and then immediately blanched and frozen at the height of its tastiness, which is why it is a good idea to keep a stash in the freezer for the off season. One could argue that you should never eat vegetables out of season, but when you have a son who eats only about five vegetables, you can't be all that seasonal. Serve with Cole Slaw (page 38).

1. Heat 1 tablespoon of the oil in a medium skillet over high heat until hot. Reduce the heat to medium; add the onion and cook, stirring occasionally, until softened, about 5 minutes. Transfer the onion to a medium bowl with a slotted spoon; set the skillet aside.

2. Add the salmon, chiles, tortilla chips, mayonnaise, and cumin to the onion in the bowl and stir until combined. Form the mixture into four 1/2-inch-thick cakes. Coat the cakes lightly in flour on all sides. Add the remaining 2 tablespoons oil to the skillet and heat over high heat until hot; reduce the heat to medium and add the salmon cakes. Sauté until well browned on both sides, 3 to 4 minutes per side.

3. Meanwhile, cook the corn in water following package directions. Drain well and return to the saucepan. Add the salsa and heat just until hot. Serve the salmon cakes topped with corn salsa.

Cooking
Ahead

Hands-on time:
15 minutes

Total preparation time:
2 hours
plus soaking time

1 pound black beans
1/4 cup extra virgin olive oil
1 medium onion, chopped
    (about 1 cup)
9 garlic cloves, minced (about
    3 tablespoons)
One 3/4-pound smoked ham
    hock or meaty ham bone
4 cups canned chicken broth
    or Chicken Stock (page 32)
2 teaspoons ground cumin
2 Turkish bay leaves
Kosher salt and freshly milled
    black pepper
12 ounces plum tomatoes,
    chopped (about 1 cup)
1 tablespoon rinsed, dried,
    and chopped fresh oregano
    or 1 teaspoon dried
1 1/2 teaspoons rinsed, dried,
    and chopped fresh thyme
    or 1/2 teaspoon dried
1 1/2 teaspoons rinsed, dried,
    and chopped fresh basil or
    1/2 teaspoon dried

Rick's Black Beans

MAKES 6 TO 8 SERVINGS

My brother-in-law Rick Adler is an awfully good cook. When we get together for our huge Adler reunion once a year, he and I end up spending a lot of time in the kitchen together preparing massive amounts of food. For some reason he didn't make it into the first cookbook (most of the rest of the family did), and every time I see him he reminds me about that, or at least his wife Katy does. I needed to correct the situation. When we all got together this year I gave him the assignment of coming up with a signature dish, and this is it. (He serves it with an herb-marinated roast pork loin which wasn't fast enough for the regular chapters or slow enough for the cook-ahead chapter, but the beans are the star anyway).

Rick soaks his beans, which speeds up the cooking process somewhat. I recently did an experiment where I cooked two pots of beans, one that had been soaked overnight and one that had not. The soaked pot took only fifteen minutes less to cook. I have heard that soaking the beans and then discarding the liquid does help with the flatulence issue, though. Rick's secret ingredient: ham hocks. They add great depth of flavor and smokiness and make the dish so hearty that you could add water to it and turn it into soup for supper if you didn't want to have it as a side dish. It will keep for several days and freezes well too. Serve with Cuban-style Roast Pork (page 272).

1. The night before cooking, pick through the beans to remove stones and discolored beans. Rinse the beans and combine them with water to cover in a bowl. Cover tightly and refrigerate overnight.

2. The next day, drain the beans and rinse them in cold water. Heat the oil in a large saucepan over high heat until hot. Reduce the heat to medium; add the onion and cook, stirring occasionally, until it is softened, about 5 minutes. Add the garlic and cook 1 minute.

3. Cut crosswise slashes through the skin of the ham hock and add it to the saucepan along with the beans, broth, cumin, and bay leaves, 1/2 teaspoon salt, and 1/2 teaspoon pepper. Bring the mixture to a boil over high heat; reduce the heat to low and simmer, covered, 1 1/4 hours.

4. Transfer the ham hock to a plate and set it aside to cool slightly. Add the tomatoes, oregano, thyme, and basil; cook until the beans are tender, about 30 minutes. When the ham hock is cool enough to handle, remove the meat. Discard the skin, fat, and bone; coarsely chop the meat and return it to the beans. When the beans are tender, remove and discard the bay leaf. Taste the beans, add salt and pepper, if desired, and serve.

2 pounds salt cod fillets,
    halved
2 leeks (white part only)
5 tablespoons extra virgin
    olive oil
2 medium onions, thinly sliced
3 garlic cloves, minced (about
    1 tablespoon)
1/2 teaspoon fennel seed
1/2 teaspoon dried thyme
1 Turkish bay leaf
4 cups canned low-sodium
    chicken broth or Chicken
    Stock (page 32)
2 large Yukon gold potatoes
    (about 1 pound), peeled
    and cut into 1/2-inch pieces
One 15-ounce can whole plum
    tomatoes, chopped
1/2 cup white wine
Two 3-inch ribbons of orange
    zest
1/2 teaspoon saffron threads
    (not powdered)
1 recipe Rouille (page 314)
1 loaf French bread, cut
    diagonally into twelve
    1/4-inch-thick slices
Kosher salt and freshly milled
    black pepper

Provençal Salt Cod Stew

MAKES 8 TO 10 SERVINGS

In the days before refrigeration, cod was salted as a way to preserve it. Today people all over the world, particularly in Mediterranean countries, continue to produce and eat salt cod simply because they love the way it tastes. Like them, I'm a big fan of salt cod's intense flavor, which I thought would work nicely in a Provençal-style fish soup.

The Provençal ingredients in this recipe include saffron, fennel, garlic, and the *rouille* garnish. Rouille is a French garlic mayonnaise flavored with red pepper and cayenne. You spread it on toasts and float them in the hot soup, which gives the soup an extra little kick.

The only problem with this recipe is that you have to start soaking the cod two days ahead of time. But if you soak it on Friday morning, before you plunge into your day, it will be ready for you to turn it into soup on Sunday. Serve with a tossed green salad.

1. Combine the salt cod and cold water to cover in a bowl; refrigerate it, covered, for 2 days, changing the water twice a day.

2. To prepare the stew, thinly slice the leeks crosswise. Soak according to step 1 on page 53. Heat 2 tablespoons of the oil in a large saucepan over high heat until hot. Reduce the heat to medium; add the onions and leeks and cook, stirring occasionally, until softened, about 5 minutes. Add the garlic, fennel, thyme, and bay leaf and cook 1 minute.

3. Drain the cod and add to the saucepan along with the broth, potatoes, tomatoes with their juice, wine, remaining 3 tablespoons oil, the orange zest, and saffron to the onion mixture. Bring the mixture to a boil over high heat; reduce the heat to low and simmer until the potatoes and fish are tender, about 20 minutes.

4. Meanwhile, prepare the Rouille. Preheat the broiler to high. Arrange the bread in one layer on a cookie sheet and broil, 4 inches from the heat source, until it is light golden, about 2 minutes a side.

5. Gently break the fish into chunks with a spoon; remove and discard the bay leaf. Taste and add salt and pepper, if desired. Ladle the stew into large bowls. Spread some of the Rouille on each of the toasts; float several toasts on top of each serving of stew.

Hands-on time:
10 minutes

Total preparation time:
5 hours 10 minutes
plus marinating time

One 8-pound bone-in fresh
pork shoulder with skin
3/4 cup fresh lime juice
6 garlic cloves, minced (about
2 tablespoons)
1 1/2 tablespoons kosher salt
2 teaspoons freshly milled
black pepper
2 tablespoons dried oregano
1 cup distilled white vinegar
1/4 cup fresh grapefruit juice
1/4 cup fresh orange juice
1 tablespoon adobo-style
seasoning

Cuban-style Roast Pork

MAKES 8 SERVINGS

When I made a Cuban sandwich on *Sara's Secrets* (consisting of roast pork, ham, Swiss cheese, and pickles), what impressed me the most was not the cheese (Who can resist melted cheese?) or the pickles (What an unusual crunchy ingredient), but the roast pork. We didn't have time to make the pork on the air; we listed it as a preprepared ingredient and used what the kitchen had cooked for us.

The kitchen made real Cuban-style pork and it was so delicious I couldn't stop eating it. I am sure it has to do with the fat content of pork shoulder, which is much higher than loin or tenderloin, the cuts you usually find at the store. Fat makes this roast much more juicy, tender, and flavorful. The overnight marinating in citrus and garlic helps, too. Serve with Rick's Black Beans (page 268) and Butter-steamed Broccoli with Soy (page 296). You can make Cuban sandwiches with the leftovers by combining the sliced pork with sliced ham, Swiss cheese, sliced pickles, and mustard on bread. Either grill the sandwich with a weight on it or cook it in a panini press.

1. Using a small sharp knife, make 1-inch-long incisions in the skin of the pork shoulder, about 2 inches apart. Combine 3 tablespoons of the lime juice, the garlic, salt, pepper, and oregano. Rub the mixture into the slashes and along the underside of the pork. Combine the remaining lime juice, the vinegar, grapefruit juice, orange juice, and adobo seasoning in a bowl large enough to hold the meat. Add the pork, skin side up. Cover and refrigerate overnight, turning occasionally. Remove from the refrigerator an hour before cooking.

2. To cook, preheat the oven to 300°F. Transfer the pork and its marinade to a roasting pan. Cover the pan with a lid or aluminum foil and roast until it is very tender, about 5 hours. Let cool slightly in the liquid. Transfer the pork to a cutting board and discard the skin and excess fat. Slice and serve.

Slow-cooked Chinese Spareribs

3 1/2 pounds (2 racks) St.
Louis–style spareribs (see
page 275)
3 cups canned chicken broth
or Chicken Stock (page 32)
1/2 cup rice wine or medium-
dry sherry
1/4 cup soy sauce
2 tablespoons dark brown
sugar
3 garlic cloves, minced (about
1 tablespoon)
1-inch piece fresh ginger, cut
in half lengthwise and
thinly sliced
2 teaspoons toasted sesame
oil
2 star anise, crushed slightly
1 cinnamon stick
1/2 cup hoisin sauce

MAKES 4 SERVINGS

My family loves Chinese takeout spareribs. I don't know why it
had never occurred to me until I started this book that this was
something you could make at home.

In order to come up with a recipe, my cookbook partner, Joanne,
went down to Chinatown and picked up a sampling of ribs. Each
had a unique taste and texture. The one thing they had in
common was a faint hint of licorice—from star anise, a popular
Asian spice.

We tried to put together the best attributes of all of them in this
recipe. We braised the ribs first in an aromatic liquid, which
included star anise, then removed them from the liquid when they
were quite tender and finished them with hoisin glaze. Serve with
Butter-steamed Broccoli with Soy (page 296) and Simple Boiled
Rice (page 40).

1. Preheat the oven to 300°F. Place the ribs in a roasting pan.

2. Bring the broth, wine, soy sauce, brown sugar, garlic, ginger, sesame oil,
star anise, and cinnamon stick to a boil in a medium saucepan over high
heat. Pour the hot broth mixture over the ribs. Cover the pan tightly with
a lid or aluminum foil and bake in the center of the oven for 2 hours.
Uncover the pan and cook the ribs 2 hours longer, turning occasionally,
until very tender. If not serving immediately, wrap and refrigerate at this
point; bring to room temperature before step 3.

3. Preheat the broiler to high. Transfer the ribs to a broiler pan and
discard the cooking liquid. Brush 1/4 cup of the hoisin sauce on the top

274

side of the ribs. Broil, 4 inches from the heat source, until the sauce bubbles and the ribs begin to brown on the edges, about 3 minutes. Turn the ribs, brush with the remaining 1/4 cup hoisin sauce, and broil on the other side until the sauce bubbles, about 3 minutes.

WHEN you go to your butcher or supermarket to buy pork ribs, you will find more choices than you might expect. How do you know what you want? Here are some clues about the major players.

Spareribs are the lean, lower portion of the rib bones held together by a piece of cartilage and bone. They are the most familiar type of pork ribs and likely to be the least expensive. Usually sold in whole or half racks, they are a lot easier to serve if you get your butcher to cut through the cartilage and bone between every rib or every two ribs.

St. Louis–style ribs are spareribs that have had the cartilage and bone removed from the bottom. They can be cooked as a whole rack yet are easy to divide into portions because you can easily cut between the ribs.

Country-style ribs are made from the blade end of the pork loin and often don't have a rib bone at all. They are much meatier than the other choices but don't really look like spareribs once cooked and aren't easy to eat with your fingers.

Baby back ribs are a restaurant cut that is really what's left of a pork loin after a boneless roast has been removed. They are smaller, a bit meatier, and easier to handle than spareribs.

SELECTING
SPARERIBS

Ropa Vieja

2 1/2 pounds skirt or flank
    steak, cut into 6 pieces
Kosher salt and freshly milled
    black pepper
3 tablespoons extra virgin
    olive oil
2 large onions, thinly sliced
    (about 4 cups)
3 garlic cloves, minced (about
    1 tablespoon)
1 cup white wine
3 cups canned chicken broth
    or Chicken Stock (page 32)
1 Turkish bay leaf
1 medium red bell pepper,
    sliced (about 2 cups)
1 medium green bell pepper,
    sliced (about 2 cups)
1 tablespoon ground cumin
1 teaspoon dried oregano
1 1/2 cups canned crushed
    tomatoes with their liquid
2 tablespoons tomato paste
1/2 cup sliced pimiento-stuffed
    olives, drained
1/4 cup liquid from olive jar
3 tablespoons drained, bottled
    capers

MAKES 6 SERVINGS

The Cubans affectionately call this stew *ropa vieja,* or "old clothes," because the finished product—composed of shredded meat, peppers, and onions—looks to them like a mess of colorful rags. But its taste? Delicioso! Serve with Simple Boiled Rice (page 40) and a tossed green salad.

1. Season the meat with 1/2 teaspoon salt and 1/4 teaspoon pepper. Heat 1 tablespoon of the oil in a large Dutch oven over high heat until hot; reduce the heat to medium-high. Add half of the meat and cook until browned on all sides, about 10 minutes. Transfer with tongs to a plate and repeat with the remaining meat.

2. Reduce the heat to medium, add the onions to the meat drippings in the skillet, and cook, stirring occasionally, until softened, about 5 minutes. Add the garlic and cook 1 minute. Add the wine and cook until it has reduced by half. Add the broth, the meat along with any drippings on the plate, and the bay leaf. Bring to a boil over high heat; reduce the heat to low, cover, and cook until the meat is fork tender, about 2 1/2 hours.

3. Transfer the mixture to a colander over a bowl; return the liquid to the Dutch oven and boil it over high heat until it has reduced to 1 cup. When the beef is cool enough to handle, shred it, discarding the bay leaf.

4. Meanwhile, heat the remaining 2 tablespoons of oil in a large skillet over high heat. Reduce the heat to medium-high; add the red and green peppers, cumin, and oregano and sauté for 3 minutes. Add the tomatoes and cook for another 3 minutes. Add the reserved meat cooking liquid, the tomato paste, olives, olive liquid, and capers and simmer for 2 minutes or until thickened slightly. Stir in the meat and onion mixture; taste and add salt and pepper, if desired. Cook, stirring, just until hot.

ℬraised Short Ribs

Hands-on time:
30 minutes

Total preparation time:
31/2 hours

MAKES 4 SERVINGS

This is actually an adaptation of a recipe by a very talented New York chef named Tom Valenti, who is known for his stick-to-your-ribs cooking (no pun intended). We ran the recipe in *Gourmet* many years ago when he was the chef at a place called Alison on Dominick. Now he has two of his own restaurants on the Upper West Side of Manhattan, Ouest and Cesca.

The real secret to this recipe is (fasten your seat belt) one whole bottle of red wine. I have always known that wine is a conductor of flavor, but nowhere is it more clearly illustrated than in this recipe. I make this every Thanksgiving in lieu of turkey—that's how popular it is at my house. It freezes beautifully, making it the perfect candidate for entertaining. Serve with Smashed Potatoes (page 38) and Asian Spiced Roasted Baby Carrots (page 292).

5 pounds beef short ribs (see page 281)
Kosher salt and freshly milled black pepper
1 tablespoon vegetable oil
1 large onion, coarsely chopped (about 2 cups)
2 medium carrots, coarsely chopped
3 garlic cloves, minced (about 1 tablespoon)
2 tablespoons tomato paste
1 sprig rinsed and dried fresh thyme or 1 teaspoon dried
1 Turkish bay leaf
One 750-ml bottle red wine
Two 14- or 14 1/2-ounce cans low-sodium chicken broth or 3 1/2 cups Chicken Stock (page 32)
1/2 recipe Horseradish Sauce (page 316)
2 tablespoons unbleached all-purpose flour
2 tablespoons unsalted butter, softened

1. Pat the ribs dry and season them on all sides with salt and pepper. Heat the oil in a Dutch oven or a deep flameproof roasting pan that will just hold the ribs in one layer over high heat until hot. Reduce the heat to medium-high, add the ribs, and brown them on all sides, 8 to 10 minutes. Transfer the ribs with tongs to a platter or bowl.

2. Preheat the oven to 375°F. Reduce the heat under the Dutch oven to medium; add the onion and carrots and cook, stirring occasionally, until golden, about 8 minutes. Add the garlic and cook for 1 minute. Add the tomato paste, thyme, and bay leaf and cook for 2 minutes. Transfer the vegetables to the platter with the ribs. Add the wine to the Dutch oven and bring it to a boil over high heat. Reduce the heat to low and simmer it until it is reduced by three fourths (to about 1 cup). Add the broth and bring it to a boil. Add the ribs and vegetables along with any juices that have accumulated on the platter. Cover the Dutch oven tightly, place it in the center of the oven, and braise for 2 1/2 hours or until the meat is tender and falling off the bones. Meanwhile prepare the Horseradish Sauce.

3. Transfer the ribs to a plate with tongs and let stand until they are cool enough to handle. Strain the broth into a bowl. Discard the solids and return the liquid to the Dutch oven. Skim off any fat that floats to the surface (see sidebar about removing fat, page 289), bring the liquid to a boil, and reduce it to about 1 1/2 cups.

4. Discard the bones and any excess fat from the ribs. Knead together the flour and butter in a small bowl, add a few spoonfuls of the reduced broth to the mixture, then whisk the butter mixture back into the broth. Bring to a boil and simmer for 5 minutes. Add salt and pepper to taste. Return the ribs to the pot and cook gently until just heated through. Divide the ribs among warmed plates, spoon some of the sauce over the top, and serve with the Horseradish Sauce.

YOU will find two main kinds of beef short ribs at the supermarket or the butcher, and either would work fine in this recipe. However, it is confusing because they look very different. Short ribs are cut from the twelve ribs that extend from the back toward the belly and are found in the plate, rib section, chuck, and brisket; butchers don't usually indicate which section the ribs come from. English-style short ribs are cut parallel to the rib bones and between each rib. They are boneless and have a rectangular shape. Flanken-style short ribs are cut across the rib bones and have a longer rectangular shape. I prefer the flanken style because the attached bones give the final braised rib more flavor. Either kind is going to come with a fair amount of fat, which I remove after cooking.

A
SHORT-RIB
PRIMER

2 tablespoons vegetable oil
2 pounds tri tip sirloin, cut
    into 1/4-inch cubes
1 large onion, chopped (about
    2 cups)
6 garlic cloves, minced (about
    2 tablespoons)
1 tablespoon pure ancho chile
    powder or to taste
1 tablespoon ground cumin
1 tablespoon dried oregano
2 jalapenos, chopped, with
    seeds
One 28 ounce can diced
    tomatoes
One 14- or 14 1/2-ounce can
    chicken broth or 1 3/4 cups
    Chicken Stock (page 32)
1 cup canned beef broth
12 ounces beer
1/4 cup tomato paste
2 chipotles in adobo sauce,
    finely chopped, plus 1
    tablespoon sauce
Accompaniments: sour cream,
    chopped avocado, chopped
    red onion, store-bought
    salsa, shredded iceberg
    lettuce, and crushed tortilla
    chips

Pure Chili

MAKES 4 TO 6 SERVINGS

We had a chili championship winner on *Sara's Secrets* and his chili was so good it inspired me to do a version for this book. I learned two main things from him: (1) Tri tip sirloin is the meat to use and in cubes, not ground; and (2) pure chile powder is the way to go. Those generic jars you buy at the supermarket are a blend of chiles, cumin, oregano, and sometimes granulated garlic. If you use pure chile powder (see Sources, page 346) you will have much more control over the seasoning, and chili is all about seasoning. Serve with Simple Boiled Rice (page 40) and Cole Slaw (page 38).

1. Preheat the oven to 325°F. Heat the oil in a Dutch oven over high heat until hot. Reduce the heat to medium-high and add half the meat. Brown well, about 10 minutes, and transfer with a slotted spoon to a bowl. Add the remaining meat, brown well, and add to the bowl. Reduce the heat to medium; add the onion and cook, stirring occasionally, until softened, about 5 minutes. Add the garlic, chile powder to taste (unless you like things really hot, 1 to 4 teaspoons should do it), cumin, and oregano and cook 1 minute.

2. Add the jalapenos, tomatoes, chicken and beef broths, beer, tomato paste, and the chipotles along with the browned meat and any juices that have accumulated in the bowl. Bring the mixture to a boil over high heat; cover the Dutch oven with aluminum foil and the lid and place it in the center of the oven. Braise for 1 1/2 to 2 1/2 hours or until the meat is very tender. Ladle over rice and serve with accompaniments.

IF YOU have made your favorite pot of chili and suddenly notice that you mismeasured the chile powder or hot sauce, rendering your creation inedible, what do you do? There are two antidotes: sugar and dairy. Sometimes just a little hit of sugar will do the trick. But if not, you can reach for the cream or sour cream or just make sure that everyone tops their bowl with a generous dollop of dairy. If you have *eaten* something too spicy, drink a glass of milk or, better yet, take a spoonful or two of your favorite vanilla ice cream.

HOW
TO TURN
DOWN CHILE
HEAT

2 tablespoons sweet or hot
  paprika (see pages 183 and
  347)
2 tablespoons chili powder
3 garlic cloves, minced (about
  1 tablespoon)
1 tablespoon kosher salt
1 tablespoon ground cumin
1 1/2 teaspoons dry mustard
1/2 teaspoon cayenne pepper
  or more to taste
One 4- to 5-pound piece beef
  brisket (from the fattiest
  end)
3 cups bottled barbecue sauce
  or 1 recipe Tangy Barbecue
  Sauce (page 321, add prep
  time)
One 14- or 14 1/2-ounce can
  chicken broth or 1 3/4 cups
  Chicken Stock (page 32)
Two 12-ounce bottles of beer

Brisket Braised in Barbecue Sauce

MAKES 8 SERVINGS

Brisket is a tough cut of meat from the breast of the beef that turns into a meltingly flavorful entrée when braised slowly for hours—and while it's in the oven you don't have to do a thing to it. It becomes even tastier after several days, which allows you to cook it over the weekend and serve it in the middle of the week. Just slice the meat a quarter inch thick against the grain and warm it gently in the barbecue sauce (my own or your favorite bottled brand). Serve with buttered noodles and a tossed green salad.

1. Several hours or a day before cooking, combine the paprika, chili powder, garlic, salt, cumin, mustard, and cayenne in a small bowl and mix well. Rub the mixture all over the brisket. Place it in a nonreactive baking dish, cover, and refrigerate until ready to cook.

2. Preheat the oven to 325°F. Prepare the Tangy Barbecue Sauce, if using. Heat the barbeque sauce in a large Dutch oven; stir in the broth and beer and bring to a boil. Add the brisket and cover the Dutch oven with aluminum foil and the lid. Braise in the oven for 4 to 5 hours or until fork tender.

3. Transfer the brisket to a platter and cover loosely with aluminum foil. Skim off and discard any fat from the surface of the sauce in the Dutch oven. Bring the sauce to a boil over high heat, reduce the heat to medium-low, and simmer until the sauce has thickened, about 30 to 35 minutes. Meanwhile, thinly slice the brisket on an angle, cutting against the grain; stir any broth from the platter into the sauce. Arrange the slices on the platter; liberally spoon some sauce over the brisket. Serve with the remaining sauce.

A WHOLE untrimmed brisket weighs eight to twelve pounds and includes a layer of fat and connective tissue called the deckle, which is usually removed before cooking. The whole brisket is favored by Texans for their famous barbecued brisket. It divides into two distinct muscles. The flat cut (also called first cut or thin cut) is the leanest part, weighing in at about four pounds. The point cut is cheaper and fattier than the flat cut and weighs four to five pounds. The meat will be moister if you use the point cut. Whichever cut you use, trim the top fat or fat cap until it is only one quarter to one third inch thick.

SELECTING BRISKET

1/3 cup Wondra or unbleached
   all-purpose flour
Kosher salt and freshly milled
   black pepper
5 tablespoons vegetable oil
2 pounds lean leg of lamb, cut
   into 1 1/2-inch cubes
2 medium onions, finely
   chopped
One 3-inch cinnamon stick
5 whole cloves
1 Turkish bay leaf
6 garlic cloves, chopped (about
   2 tablespoons)
1 large jalapeño or 2 serrano
   chiles, thinly sliced (seeds
   removed if desired)
1 1/2 tablespoons salt-free
   packaged garam masala,
   curry powder, or Todd's
   Garam Masala (page 21,
   add prep time)
1 1/2 teaspoons finely grated
   fresh ginger (use a
   Microplane)
1 cup chopped, drained
   canned tomatoes
1/2 cup plain yogurt,
   preferably Greek (see Note,
   page 97)

Indian Braised Lamb
with Spinach

MAKES 6 TO 8 SERVINGS

Whenever we go to an Indian restaurant my husband invariably orders lamb saag, lamb cubes braised with spinach in a curry sauce thickened with a little yogurt. This is my version. You can usually find cut-up cubes of lamb leg at the supermarket, labeled either "lamb stew" or "lamb for kabobs." The rest of the ingredients are readily available, too, except perhaps for the masala, which is an Indian spice mix. (Todd's Garam Masala [page 21] is a great homemade version, but you can also substitute your favorite brand of curry powder.) If you don't want to bother with fresh spinach, you can work with the frozen kind. If you don't like heat, leave out the chiles. This is one of those dishes that gets better the next day and also freezes very well. Serve with Simple Boiled Rice (page 40).

1. Preheat the oven to 325°F. Combine the flour with 1/2 teaspoon salt and 1/4 teaspoon pepper in a shallow bowl. Heat 2 tablespoons of the oil in a large Dutch oven over high heat until hot. Toss half of the lamb in the flour mixture, shaking off the excess. Reduce the heat to medium-high, add the floured lamb, and brown on all sides, about 8 minutes total. Remove the lamb with a slotted spoon to a bowl. Repeat with another 2 tablespoons oil and the remaining lamb.

2. Reduce the heat to medium; add the remaining 1 tablespoon oil, the onions, cinnamon stick, cloves, and bay leaf to the Dutch oven and cook, stirring occasionally, until softened, about 5 minutes. Add the garlic, chiles, garam masala, and ginger and cook 1 minute. Add 1 cup water, the tomatoes, yogurt, and lamb, along with any juices that have accumulated in the bowl. Bring the mixture to a boil.

3. Cover the pot with aluminum foil and the lid and braise in the center of the oven for 1 1/2 hours or until the lamb is very tender. Add the spinach to the pot and stir well. Cover and braise for 10 minutes more. Remove the bay leaf, cloves, and cinnamon stick. Add the lemon juice and add salt and pepper to taste.

One 5-ounce bag rinsed baby spinach or 6 to 8 ounces loose spinach, coarse stems discarded and leaves rinsed well

1 tablespoon fresh lemon juice

1/3 cup Wondra or unbleached
all-purpose flour
Kosher salt and freshly milled
black pepper
4 tablespoons extra virgin
olive oil
Four 1-pound lamb shanks
1 large onion, thinly sliced
(about 2 cups)
6 garlic cloves, minced (about
2 tablespoons)
2 cups white wine or
vermouth
6 plum tomatoes, quartered
lengthwise
1 small eggplant (about 3/4
pound), cut into 1 1/2-inch
chunks
2 tablespoons tomato paste
1 1/2 teaspoons herbes de
Provence (or 1/2 teaspoon
each dried basil and thyme
and 1/4 teaspoon each
savory and crumbled
rosemary)
2 small zucchini (about 10
ounces), sliced 1/2 inch thick
1/2 cup rinsed, dried, and
shredded fresh basil leaves

Braised Lamb Shanks
with Ratatouille Sauce

MAKES 4 SERVINGS

Ratatouille is a wonderful vegetable stew from the south of
France consisting of all the typical Provençal vegetables—
eggplant, zucchini, tomatoes, and garlic. It is delicious alongside
lamb, which got me to thinking it might be a good idea to stew
the vegetables and the meat together. Sure enough, the two
make beautiful music together. Serve with buttered noodles.

1. Preheat the oven to 325°F. Combine the flour with 1/2 teaspoon salt
and 1/4 teaspoon pepper in a resealable plastic bag. Heat 2 tablespoons of
the oil in a 6-quart Dutch oven over high heat until hot.

2. Shake the lamb shanks in the flour, one at a time, until they are well
coated; remove from the bag and shake off any excess flour mixture.
Reduce the heat under the Dutch oven to medium-high; add the lamb and
brown on all sides, about 10 minutes. Transfer the shanks to a plate with
tongs. Reduce the heat to medium; add the remaining oil, the onion, and
garlic and cook, stirring occasionally, until softened, 5 minutes. Add the
wine and simmer until reduced by half. Add the lamb to the pan along
with the tomatoes, eggplant, tomato paste, herbes de Provence, and 1
teaspoon salt. Bring the mixture to a boil over high heat. Cover the pot
with aluminum foil and the lid and braise in the center of the oven until
the lamb is almost tender, about 2 1/2 hours. Remove and discard the
excess fat (see sidebar).

3. Remove and reserve 1 cup of the vegetables with cooking liquid from
the pan. Add the zucchini to the Dutch oven. Cover, return to the oven,
and cook until the zucchini are tender, about 20 minutes. Meanwhile,
puree the reserved vegetable and cooking liquid mixture in a blender.

4. When the zucchini is tender, remove the lamb shanks to a large shallow baking dish. Stir the pureed vegetables into the sauce. Add salt and pepper to taste and spoon the sauce over the lamb. Serve each shank with some of the vegetables and sauce. Top each portion with basil.

MOST slow-cooking dishes give off a fair amount of fat as the meat cooks down. The fat floats to the top of the pot and sits there like an oil slick, sometimes as thick as half an inch. The easiest way by far to remove this fat is to let the dish cool and refrigerate it overnight. The next day the fat will have hardened and will be very easy to scoop off. The added benefit of letting the stew or braised item chill overnight is that it will develop more flavor.

If you do not have time to chill your dish, however, there are other quick ways to skim off the fat. Tip the pan slightly so the fat collects on one side of the pot and simply skim it off with a spoon. When you have gotten down to a small fat layer on top of the stew, gently run paper towels over the top, discarding the towels as they are soaked, until you have removed all the fat.

I have also had good success with a fat separator, a kitchen tool that looks like a measuring cup with a long spout. The idea is that when you pour the cooking liquid into the cup, the fat will rise to the top of both the long sprout and the cup. You just pour off the little layer of fat from the top of the spout and then keep pouring the liquid into a clean pot until you reach the fat layer in the cup.

HOW
TO REMOVE
FAT

Side
Dishes
Take Center
Stage

Asian Spiced Roasted Baby Carrots

V

MAKES 4 SERVINGS

1 pound peeled baby carrots
1 tablespoon vegetable oil
1/4 teaspoon kosher salt
2 tablespoons soy sauce
1 tablespoon unsalted butter, sliced
2 teaspoons finely grated fresh ginger (use a Microplane)
2 teaspoons ground cumin
2 teaspoons sherry vinegar
1 teaspoon toasted sesame oil
1/4 teaspoon freshly milled black pepper

Those handy little packages of peeled, shaped "baby" carrots that have been showing up in supermarkets in recent years really cut down on prep time. Simply tossing them with oil, salt, and pepper and then roasting them in a hot oven intensifies their flavor. But add Asian elements such as ginger and toasted sesame oil, and you've truly got something.

1. Preheat the oven to 450°F. Combine the carrots, vegetable oil, and salt in a medium bowl. Spread the carrots on a rimmed baking sheet and roast, stirring once, until tender and starting to brown, 20 to 25 minutes.

2. Meanwhile, combine the soy sauce, butter, ginger, cumin, vinegar, sesame oil, and pepper in a large bowl.

3. When the carrots are tender, add them to the soy sauce mixture and toss until the butter melts and the carrots are completely coated; serve immediately.

Grated Carrot Salad

V

Hands-on time:
15 minutes

Total preparation time:
15 minutes

MAKES 4 TO 6 SERVINGS

If you have a grating disk on your food processor, this makes a perfect weeknight salad. Tossed with cumin and paprika–flavored oil, raisins, olives, and lemon juice, it is a refreshing change from the usual green salad or cole slaw.

1. Heat the oil in a small skillet over medium-low heat. Add the cumin seeds and cook until they turn a shade darker and become fragrant, about 4 minutes. Remove the pan from the heat, stir in the paprika, and let the mixture cool.

2. Meanwhile, coarsely grate the carrots, preferably using the coarse grating disk on a food processor. Toss the carrots with the cooled oil mixture, the raisins, olives, cilantro, lemon juice to taste, the sugar, and salt. Serve at room temperature or refrigerate, covered, and serve cold.

3 tablespoons extra virgin olive oil
1 teaspoon cumin seeds
1 teaspoon paprika
1 pound carrots (about 8 medium)
1/3 cup golden raisins
1/3 cup chopped pimiento-stuffed green olives
1/4 cup rinsed, dried, and chopped fresh cilantro
2 to 3 teaspoons fresh lemon juice, or to taste
1 teaspoon sugar
1/2 teaspoon kosher salt

Southwestern Sweet Potato Sauté

V

MAKES 4 TO 6 SERVINGS

*2 large sweet potatoes (about
24 ounces total), peeled*
3 tablespoons vegetable oil
1 teaspoon ground cumin
*1/2 to 1 chipotle in adobo
sauce, finely chopped*
*1/4 cup pepitas (hulled
pumpkin seeds)*
*Kosher salt and freshly milled
black pepper*

Discovering the grating disk on my food processor many years ago
was a eureka moment for me—ten minutes later I was grating and
then sautéing every vegetable I could put my hands on. Talk about
convenient! Baking a whole sweet potato takes about an hour,
but sautéing the grated potato takes only fifteen minutes from
start to finish—and you end up concentrating the flavor to boot.
This recipe dresses up your potato with Southwestern ingredients,
but there's no reason not to go Asian (add ginger and soy) or
Italian (add sage, brown butter, and pine nuts) as the mood strikes
you. For that matter, you could swap out the sweet potato and
use butternut squash instead.

1. Coarsely grate the sweet potatoes, preferably using the grating disk of a
food processor. (You should have about 5 cups.)

2. Heat the oil in a large skillet over high heat until hot. Reduce the heat
to medium-high; add the sweet potatoes and cumin and sauté, stirring
constantly, until the potatoes are almost tender, 3 to 5 minutes. Add the
chipotle, pepitas, and salt and pepper to taste. Cook for 2 minutes more or
until the sweet potatoes are tender.

Oven Fries

Hands-on time:
10 minutes

Total preparation time:
30 minutes

V

MAKES 4 SERVINGS

Everyone loves French fries, but who's going to make them at home? They're messy and require too much babysitting—and besides, they're hardly the healthiest side dish on the planet. So here is the baked alternative—crispy as you please, but much less fatty than the fried kind. Try them once and see if your family doesn't love them.

2 large baking potatoes, scrubbed (about 1 1/2 pounds)
2 tablespoons extra virgin olive oil
Kosher salt

1. Preheat the oven to 500°F. Generously grease a large baking sheet.

2. Cut the potatoes lengthwise into 1/3-inch-thick French fries. Toss them with the oil and 1/4 teaspoon salt in a large bowl. Spread them on the pan and roast them in the lower third of the oven for 15 minutes. Turn them over and roast until golden on all sides, about 10 minutes. Sprinkle with salt to taste and serve.

Butter-steamed Broccoli
with Soy

V

MAKES 4 SERVINGS

1 large head broccoli
3 tablespoons unsalted butter
1 tablespoon soy sauce
Kosher salt and freshly milled
black pepper

One of the first restaurants I worked in was Cybele's in Boston's Faneuil Hall. We were on a very tight budget, so instead of making one or two special vegetables for each dish we would serve a one-size-fits-all starch and vegetable and plop them on every plate. I developed this quick and easy way to cook vegetables, which involves just one large skillet. I put the sliced carrots, green beans, cauliflower florets—whatever we had—into the pan with a couple of pats of butter and a little bit of water. I would cover the pan, simmer the vegetables until they were almost tender, then remove the lid and cook until the water evaporated and the vegetables were glazed in that butter. It was a very quick process suitable to a fast-moving restaurant or a quick home-cooked weeknight meal. Try this method with any of your favorite vegetables.

1. Cut the broccoli into florets, reserving stems for another use. Combine the broccoli with the butter, soy sauce, and 1/4 inch water in a skillet just large enough to hold the broccoli in one layer. Bring the mixture to a boil over high heat. Reduce the heat to low, cover, and simmer for 3 minutes.

2. Remove the cover and simmer the broccoli until most of the liquid has evaporated, 1 to 2 minutes longer. Add salt and pepper to taste. Stir until all the florets are nicely coated with the butter mixture and serve.

Charred Onions and Peppers

V

MAKES 4 SERVINGS

Hands-on time:
10 minutes

Total preparation time:
15 minutes

It doesn't get much simpler than this side dish, particularly if you pick up sliced onions and peppers from your supermarket's salad bar.

1. Place an oven rack 6 inches from the broiler; preheat the broiler to high. Lightly oil a rimmed baking sheet.

2. Combine the chutney and mustard in a large bowl; add the onions and peppers and toss until completely coated. Spread the vegetable mixture on the baking sheet and broil until crisp-tender and browned on the edges, about 5 minutes, stirring once. Add salt and pepper to taste. Transfer the mixture to a serving bowl and serve.

1/2 cup mango chutney (preferably Major Grey's)
3 tablespoons Dijon mustard
2 medium onions, sliced (about 3 cups)
1 each red, yellow, and green medium bell peppers, sliced (about 3 cups)
Kosher salt and freshly milled black pepper

Creamed Corn

V

MAKES 4 SERVINGS

8 to 9 ears fresh corn
3 tablespoons unsalted butter
1 small onion, finely chopped
    (about 1/2 cup)
4 scallions (white and light
    green parts), finely
    chopped (about 1/2 cup)
2 tablespoons rinsed, dried,
    and shredded fresh basil
1 tablespoon fresh lemon juice
Kosher salt and freshly milled
    black pepper

You can make creamed corn without cream and still get just what you want from the dish: the texture of cream and the flavor of corn. In fact, creamed corn without cream is a distinct improvement on creamed corn with cream. Relying on the corn's own starch for thickening guarantees that the dish will be plenty creamy. And without cream to mask the flavor, the dish tastes much more like the essence of corn. (And that's not even to mention the savings in calories.) You can put an Indian twist on this simple recipe by substituting 3 tablespoons chopped fresh cilantro, 1 large jalapeño chile, chopped, and 1 1/2 teaspoons finely grated fresh ginger (use a Microplane) for the basil and lemon juice. Or for a Mexican twist, substitute 1 tablespoon chopped chipotles in adobo (smoked jalapeños in a vinegary tomato sauce), 1 1/2 teaspoons ground cumin, and 1 1/2 teaspoons chopped fresh oregano. It would also be great with 4 slices cooked bacon, crumbled, and 1 large (8 ounces) ripe tomato, chopped.

1. Cut the corn kernels from the cobs (you should have about 6 cups). Transfer 2 cups to a blender and puree until very smooth. Press the mixture through a strainer into a bowl; reserve the puree.

2. Melt the butter in a large skillet over medium-low heat. Add the onion and cook, stirring occasionally, until softened, about 8 minutes.

3. Add the whole corn kernels and cook 3 minutes. Add 1/2 cup water, bring to a simmer, and cook for 3 minutes. Stir in the corn puree and scallions and simmer 2 minutes more. Add the basil, lemon juice, and salt and pepper to taste.

Tomato Gratin

v

MAKES 6 TO 8 SERVINGS

2 pounds firm-ripe plum
    tomatoes, quartered
    lengthwise
Kosher salt
3 tablespoons extra virgin
    olive oil
2 large garlic cloves, minced
    (about 1 tablespoon)
1 teaspoon red pepper flakes,
    optional
Freshly milled black pepper
18 round butter-flavored
    crackers, about 1 1/4 inches
    in diameter (Look for a kind
    without trans fat)
1 1/2 ounces Parmigiano-
    Reggiano cheese, finely
    grated (about 1/2 cup; see
    grating information, page
    10)
2 tablespoons rinsed, dried,
    and chopped fresh herbs
    such as oregano, marjoram,
    thyme, or basil or a mixture

This dish tastes best when the tomato season is at its height—late August here in the Northeast. As with almost any recipe featuring tomatoes, I presalt them to remove their excess liquid and concentrate their flavor. You can top them off with any kind of cracker—even plain old bread crumbs would be fine—but I like using Ritz crackers because their buttery taste reminds me of my grandmother Ruth Moulton. This is the kind of dish she would have served.

1. Preheat the oven to 425°F. Sprinkle the tomatoes liberally with salt and let drain in a colander for 15 minutes. Transfer to paper towels and gently pat dry. While the tomatoes are draining, combine the oil, garlic, and red pepper flakes, if using.

2. Lightly oil a baking dish large enough to hold the tomatoes in a single layer. Arrange the tomatoes in the dish, skin side down; drizzle the garlic oil over them and sprinkle with black pepper.

3. Put the crackers in a zippered plastic bag and crush with a rolling pin. Add the cheese and herbs to the crumbs in the bag and shake to combine; sprinkle the crumb mixture evenly over the tomatoes.

4. Bake the gratin in the upper third of the oven 12 to 15 minutes, until the crumb topping browns and the tomatoes are heated through.

STORE tomatoes at room temperature until they are fully ripe. Do not put them in the fridge unless they threaten to become overripe, because you will arrest the ripening process and kill their flavor and texture. It is also best to store them with the stem end up. The stem end is the most fragile area of the tomato, and allowing the tomato to rest on it can cause bruising and deterioration.

STORING
TOMATOES

Radish and Orange Salad
with Peppery Orange Dressing

v

MAKES 4 SERVINGS

Radishes don't get nearly enough love in this country and I have no idea why. They are both peppery and sweet, crunchy, and quite refreshing. Teamed up with oranges, arugula, and olives, they make a great side salad.

By the way, the best way to slice radishes is with a food processor fitted with the slicing disk. But using a knife, you could halve them lengthwise (so they don't roll around), lay them flat on the counter, and slice them crosswise.

1. Grate 1 teaspoon zest from one of the oranges and reserve. Peel the oranges using a serrated knife and slice them crosswise into 1/4-inch-thick rounds (see sidebar).

2. Rinse and trim the radishes and slice them into rounds. (Using a food processor with a slicing disk will speed up the process.) Whisk together the lemon juice, reserved orange zest, salt, sugar, and cayenne; gradually whisk in the oil.

3. Line a platter with arugula and arrange the orange slices, overlapping if necessary, in a circle on top of the arugula. Mound the radishes in the center and top them with the olives. Drizzle the salad with the dressing just before serving.

Hands-on time:
20 minutes

Total preparation time:
25 minutes

2 navel oranges, rinsed and dried
12 large radishes (about 8 ounces)
2 tablespoons fresh lemon juice
1/2 teaspoon kosher salt
1/4 teaspoon sugar
1/8 teaspoon cayenne pepper
1/3 cup extra virgin olive oil
1 bunch arugula or watercress, rinsed and dried, tough stems discarded
1/2 cup pitted, brine-cured olives such as kalamata

HOW TO PEEL AND SLICE AN ORANGE

THIS is a technique I learned in cooking school that I use not only for oranges, grapefruits, and all citrus but also for any unwieldy roundish fruit or vegetable: First cut off the top and bottom of the orange and lay it flat on a cutting board, cut side down. Then, starting at the top and working your way down with a serrated knife, cut off the peel and pith in strips, all the way down to the flesh of the orange. You will probably have to flip it over to make sure you cut all the peel and pith off the bottom half. Then you can simply slice the orange crosswise into neat slices. I peel butternut squash, eggplant, and pineapple this way too. Resting them on a flat surface is a lot easier to negotiate than trying to peel them in the air with a knife or a vegetable peeler.

Sautéed Beets
with Balsamic Vinegar

V

MAKES 6 SERVINGS

My husband would not be sorry if this were an all-beet cookbook. "The niche is wide open," he pointed out when we were still in the planning stages. "If you focus you can establish yourself as the George Washington Carver of the beet." Though I've declined to take advantage of this opportunity, I am well aware that my husband loves beets. I love them less, not least because there's almost no way to cook them without having your hands turn purple. So I came up with this recipe. The beets seem to bleed less when you peel them first, and grating them slashes the cooking time from forty minutes to three or four.

1. Peel the beets. To grate beets in a food processor, cut them into pieces that will fit through the feed tube and grate using the grating disk. Or, grate using the coarse side of a four-sided hand grater.

2. Heat the oil in a large skillet over high heat until hot. Reduce the heat to medium-high, add the beets, and sauté, stirring frequently, for 3 to 4 minutes, until the beets are just crisp-tender. Add the balsamic vinegar and salt and pepper to taste.

Hands-on time:
15 minutes

Total preparation time:
15 minutes

1 3/4 pounds beets
2 tablespoons vegetable oil
3 tablespoons balsamic vinegar
Kosher salt and freshly milled black pepper

Grilled Radicchio Salad

V

MAKES 4 SERVINGS

1/4 cup pine nuts, optional

2 heads radicchio (about 1 1/2 pounds), rinsed and dried

4 tablespoons extra virgin olive oil

Kosher salt and freshly milled black pepper

2 tablespoons balsamic vinegar, preferably aged

I'm not a big fan of raw radicchio—it's very bitter. Grill it, though, and you're talking about a different animal completely, something mellow and almost sweet. Topped with a little balsamic vinegar, grilled radicchio makes a wonderful warm salad.

1. If using pine nuts, preheat the oven to 350°F. Toast the pine nuts on a rimmed baking sheet until they are golden, about 10 minutes.

2. Meanwhile, preheat a grill, grill pan, or broiler to medium-high. Cut each radicchio into 6 wedges, drizzle with 2 tablespoons of the oil, and sprinkle with salt and pepper on all sides. Arrange the wedges in one layer on a grill, grill pan, or shallow baking pan for broiling.

3. Grill or broil the radicchio for 6 to 8 minutes on each side or until tender and caramelized. Transfer it to a platter or plates and drizzle with the remaining 2 tablespoons oil, the balsamic vinegar, and pine nuts, if using.

Mediterranean Orzo Pilaf

Hands-on time:
15 minutes

Total preparation time:
25 minutes

MAKES 4 TO 6 SERVINGS

I love risotto for its creaminess—but not on a weeknight. It just doesn't work unless you stand over it like a schoolmarm. Orzo, on the other hand, is nearly as creamy and a lot less fussy. And with the addition in step 2 of cooked shrimp or scallops, you could turn it into a main dish that will stick to your ribs.

1. Heat the oil in a large skillet over high heat until hot. Reduce the heat to medium; add the onion and cook, stirring occasionally, until softened, about 5 minutes. Add the garlic and cook 1 minute. Stir in the chicken broth and orzo; bring to a boil over high heat. Reduce the heat to low and simmer, stirring occasionally, until all the liquid has been absorbed and the orzo is tender, 8 to 10 minutes.

2. Stir in the artichoke hearts, olives, dill, lemon zest, and salt and pepper to taste. Cook until the artichokes are heated through, about 1 minute.

2 tablespoons extra virgin olive oil

1 small onion, finely chopped (about 1/2 cup)

1 garlic clove, minced (about 1 teaspoon)

2 1/2 cups canned chicken broth or Chicken Stock (page 32)

8 ounces orzo

One 6 1/2-ounce jar marinated artichoke hearts, drained and coarsely chopped

1/3 cup pitted, brine-cured olives such as kalamata, chopped

2 tablespoons rinsed, dried, and chopped fresh dill

1/2 teaspoon grated lemon zest

Kosher salt and freshly milled black pepper

Hands-on time:
5 minutes

Total preparation time:
25 minutes

One 14- or 14 1/2-ounce can
  chicken broth or 1 3/4 cups
  Chicken Stock (page 32)
3/4 cup basmati or jasmine
  rice, rinsed
Two 4-inch pieces lemongrass,
  split lengthwise and
  smashed with the flat side
  of a chef's knife, optional
One 2-inch piece fresh ginger,
  peeled, split lengthwise,
  and smashed with the flat
  side of a chef's knife
Kosher salt
One 13 1/2- or 14-ounce can
  unsweetened coconut milk,
  low-fat if preferred

Coconut Rice

MAKES 4 TO 6 SERVINGS

Boil your rice in water and you get rice. Boil it in coconut milk and you get something special. Coconut rice is the perfect accompaniment to any Asian-style dish, including this book's Mustard-chutney Roasted Chicken Thighs (page 157). Happily, you can find unsweetened coconut milk in the Asian section of most supermarkets today. Right next to it will be the low-fat version, which offers fewer calories and, yep, less flavor.

1. Bring the broth to a boil in a heavy saucepan over high heat. Stir in the rice, lemongrass, if using, the ginger, and 1/4 teaspoon salt. Cover, reduce the heat to low, and cook until the broth has been absorbed, about 8 to 10 minutes.

2. Add the coconut milk; cover, return to a boil over low heat, and cook, stirring frequently, until the rice is tender and most of the coconut milk has been absorbed, 8 to 10 minutes longer. Remove the lemongrass and ginger; taste and add more salt, if desired.

Greek Spinach Rice

MAKES 4 SERVINGS

During the late seventies, when my husband and I lived in Boston, one of our favorite spots was a Greek restaurant in Cambridge's Central Square that served this dish. It is essentially rice pilaf fortified with spinach, lemon, and dill. It would be the perfect accompaniment to some simple sautéed fish, scallops, or roast chicken.

1. Heat 2 tablespoons of the oil in a medium saucepan over high heat. Reduce the heat to medium; add the onion and cook, stirring occasionally, until softened, about 5 minutes. Add the garlic and cook 1 minute. Add the rice and cook, stirring, until it is coated with oil, about 1 minute. Add 1 1/2 cups of the chicken broth and the bay leaf; bring to a boil over high heat. Reduce the heat to low, cover, and simmer until all the liquid has been absorbed and the rice is tender, about 17 minutes. Let the rice stand for 5 minutes (do not stir it).

2. Meanwhile, heat the remaining tablespoon of oil in a medium skillet over medium-high heat. Add the spinach and pepper flakes, if using, and cook, stirring, until the spinach has just wilted, about 2 minutes. Add salt and pepper to taste. After the rice has rested, fluff it with a fork, discard the bay leaf, and stir in the spinach, dill, and lemon juice. Add enough of the remaining chicken broth to make the rice a little creamy and serve.

3 tablespoons extra virgin
   olive oil
1 small onion, finely chopped
   (about 1/2 cup)
1 garlic clove, minced (about
   1 teaspoon)
3/4 cup long-grain white rice
2 cups canned chicken broth
   or Chicken Stock (page 32)
1 small Turkish bay leaf
One 5-ounce package rinsed
   spinach
1/2 teaspoon red pepper
   flakes, optional
Kosher salt and freshly milled
   black pepper
2 tablespoons rinsed, dried,
   and chopped fresh dill
2 teaspoons fresh lemon juice

Quick
Sauces

Quick Herb Sauce

𝒱

MAKES ABOUT 1 1/8 CUPS

1 cup packed, rinsed, and
    dried fresh basil leaves
1 cup mayonnaise
1/4 cup packed, rinsed, and
    dried fresh flat-leaf parsley
    leaves
2 scallions (white and light
    green parts), coarsely
    chopped (about 1/4 cup)
1 large garlic clove, minced
    (about 1 1/2 teaspoons)
1 teaspoon grated lemon zest
Kosher salt and freshly milled
    black pepper

Normally you want to treat fresh herbs gently. Dry them well and chop them with a very sharp knife so they don't get bruised and wet. This sauce is an exception—in order to get the complete essence out of the herbs, I throw them into a blender with some mayonnaise and pulverize them. The herbs thin down the mayonnaise, turn it a bright green, and infuse it with big flavor. I have used this sauce as a spread for my Fried Clam (page 94) and Fried Green Tomato Sandwiches (page 87) and as a dressing for the Turkey Club Salad (page 75), but it would also make an excellent sauce for crudités or for sautéed fish, chicken, or shellfish.

1. Combine the basil, mayonnaise, parsley, scallions, garlic, and lemon zest in a blender and puree until very smooth. Add salt and pepper to taste.

2. Cover and refrigerate until ready to serve.

THE BEST way to store soft leafy herbs such as basil, parsley, cilantro, dill, and tarragon is to stand them root end down in a glass or measuring cup of cool water. If your house is cool, you can just keep them on the counter; if it is not, store the herbs in the glass in the fridge. Store woody herbs, such as rosemary, bay leaves, or thyme, in a loose plastic bag in the fridge. Chives, which are neither leafy nor woody, keep well wrapped in a paper towel in a plastic bag in the fridge.

STORING FRESH HERBS

Rouille

V

MAKES ABOUT 1 1/2 CUPS

1 cup mayonnaise
1/2 cup jarred roasted red
    peppers in water, well
    drained, or Roasted Peppers
    (page 30), using red bell
    peppers
1 teaspoon fresh lemon juice
2 garlic cloves, minced (about
    2 teaspoons)
1/4 teaspoon cayenne pepper
Kosher salt and freshly milled
    black pepper

We almost never encounter *rouille*—a garlicky, spicy red pepper sauce from the south of France—except as the garnish for the hearty seafood soup called *bouillabaisse*. As far as I'm concerned it's too tasty to remain so narrowly confined. I have used it as the finishing touch to Provençal Salt Cod Stew (page 270) and as a topping for Fried Clam Sandwiches (page 94). I also recommend it with baked or grilled lamb, chicken, or shrimp.

1. Combine the mayonnaise, peppers, lemon juice, garlic, and cayenne in a blender and puree until smooth. Add salt and pepper to taste.

2. Cover and refrigerate until ready to serve.

Italian Tuna Sauce

Hands-on time:
5 minutes

Total preparation time:
5 minutes

MAKES ABOUT 1 1/3 CUPS

In the abstract, veal and tuna might not seem to be as natural a combination as, say, peanut butter and jelly. But a single mouthful of Italy's *vitello tonnato*—or veal with tuna sauce—and you're immediately struck by how brilliantly the bland poached veal and the tart tuna team up. In fact, the sauce is great on all sorts of food, including grilled chicken, any fish, leftover turkey, pork chops, sliced tomatoes and cucumbers, even grilled bread. The calorie-conscious can make this recipe using tuna packed in water, but tuna in oil has much more flavor.

1/2 cup low-fat mayonnaise
One 3-ounce can tuna, packed in oil, drained
2 tablespoons canned chicken broth or Chicken Stock (page 32)
1 tablespoon fresh lemon juice
1 tablespoon drained, bottled capers
Kosher salt and freshly milled black pepper

1. Combine the mayonnaise, tuna, broth, lemon juice, and capers in a blender and puree until very smooth. Add salt and pepper to taste.

2. Cover and refrigerate until ready to serve.

Horseradish Sauce

v

MAKES ABOUT 1 CUP

About 1/4 cup bottled
   horseradish
1/2 cup sour cream
1/4 cup mayonnaise
1/2 teaspoon dry mustard
Kosher salt and freshly milled
   black pepper

Horseradish, like mustard, is one of those condiments that can perk up just about any dish. I usually think of braised beef, but then pork of all kinds comes to mind, and even salmon. It seems to work well with fattier items. I have suggested it as a topping to the Potato Pancakes with Smoked Salmon and Fried Eggs (page 108) or as the dressing for Kielbasa and Celery Root Salad (page 77). It would also be the perfect accompaniment to Braised Short Ribs (page 279) or any beef stew.

1. Place the horseradish in a small strainer over a cup and press until the horseradish is quite dry. Measure and set aside 2 tablespoons drained horseradish and 2 tablespoons of the vinegar from the horseradish. Strain more if you don't have enough.

2. Whisk together the sour cream, mayonnaise, reserved horseradish and its vinegar, the mustard, and salt and pepper to taste.

3. Cover and refrigerate until ready to serve.

Mediterranean Salsa Verde

MAKES A SCANT 1 CUP

Think of this sauce as an intense parsley vinaigrette. It is perfect on a seared steak, but it would make you equally happy if it were drizzled over fish, chicken, or grilled vegetables. In this book it is featured on my Cauliflower "Steak" with Sautéed Peppers (page 224). By the way, the anchovies impart depth of flavor, not fishiness, but leave them out if you can't stand them.

1. Combine the parsley, scallions, capers, vinegar, lemon juice, anchovies, if using, mustard, and garlic in a food processor fitted with the chopping blade; process until the mixture is finely chopped.

2. With the motor running, gradually add the oil through the feed tube until the mixture thickens. Add salt and pepper to taste.

3. Cover and refrigerate until ready to serve. Stir before using.

1/2 cup packed rinsed and dried fresh flat-leaf parsley leaves
3 scallions (white and light green parts), cut into 1-inch pieces (about 1/3 cup)
2 tablespoons drained, bottled capers
1 tablespoon red wine vinegar
1 tablespoon fresh lemon juice
2 anchovies, rinsed and coarsely chopped, optional
2 teaspoons Dijon mustard
1 garlic clove, coarsely chopped (about 1 teaspoon)
1/2 cup extra virgin olive oil
Kosher salt and freshly milled black pepper

Mexican Tomatillo Salsa

V

MAKES A SCANT 1 CUP

3 fresh tomatillos, husked,
    rinsed, and quartered
4 scallions (white and light
    green parts), coarsely
    chopped (about 1/2 cup)
1/3 cup rinsed, dried and
    coarsely chopped cilantro
    (stems and all)
2 tablespoons vegetable oil
1 tablespoon fresh lime juice
1/2 jalapeño or 1 serrano chile,
    seeds removed, if desired
1 small garlic clove, minced
    (3/4 teaspoon)
Kosher salt and freshly milled
    black pepper

After you remove the papery husk of the Mexican tomatillo,
you're looking at a vegetable with a strong resemblance to a small
green tomato. It doesn't taste like a tomato, though. Rather, it has
a faintly lemony flavor, pleasingly sour, all its own. Tomatillos are
actually related to the cape gooseberry, not the tomato, and they
are native to Mexico. Tomatillos are a key ingredient in the
Mexican green salsa that is served with many dishes alongside red
(or tomato-based) salsa. I have specified Mexican Tomatillo Salsa
as the topping for Sautéed Soft-shell Crabs (page 210) and for the
Fried Eggs and "Refried" Beans Burritos (page 110), but it would
also be delicious with any grilled or sautéed fish or chicken.

1. Combine the tomatillos, scallions, cilantro, oil, lime juice, jalapeño, and
garlic in a food processor and pulse until the ingredients are almost
smooth with a few small chunks. Add salt and pepper to taste.

2. Cover and refrigerate until ready to serve.

Sautéed Cherry Tomato Sauce

V

Hands-on time:
10 minutes

Total preparation time:
30 minutes

MAKES ABOUT 4 CUPS

Tomatoes at their best are so good they make you glad to be alive. Unfortunately, unless it's the height of the season in late summer, a good full-sized tomato is hard to find. That's why I often reach for cherry tomatoes when I want to prepare a quick tomato sauce. They're just more reliable in terms of flavor and texture than the full-sized guys. Using cherry tomatoes in a sauce, however, means that unless you puree and strain it, the sauce will end up with a more "rustic" texture than one using full-sized tomatoes because the cherries produce a higher ratio of skin to pulp. That's not a problem for me. I like it rustic.

I recommend using this sauce as a topping for Ricotta Gnocchi (page 140), but you could put it on top of pizza or use it with any pasta dish that calls for tomato sauce.

*6 garlic cloves, peeled and
    sliced
1 medium onion, cut into 8
    pieces
1/4 cup extra virgin olive oil
3 pints cherry tomatoes (about
    14 ounces each), rinsed
Kosher salt and freshly milled
    black pepper*

1. Purée the garlic in a food processor fitted with the chopping blade. Add the onion and pulse 3 to 4 times, until finely chopped. Heat the oil in a large skillet over high heat until hot. Reduce the heat to medium; add the onion and garlic and cook, stirring occasionally, until they are softened, about 5 minutes.

2. Meanwhile, place 1 pint of the cherry tomatoes in the food processor bowl and pulse 3 to 4 times, until coarsely chopped. Transfer to a bowl and repeat with the remaining 2 pints of tomatoes. Add the chopped cherry tomatoes to the onion and simmer, stirring frequently, until they form a sauce, about 15 to 20 minutes. Add salt and pepper to taste and serve over Ricotta Gnocchi or other pasta.

Hands-on time:
5 minutes

Total preparation time:
5 minutes

Parsley Pesto

𝒱

MAKES 1 1/4 CUPS

3 cups packed rinsed and dried
fresh flat-leaf parsley sprigs
1/2 cup walnut pieces
1 ounce Parmigiano-Reggiano
cheese, coarsely grated
(about 1/3 cup; see grating
information, page 10)
2 garlic cloves, sliced (about 2
teaspoons)
1/3 cup extra virgin olive oil
Kosher salt and freshly milled
black pepper

This recipe has all the elements of traditional pesto with a couple of crucial substitutions—parsley instead of basil and walnuts instead of pine nuts. Still, it goes wherever a basil pesto would. Toss it with cooked spaghetti or linguine. Use it as a topping for roast chicken or for pizza, as a sauce for sautéed or grilled fish (Sautéed Scallops and Asparagus with Parsley Pesto, page 247), or as a filling for baked mushrooms (Giant Stuffed Mushrooms, page 218).

1. Combine the parsley, walnuts, cheese, and garlic in a food processor fitted with the chopping blade. Process until finely chopped. With the processor running, gradually add the oil. Add salt and pepper to taste.

2. Cover and refrigerate until ready to serve.

Tangy Barbecue Sauce

V

MAKES ABOUT 3 CUPS

Hands-on time:
10 minutes

Total preparation time:
20 minutes

Apparently almost everyone who's ever eaten barbecue has invented his or her own customized barbecue sauce. I know because I read through dozens and dozens of these recipes before I invented my own. This one is much less sweet than the usual, so feel free to add more sugar or maple syrup. Likewise, add more cayenne if you want more heat. I use this sauce with Brisket Braised in Barbecue Sauce (page 284) and Barbecued Kielbasa (page 170), but it is fairly all-purpose. It creates a finger-licking glaze if you brush it onto chicken, pork chops, or ribs when they're almost done grilling.

2 cups ketchup (24-ounce bottle)
1/4 cup dark brown sugar
1/4 cup plus 2 tablespoons cider vinegar
1/2 small onion, very finely chopped (about 1/4 cup)
1/4 cup Worcestershire sauce
1/4 cup Dijon mustard
1/4 cup Grade B maple syrup
2 teaspoons chili powder
2 teaspoons hot sauce, or to taste
2 teaspoons dry mustard
2 garlic cloves, minced (about 2 teaspoons)
1/2 teaspoon cayenne pepper
Kosher salt and freshly milled black pepper

1. Whisk together the ketchup, brown sugar, vinegar, onion, Worcestershire sauce, Dijon mustard, maple syrup, chili powder, hot sauce, dry mustard, garlic, and cayenne in a medium saucepan. Bring to a boil over high heat; reduce the heat to low and simmer, stirring occasionally, for 8 minutes. Add salt and pepper to taste.

2. Cover and refrigerate until ready to use.

Harissa

V

MAKES ABOUT 1 CUP

Hands-on time:
5 minutes

Total preparation time:
5 minutes

One 12-ounce jar roasted red peppers in water, well drained, or two Roasted Peppers (page 30, add prep time)
1 tablespoon extra virgin olive oil
2 garlic cloves, minced (about 2 teaspoons)
1 teaspoon cumin seed
1/2 teaspoon coriander seed
1/2 teaspoon caraway seed
1/2 teaspoon red pepper flakes
Kosher salt and freshly milled black pepper

Harissa is Tunisian chili paste that is used as a condiment, most often with couscous dishes. It will improve any dish that needs a little heat, such as the Moroccan Vegetable Stew (page 236). It would also perk up a thick fish soup or dried bean dish, or add a refreshing flash of fire to grilled meat, fish, or poultry.

1. Combine the peppers, oil, garlic, cumin, coriander, caraway, and pepper flakes in a blender or food processor fitted with a chopping blade; puree until smooth. Add salt and black pepper to taste.

2. Cover and refrigerate until ready to serve.

Sesame Miso Sauce

V

MAKES ABOUT 1 CUP

Hands-on time:
10 minutes

Total preparation time:
10 minutes

Miso is fermented soybean paste, it has great depth of flavor and creaminess of texture. Flavored with rice vinegar, ginger, and sesame, it makes a wonderful sauce for any mild protein that needs a flavor partner, such as Soba Noodle and Chicken Salad (page 74). It is also a great accompaniment to vegetable dishes such as Grilled Shiitake, Sweet Potato, and Eggplant Kabobs (page 220).

1. Combine 3 tablespoons water with the vegetable oil, vinegar, miso, ginger, tahini, and wine in a blender and blend until smooth.

2. Cover and refrigerate until ready to serve. May be kept for up to 5 days; shake before using.

3 tablespoons vegetable oil
2 tablespoons seasoned rice wine vinegar
2 tablespoons white or red miso
2 tablespoons finely grated fresh ginger (use a Microplane)
1 1/2 tablespoons well-stirred tahini or 2 teaspoons toasted sesame oil
1 tablespoon rice wine or dry sherry

MISO, also known as bean paste, is a staple of Japanese cuisine made from salted and fermented soybeans and a grain, usually rice or barley. It has a creamy consistency, much like peanut butter, and comes in a wide variety of flavors and colors. The lighter-colored versions are used in more delicate soups and sauces, and the darker-colored varieties give body and flavor to heavier dishes. You can find it packaged in tubs, jars, and tubes in Asian stores and increasingly at the supermarket. It will keep for several months in the fridge. For years I experienced miso only in Japanese restaurants in the ubiquitous miso soup, but now it has become a staple in my pantry.

WHAT
IS
MISO?

Tahini Sauce

Hands-on time:
10 minutes

Total preparation time:
10 minutes

V

MAKES ABOUT 2/3 CUP

*1/4 cup well-stirred tahini
paste*
1/4 cup vegetable oil
1 tablespoon fresh lemon juice
*1 garlic clove, minced (about
1 teaspoon)*
*2 tablespoons rinsed, dried,
and chopped fresh flat-leaf
parsley*
*Kosher salt and freshly milled
black pepper*

The Middle Eastern equivalent of American peanut butter, tahini paste, made from ground sesame seeds, has been widely available on our shores only for the last ten years or so. I love it. In this book, I've paired it with a familiar partner, Sautéed Falafel (page 232). However, this sauce is also great with grilled fish, fowl, or lamb shish kabob. And it's wonderful tossed with noodles or used as a dipping sauce with crudités.

1. Whisk together the tahini paste, oil, 3 tablespoons water, the lemon juice, and garlic. Stir in the parsley and salt and pepper to taste.

2. Cover and refrigerate until ready to serve.

Peanut Sauce

V

Hands-on time:
10 minutes

Total preparation time:
10 minutes

MAKES ABOUT 1 1/2 CUPS

Many years ago I hired my friend Rosa Ross, a cooking teacher and author who specializes in Chinese cuisine, to teach me some recipes for a Chinese New Year's party we were throwing at *Gourmet.* One of the recipes was Summer Rolls with Peanut Dipping Sauce. The dipping sauce was completely addictive and is still my favorite after all these years. Here is my adapted version. It is the perfect accompaniment to Ramen Noodles and Asian Vegetables (page 256). It would also make a nice sauce for skewered chicken, pork, or vegetables or even sautéed shrimp. Or you can toss it with linguine, shredded cooked chicken (rotisserie chicken would work well here), and defrosted frozen peas.

1/2 cup smooth unsalted peanut butter
1/2 cup hoisin sauce
2 scallions (white and light green parts), coarsely chopped (about 1/4 cup)
1 1/2 tablespoons fresh lime juice
1 tablespoon soy sauce
2 teaspoons finely grated fresh ginger (use a Microplane)
Hot pepper sauce

1. Combine the peanut butter, hoisin sauce, scallions, lime juice, 1/4 cup water, the soy sauce, ginger, and hot sauce to taste in a food processor and puree until smooth. Add additional water, if necessary, to thin the sauce to a pourable consistency.

2. Cover and refrigerate until ready to serve.

Easy
Desserts

Hands-on time:
10 minutes

Total preparation time:
15 minutes
plus freezing time

Eight packaged 3-inch round
chocolate chunk brownie
cookies or four 3-inch
square brownies
1 cup raspberry sorbet
1/3 cup dried egg whites (see
Note)
1 teaspoon vanilla extract
1/4 teaspoon table salt
1/2 cup sugar

Baked Alaskan

𝒱

MAKES 4 SERVINGS

Everybody knows baked Alaska, but Baked *Alaskan?* What can I say—this is a shout-out to Ad-Rock of the Beastie Boys, who saluted *Sara's Secrets* in the liner notes to *To the 5 Boroughs,* the Beasties' 2004 album. In the middle of a song called "Rhyme the Rhyme Well," Ad-Rock goes searching for a rhyme for "Yo, what's crackin'" . . . and comes up with "Serving emcees on a platter like Baked Alaskan." And he's absolutely right. Baked Alaska, that famously mind-boggling confection of flaming ice cream and cake, is always delivered to your table on a platter.

Pyrotechnics aside, baked Alaska happens to be delicious. But it is not the sort of thing you would make at home and certainly not on a weeknight. Here's a quick version of a *Gourmet* recipe for individual baked Alaskas that makes big use of one of my favorite flavor combos—chocolate and raspberry. You can set up the frozen ice cream sandwiches days ahead of time (as long as they are well wrapped), and then whip up the egg whites and sugar at the last minute. After you have frosted the sandwiches, stick them in the oven and count the minutes (there are only six) until you're digging into a most delectable dessert.

1. Assemble the ice cream–filled cookies. Place 4 cookies upside down on a work surface, or split the brownies and place the bottoms, cut side up, on a work surface. Spoon 1/4 cup sorbet on each cookie and spread to the edge. Top with another cookie or the brownie top right-side up. Wrap and freeze just until the ice cream is hard, about 25 minutes. If making ahead, set out at room temperature for 10 minutes before frosting and baking.

2. Just before serving, preheat the oven to 450°F. Combine 3/4 cup plus 2 tablespoons warm water, the egg whites, vanilla, and salt. Beat with an electric mixer until frothy. Gradually beat in the sugar until soft peaks form when the beaters are raised, 3 to 4 minutes.

3. Remove the filled cookies from the freezer and place 3 inches apart on an oiled rimmed baking sheet. Frost each with some of the beaten egg whites. Bake in the center of the oven for 6 minutes or until nicely browned. Serve immediately.

Note: I recommend using dried egg whites such as Just Whites because the egg whites in this recipe are not heated enough to eliminate the risk of salmonella.

Chocolate Fondue

𝒱

MAKES 4 SERVINGS

2/3 cup heavy cream

6 ounces bittersweet
chocolate, coarsely chopped

4 teaspoons fruit-flavored
liqueur such as
Kirschwasser, Grand
Marnier, Poire William, or
vanilla extract, optional

About 24 dipping items such
as cherries, strawberries, or
bite-size pieces of
pineapple, apple, banana,
pound cake, angel food
cake, Rice Krispies treats, or
small cookies

Wasn't it the Smothers Brothers who sang about falling into a vat of chocolate? Dreamy, right? Well, short of total immersion, there is always chocolate fondue, which is simply a fondue pot full of warm melted chocolate into which you can dip whatever tickles your fancy. In fact, this recipe doesn't even require an official fondue pot. Just keep the sauce in a metal bowl set over a saucepan of hot water and set the saucepan on a trivet in the center of the table. Or you can transfer the chocolate to four individual ramekins, which allows everyone to have a personal chocolate fondue. Theoretically, the ramekin crew would have to eat extra quickly because the chocolate cools off and hardens faster in smaller portions—but no one's ever lingered over it long enough to know for sure.

1. Heat the cream in a small saucepan over low heat until bubbles begin to form at the edge. Remove the pan from the heat and add the chocolate. Let stand 2 to 3 minutes or until the chocolate has melted and then stir until combined. Stir in the liqueur, if using. Transfer to a fondue pot and keep warm.

2. Serve with fresh fruit and other dipping items of your choice.

Chocolate Bread Pudding

Hands-on time:
20 minutes

Total preparation time:
70 minutes

V

MAKES 6 SERVINGS

I've never met a bread pudding I didn't like. In the interest of keeping this version simple, I used bottled chocolate milk and packaged bread when I first started to test it. The bread worked out fine, but none of the milks was chocolatey enough. Switching gears, I resorted to ganache. A pillar of classical French baking composed of melted chocolate and cream, it is usually employed as the base of truffles, cake frosting, and anything else that requires the essence of chocolate. For this recipe I lightened up the ganache a bit by replacing the cream with milk, but it still makes my bread pudding as deeply chocolatey as I wanted it to be.

3 cups milk
8 ounces bittersweet chocolate, coarsely chopped
One 13- to 14-inch loaf soft-crust supermarket Italian bread, cut into small cubes
3 large eggs
3/4 cup sugar
2 teaspoons vanilla extract
1/4 teaspoon table salt
Sweetened whipped cream or ice cream, optional

1. Heat 1 cup milk in a small saucepan over low heat until bubbles begin to form at the edge. Remove the pan from the heat and add the chocolate. Let stand 2 to 3 minutes or until the chocolate has melted; stir to combine.

2. Arrange the bread cubes in a buttered 9 × 13-inch glass baking dish. Whisk the eggs in a medium bowl until frothy; whisk in the remaining 2 cups milk, the sugar, vanilla, and salt until combined; stir in the chocolate mixture. Reserve 1 cup of the mixture; pour the rest evenly over the bread. Set aside, covered, for 30 minutes.

3. Preheat the oven to 425°F. Uncover the baking dish and pour the reserved chocolate mixture evenly over the bread. Bake in the center of the oven until the bread has puffed and is set throughout, about 20 minutes. Serve with whipped cream or ice cream, if desired.

Berry Rice Pudding

V

MAKES ABOUT 6 SERVINGS

1 1/2 cups cooked leftover
long-grain white rice or
Simple Boiled Rice (page 40)
1/2 cup ginger marmalade
1/2 cup heavy cream
2 teaspoons vanilla extract
1 pint blueberries, rinsed and
dried
1 pint raspberries, rinsed and
dried

I love rice pudding, as does the husband, but I am certainly not going to make it from scratch on a weeknight. However, there is a good chance you have leftover rice every so often from a take-out meal, and this would be a very tasty way to recycle it.

1. Combine the rice, marmalade, 2 tablespoons of the cream, and the vanilla in a large bowl. Beat the remaining cream in a small bowl with an electric beater until soft peaks form. Stir the whipped cream into the rice mixture.

2. Reserve 8 large blueberries and 8 large raspberries. Gently stir the remaining berries into the rice mixture and transfer to a serving bowl. Garnish with the reserved berries and serve or cover and refrigerate until ready to serve.

Blueberry Yogurt Pie

V

MAKES 6 SERVINGS

When Joanne came up with the idea for this recipe, I was worried because yogurt is so watery and so tart. I just didn't see how we were going to get the right texture or flavor. Then Joanne reminded me about Greek yogurt, which is much thicker and richer than the regular varieties and more readily available at the supermarket than it used to be. Wow, what a delicious ingredient! It was such a great partner to the blueberries that this pie turned out to be one of my favorite desserts.

1. Stir the gelatin into 3 tablespoons water in a small saucepan and set aside 5 minutes to soften. Heat over very low heat, stirring constantly, just until the gelatin has dissolved. Whisk the gelatin mixture into 1/4 cup of the cream in a small bowl. Combine the yogurt, sugar, and vanilla in a large bowl. Gradually whisk in the gelatin mixture. Refrigerate until ready to assemble the filling, about 5 minutes.

2. Beat the remaining 3/4 cup cream in a small bowl with an electric beater until stiff peaks form. Fold the whipped cream and 1 3/4 cups of the berries into the chilled yogurt mixture. Spoon the mixture into the pie shell, mounding in the center. Sprinkle the remaining 1/4 cup blueberries over the top, and refrigerate at least 30 minutes before serving.

Hands-on time:
15 minutes

Total preparation time:
15 minutes
plus chilling time

1 envelope unflavored gelatin
1 cup heavy cream
2 cups plain whole-milk Greek yogurt or drained regular plain whole-milk yogurt (see Note, page 97)
1/2 cup sugar
1 teaspoon vanilla extract
1 pint blueberries
One 6-ounce prepared vanilla wafer or graham cracker crumb crust

*M*angos
with Coconut Rum Sauce

V

MAKES 4 SERVINGS

2 ripe mangos
1 cup unsweetened coconut
 milk
1 1/2 teaspoons grated lime
 zest
2 to 3 tablespoons lime juice
3 tablespoons dark rum,
 optional
2 tablespoons sugar
1 1/2 teaspoons vanilla extract
4 lime slices, optional

Coconut milk is one of the flavors that defines the cuisines of Thailand and South India, but almost always in savory dishes. Here it stars in a dessert, an idea so obvious in retrospect that Joanne and I were slapping our foreheads and wondering why we hadn't thought of it before. Coconut milk is super creamy and delicious all by itself and as close as your local supermarket. We simply added flavoring—lime, rum, vanilla, and sugar—and it was ready to go. It is the perfect sauce for fresh-cut fruit or any kind of berry.

1. On a cutting board, hold mangos with one of the narrower sides facing up. Keeping in mind that the large flat oval pit follows the outside shape of the fruit, start 1/4-inch to the side of the stem and slice along each side of the pit to cut off the "cheeks." Peel the mango "cheeks" and arrange them in a 9-inch shallow baking dish or quiche dish, leaving a space in the center. Slice each "cheek" crosswise to make 5 pieces. Peel and trim off the bands of fruit around the mango seeds. Coarsely chop the fruit and mound it in the center of the dish.

2. Meanwhile, whisk together the coconut milk, lime zest, lime juice to taste, rum, if using, the sugar, and vanilla; pour a little into the open spaces between the mangos. Garnish the mangos with lime slices, if desired, and serve with the remaining sauce.

Pineapple Flambé

V

MAKES 4 SERVINGS

For many home cooks the prospect of tackling a pineapple is about as inviting as tackling an armadillo. Luckily, we live in the twenty-first century, where getting your hands on a pineapple that's already been peeled, cored, and cut into rings is as easy as strolling into your local supermarket.

1. Combine the sour cream, ginger, and sugar in a small bowl. Transfer the ginger cream to a serving bowl and refrigerate, covered, until ready to serve.

2. Melt 1 tablespoon of the butter in a large skillet over medium heat. Add half the pineapple and brown the slices on both sides. Transfer pineapple to a plate and set aside; repeat with remaining butter and pineapple slices.

3. Return the reserved pineapple to the skillet; sprinkle with brown sugar and cook, turning the slices once, just until the sugar melts, 2 to 3 minutes. Add the brandy and heat until vapors rise from the pan. Ignite the brandy by carefully holding a lighted match near the edge of the pan. Stir until the flames have gone out.

4. Arrange the pineapple and brandy mixture on 4 heatproof dessert plates and serve with the ginger cream.

Hands-on time:
15 minutes

Total preparation time:
15 minutes

3/4 cup sour cream
3 tablespoons finely chopped crystallized ginger
1 teaspoon sugar
2 tablespoons unsalted butter
1 peeled, cored fresh pineapple (8 slices)
1/4 cup packed light brown sugar
1/4 cup brandy

$\mathcal{S}$*tuffed Strawberries*

$\mathcal{V}$

MAKES 4 SERVINGS

*8 large strawberries (about
1 pound)*

*2 ounces low-fat cream cheese
(about 1/4 cup), softened*

1 teaspoon sugar

*3/4 ounce bittersweet or
semisweet chocolate, finely
chopped*

*2 tablespoons chopped
candied orange zest*

I'm a big fan of the wonderful Italian pastry called cannoli—especially the filling of fresh ricotta, candied zest, and chocolate. My dessert swaps the cannoli's crunchy cylinder of deep-fried dough for a large succulent strawberry. I've also replaced the ricotta in the filling with low-fat cream cheese, because ricotta is too wet for this recipe. (You can use full-fat cream cheese if you want, but I think the low-fat is actually quite satisfying, and who needs the extra calories?) The creamy filling and chocolate chunks are a great counterpoint to the tart strawberries.

1. Cut each strawberry in half lengthwise through the cap. Arrange the strawberry halves, cut side up, on a serving plate. Trim a thin slice from the bottom if necessary to make each half sit evenly. Using a small spoon or melon baller, scoop out a hollow in the center of the cut side of each strawberry. Reserve the strawberry scraps for another use (or eat them).

2. Combine the cream cheese and sugar in a small bowl; stir in the chocolate and orange zest. Divide the cream cheese mixture among the hollows in the strawberries and serve or refrigerate, covered, for up to 1 hour.

Quick Grape Crumble

V

MAKES 4 SERVINGS

Hands-on time:
20 minutes

Total preparation time:
40 minutes

Most people don't know it, but cooked grapes are delicious. The process tames the grapes' acidity and intensifies their sweetness. That's why I decided to put them into this baked dessert with a crispy topping of sweetened oats and almonds. It took my family by surprise, particularly my sweetaholic daughter Ruth, who had never before considered the grape dessert-worthy.

1. Preheat the oven to 375°F. Combine the grapes, jelly, and port wine in a saucepan. Cook over medium heat, stirring occasionally until the grapes burst, about 10 minutes. Whisk together the cornstarch, lemon juice, and 1 tablespoon water. Add the mixture to the grapes and cook, stirring constantly, until the grape filling boils and thickens. Transfer the filling to a shallow 1-quart baking dish or 8-inch round pan.

2. Meanwhile, prepare the topping. In a mini food processor or blender, pulse the flour, brown sugar, cinnamon, and salt once or twice to combine. Add the butter and pulse 2 to 3 times just until coarse crumbs form. Stir in the oats and almonds and sprinkle the mixture evenly over the grape filling. Bake in the center of the oven for 20 to 25 minutes, until the crust is golden.

2 cups seedless red or green grapes or a mix
1/4 cup red currant jelly
2 tablespoons port wine, white grape juice, or water
1 tablespoon cornstarch
1 tablespoon fresh lemon juice
1/4 cup unbleached all-purpose flour
1 tablespoon packed light brown sugar
1/2 teaspoon ground cinnamon
1/4 teaspoon table salt
6 tablespoons cold unsalted butter, cut into pieces
1/2 cup rolled oats
1/2 cup sliced or slivered almonds

Gingerbread Pancakes
with Butterscotch Apples

V

MAKES 4 SERVINGS

2 tablespoons unsalted butter

2 large Golden Delicious apples (about 1 pound), peeled and sliced

1/4 cup packed light brown sugar

1 tablespoon fresh lemon juice

1 1/4 teaspoons ground cinnamon

1/2 teaspoon table salt

1 1/2 teaspoons vanilla extract

3/4 cup unbleached all-purpose flour

1/4 cup granulated sugar

1 1/2 tablespoons ground ginger

1/2 teaspoon baking powder

1 large egg

3 tablespoons molasses

3 tablespoons vegetable oil, plus more for cooking the pancakes

If it makes sense sometimes to eat breakfast for dinner, why not breakfast for dessert? These pancakes are perfect for the fall, when apples are in season and gingerbread spices are on the mind. My apple of choice is the Golden Delicious because when cooked, it becomes honeyed and intense, but you can use any apple that holds its shape. Don't try this with McIntosh; they disintegrate into mush.

1. Preheat the oven to 200°F. Melt the butter in a large skillet over medium heat. Add the apples and cook, stirring occasionally, until tender, about 10 minutes. Stir in the brown sugar, 2 tablespoons water, the lemon juice, 1/4 teaspoon cinnamon, and 1/4 teaspoon salt. Cook until the mixture bubbles. Remove from the heat and stir in the vanilla; transfer to a serving dish and set aside.

2. Meanwhile, in a small bowl stir together the flour, granulated sugar, ginger, remaining 1 teaspoon cinnamon, the baking powder, and remaining 1/4 teaspoon salt in a small bowl. Combine 1/4 cup water, the egg, molasses, and 3 tablespoons oil in a glass measuring cup; add to the flour mixture and stir with a fork until the mixture is just combined but not smooth. Add additional water if necessary to reach the consistency of pancake batter.

3. Brush a nonstick skillet with a little oil; heat over medium-low heat. Add the gingerbread mixture to the skillet a generous tablespoonful at a time and spread to make a 2 1/2-inch round; cook until lightly browned, about 3 minutes. Turn and brown on the other side, 3 to 4 minutes. Repeat until all the batter has been used. Keep the pancakes warm in the oven until all have been cooked.

4. To serve, divide the pancakes among 4 dessert plates and top each serving with some of the apples.

Basic Yellow Cake

v

MAKES 6 TO 8 SERVINGS

3/4 cup sugar
6 tablespoons unsalted butter,
softened
2 large eggs
1 tablespoon vanilla extract
1 1/2 cups self-rising cake flour
(see sidebar)
1/2 cup milk

What an exciting idea to be able to whip up a cake from scratch on a weeknight in only ten minutes. You just need a food processor and six very simple ingredients that you probably already have on hand. You can eat the cake as is or accompanied by berries tossed with a little sugar. Or, sprinkle some chocolate chips on top of the cake right when it comes out of the oven, let them melt, and then spread them over the cake for a quick frosting.

1. Preheat the oven to 350°F. Grease an 8-inch round cake pan.

2. Combine the sugar and butter in the bowl of a food processor fitted with a chopping blade. Process until fluffy, about 1 minute. Add the eggs and vanilla and process until combined. Add the flour and milk; pulse once or twice, just until the flour is moistened. The mixture doesn't have to be smooth.

3. Transfer the batter to the baking pan and bake in the upper third of the oven until the center springs back when gently pressed, about 35 minutes. Cool on a rack in the pan for 5 minutes, then cut into wedges and serve warm or invert onto a rack to cool completely.

IF YOU don't have self-rising cake flour, you can make your own by adding 1 1/4 teaspoons baking powder and 1/4 teaspoon salt for every cup of cake flour. If you don't have cake flour, you can substitute all-purpose flour by removing 2 tablespoons from each cup of unsifted all-purpose flour. If you have cornstarch, replacing the 2 tablespoons all-purpose flour removed from each cup with 2 tablespoons cornstarch will improve the texture of your cake but is not essential.

HOW TO MAKE YOUR OWN SELF-RISING CAKE FLOUR

Nectarine and Plum Upside-down Cake

V

MAKES 9 SERVINGS

Hands-on time:
15 minutes

Total preparation time:
55 minutes

This is a variation of the basic yellow cake. It takes a little longer because you have to slice and arrange the fruit, but it is really worth it. You could use all nectarines, all plums, or throw peaches into the mix.

8 tablespoons (1 stick) unsalted butter, softened

3 tablespoons light brown sugar

1 tablespoon plus 1 teaspoon vanilla extract

2 medium nectarines, each cut into 8 slices

2 large plums, each cut into 8 slices

2/3 cup granulated sugar

2 large eggs

1 1/2 cups cake flour

2 teaspoons ground cinnamon

1 3/4 teaspoons baking powder

1/2 teaspoon table salt

1/4 teaspoon ground nutmeg

1/4 cup milk

1. Preheat the oven to 350°F. Combine 2 tablespoons of the softened butter, the brown sugar, and 1 teaspoon vanilla in a small bowl. Lightly grease the sides of an 8-inch square cake pan; spread the brown sugar mixture evenly over the bottom of the pan. Arrange the nectarine and plum slices in alternating rows over the brown sugar mixture.

2. Combine the granulated sugar and the remaining 6 tablespoons butter in the bowl of a food processor fitted with a chopping blade. Process until fluffy, about 1 minute. Add the eggs and 1 tablespoon vanilla and process until combined. Add the flour mixed with the cinnamon, baking powder, salt, and nutmeg; pour the milk over all. Pulse once or twice, just until the flour is moistened. The batter doesn't have to be smooth.

3. Spoon the batter evenly over the fruit in the pan and bake until the center springs back when gently pressed, about 40 minutes. Cool on a rack in the pan for 5 minutes, then loosen the edges and invert onto a serving plate. Cut into squares and serve warm.

Pecan Pie Squares

Hands-on time:
10 minutes

Total preparation time:
30 minutes
plus 10 minutes
cooling time

16 to 18 graham crackers
(2 1/4 x 2 1/2 inches)
1 cup packed light brown
sugar
2 large eggs
1/2 cup light corn syrup
2 tablespoons unsalted butter,
melted
2 teaspoons vanilla extract
1/2 teaspoon table salt
8 ounces pecan halves (about
2 cups)

V

MAKES 12 SERVINGS

Looking to develop a recipe that would satisfy her sweet tooth on a weeknight, Joanne took all the elements of traditional pecan pie and worked them into this mini version. It is every bit as delicious as the pull-out-all-the-stops original, but takes only forty minutes to make—including just ten minutes of hands-on time. If you really want to splurge, top it with some vanilla ice cream.

1. Preheat the oven to 375°F. Line a 9 × 13-inch baking pan with aluminum foil; very generously grease the foil. Arrange the graham crackers in the pan, crumbling some to fill in any spaces.

2. Whisk together the brown sugar, eggs, corn syrup, butter, vanilla, and salt in a medium bowl; stir in the pecans and pour the mixture over the graham crackers. Bake until the filling is set in the center, about 20 minutes.

3. Set the pan on a wire rack to cool for 10 minutes before cutting into 12 squares. Serve warm or at room temperature. Store any remaining squares in the refrigerator and warm slightly before serving.

Rocky Road Bars

ᴠ

MAKES 12 BARS OR 16 SQUARES

Here are all the elements of rocky road candy—chocolate, nuts, marshmallows—in a cookie. You can custom design it by varying your choice of nuts and chocolate. I would opt for cashews, peanuts, or almonds with dark bittersweet chocolate such as Valrhona or Scharffen Berger. You just have to plan ahead, since it takes about an hour to set up in the fridge. You could make them in the morning before going to work and then—what a happy thing—you would have dessert all ready for you after dinner.

1. Melt the chocolate in the top of a double boiler or a bowl placed over hot water. Stir in the nuts and marshmallows.

2. Arrange the cookies on a small cookie sheet. Divide the chocolate mixture among the cookies, spreading to the edges. Refrigerate, uncovered, until firm, about 1 hour.

Hands-on time:
15 minutes

Total preparation time:
15 minutes
plus 1 hour
chilling time

One 3-ounce bar bittersweet or semisweet chocolate, coarsely chopped
1 cup unsalted mixed nuts
1/2 cup miniature marshmallows or regular marshmallows, each cut into 8 pieces
12 rectangular (2 x 1 1/2- inch) butter cookies or 16 square shortbread cookies

Sources

Adriana's Caravan
321 Grand Central Terminal
New York, NY 10017
http://www.adrianascaravan.com
800–316–0820

Crystallized ginger, dried porcini mushrooms, garam masala (salt free), herbes de Provence, miso, paprika (hot, sweet, and smoked), pearl couscous, piquillo peppers, rice vinegar, saffron, sherry vinegar, soba noodles, tahini, truffle oil, Turkish bay leaves

Broadway Panhandler
477 Broome Street (at Wooster)
New York, NY 10013
866–COOKWARE (266–5927)
http://www.broadwaypanhandler.com

Microplanes and other kitchen equipment

Browne Trading Company
Merrill's Wharf
262 Commercial Street
Portland, ME 04101
http://www.browne-trading.com
800–944–7848, 207–775–7560

Smoked salmon, smoked trout, salt cod

Bryant Preserving Company
PO Box 367
Alma, AR 72921
800–634–2413
fax 479–632–2505
http://www.bryantpreserving.com

Pickled okra and other condiments

Complements to the Chef
374 Merrimon Avenue
Asheville, NC 28801
828–258–0558
800–895–CHEF
http://www.complementstothechef.com

Microplanes and other kitchen equipment

D'Artagnan
280 Wilson Avenue
Newark, NJ 07105
http://www.dartagnan.com
800-327–8246, Ext. 0

Duck breasts, duck confit, organic poultry

Durham's Tracklements
212 East Kingsley Street
Kerrytown, Ann Arbor, MI
http://www.tracklements.com
800–844–7853

Smoked salmon and trout

Ethnic Grocer
695 Lunt Avenue
Elk Grove, IL 60007
http://www.ethnicgrocer.com
312–373–1777

Panko bread crumbs, polenta, saffron, soba noodles, toasted sesame oil, tahini, wasabi powder, wasabi peas

Jamison Farms
171 Jamison Lane
Latrobe, PA 15650
http://www.jamisonfarms.com
800–237–5262

Natural lamb

Kenyon's Grist Mill
Usquepaugh
West Kingston, RI 02892
http://www.kenyonsgristmill.com
401–783–4054

Stone-ground cornmeal and Johnny Cake meal

Mexgrocer
PO Box 2888
La Jolla, CA 92038
http://www.mexgrocer.com
877–463–9476

Chipotles in adobo sauce

Niman Ranch
1025 East 12th Street
Oakland, CA 94606
http://www.nimanranch.com
510–808–0340

Natural beef, pork, and lamb

Pasta and Co.
104 Pike Street, Suite 200
Seattle, WA 98101
http://www.pastaco.com
800–943–6362

Radiatore, pearl couscous

Penzey's Spices
19300 West Janacek Court
Brookfield, WI 53008
http://www.penzeys.com
800–741–7787

Herbes de Provence, paprika (hot, sweet, and smoked), Turkish bay leaves, star anise

Peppers
Rehoboth Outlets #3
1815 Ocean Outlets
Rehoboth, DE 19971
http://www.peppers.com
302–227–4608

Hot sauces, ground pure chile powders, salsas, salad dressings, barbecue sauces, spice rubs

The Kitchen Market
218 Eighth Avenue
New York, NY 10011
http://www.kitchenmarket.com
888–468–4433

Coconut milk, crystallized ginger, fish sauce, ground pure chile powders, panko bread crumbs, toasted sesame oil, wasabi

The Spanish Table
1427 Western Avenue
Seattle, WA 98101
http://www.tablespan.com
206–682–2827

Chorizo, saffron, sherry vinegar, paprika (sweet, hot, smoked)

The Spice House
1031 North Old World Third Street
Milwaukee, WI 53203
http://www.thespicehouse.com
414–272–0977, 847–328–3711

Paprika (sweet, hot, smoked), saffron, star anise, tahini, wasabi powder

Tienda
4514 John Tyler Highway
Williamsburg, VA 23188
http://www.tienda.com
888–472–1022

Chorizo, paprika (sweet, hot, smoked), saffron, piquillo peppers

Uwajimaya
600 5th Avenue South, Suite 100
Seattle, WA 98104
http://www.uwajimaya.com
206–624–6248

Panko, rice vinegar, wasabi

Vermont Maple Sugar Makers
  Association
Vermont Agency of Agriculture,
  Food & Markets
116 State Street, Drawer 20
Montpelier, VT 05620
802–828–3461
http://www.VTmaple.org

A guide to Vermont maple syrup producers who sell by mail; look for grade B

Zingerman's
422 Detroit Street
Ann Arbor, MI 48104
http://www.zingermans.com
888–636–8162 (mail order),
734–663–DELI (store)

Chorizo, garam masala (salt free), salami, smoked fish, varietal vinegars

Index

Middle Eastern Pizza, 188–89
Todd's Keema Matar, 184–85
Lasagna
Quick Asparagus Lasagna, 126–27
Roasted Red Pepper and Prosciutto
Lasagna, 128
Leeks
Crispy Polenta Slices with Gorgonzola
and Leeks, 240
Smashed Potato, Leek, and Cabbage
Soup with Corned Beef, 53
Lemon
Baked Whole Fish with Rosemary,
Olive Oil, and Lemon, 193–94
Lemon Chicken, 149
Seared Scallops with Shredded
Zucchini and Lemon Cream, 213
Lentil
Sausage, Lentil, and Spinach Stew, 173
Linguine with White Bean, Sun-dried
Tomato, and Olive Sauce, 260

Macaroni and Cheese, Bette's, 125
Mangos with Coconut Rum Sauce, 334
Marshmallow
Rocky Road Bars, 345
Matzo Brie with Creamed Spinach and
Crispy Onions, 113
Meat, 168–89. *See also* Beef; Ham; Lamb;
Meatballs; Pork; Sausage; Veal
how to remove fat, 289
Middle Eastern Pizza, 188–89
slicing meat thin, 61
Todd's Keema Matar, 184–85
Meatballs
Escarole and White Bean Soup with
Large Meatballs, 58
Middle Eastern Meatball Sandwiches
with Cucumber Yogurt Sauce,
97
Meatless Moussaka, 245
Meatloaf Burgers, 181
Mediterranean Orzo Pilaf, 307
Mediterranean Salsa Verde, 317
Mesclun
Smoked Chicken or Turkey Salad,
71
Turkey Cutlets Milanese, 160–61
Mexican Chicken Salad, 70
Mexican Tomatillo Salsa, 318
Middle Eastern Meatball Sandwiches
with Cucumber Yogurt Sauce, 97

Middle Eastern Pizza, 188–89
Mint
Chilled Pea Soup with Mint, Curried
Shrimp, and Peanuts, 46–47
Thai-style Steak Salad with Spicy
Mint Dressing, 80
Miso
about, 323
Sesame Miso Sauce, 323
Monterey Jack cheese
Eggs Baked in Ham with Sofrito,
104
Moroccan Vegetable Stew, 236
Moussaka, Meatless, 245
Mozzarella cheese
Baked Eggplant, Tomato, and Feta
Stacks, 221
French-toasted Mozzarella and
Prosciutto Sandwiches, 90
Roasted Red Pepper and Prosciutto
Lasagna, 128
Muenster cheese
Giant Stuffed Mushrooms, 218–19
Mushrooms
Det Burgers, 179–80
Green Bean Casserole Moderne,
230–31
Exotic Mushroom Pot Pie, 216–17
Giant Stuffed Mushrooms, 218–19
Grilled Shiitake, Sweet Potato, and
Eggplant Kabobs, 220
Mushroom Strata, 111
Porcini Mushroom Sauce, 263
portobello gills, removing, 219
Mussels
cultivated or wild, 209
Pearl Couscous and Shellfish Stew,
138–39
Steamed Mussels in Curried Coconut
Broth, 208
Mustard-chutney Roasted Chicken
Thighs, 157

Nacho Pie, 246
Napa cabbage
Asian Turkey Burgers with Wasabi
Sauce, 164
Korean-style Beef with Spicy
Cabbage, 176–77
Nectarine and Plum Upside-down Cake,
343
Niçoise Salad, Shrimp, 66–67

Nuts. *See also* Pecans; Walnuts
primer for, 89
roasting, 89
Rocky Road Bars, 345

Olives
Grilled Lamb with Onion Kabobs
with Olive Aioli, 186
Linguine with White Bean, Sun-dried
Tomato, and Olive Sauce, 260
Onions
Charred Onions and Peppers, 297
Grilled Lamb with Onion Kabobs
with Olive Aioli, 186
Italian-style Onion Soup with a
Poached Egg and Parmigiano-
Reggiano Cheese, 44–45
Matzo Brie with Creamed Spinach
and Crispy Onions, 113
Oranges
how to peel and slice and orange, 304
Radish and Orange Salad with
Peppery Orange Dressing, 303
Orzo and Basmati Pilaf with Spring
Vegetable Ragout, 132–33
Oven-baked Chowder, 48
Oven Fries, 295

Pancakes
Gingerbread Pancakes with
Butterscotch Apples, 338–39
Potato Pancakes with Smoked Salmon
and Fried Eggs, 108
Pancetta
Farfalle with Cauliflower and Sautéed
Bread Crumbs, 120
Panko Bread Crumbs, 24
Lemon Chicken, 149
Paprika
about, 183
Bacon and Paprika Sauce, 182–83
Parmesan cheese (Parmigiano-Reggiano)
Antipasto Salad with Parmigiano-
Reggiano Dressing, 79
Creamy Baked Polenta, 259
Crispy Pumpkin Ravioli, 129–31
Escarole and White Bean Soup with
Large Meatballs, 58
Fusilli with Broccoli and Prosciutto,
121
Italian Croutons, 27